THE COMPACT SURVEY OF THE BIBLE

THE COMPACT SURVEY OF THE BIBLE

John Balchin•Peter Cotterell•Mary Evans
Gilbert Kirby•Peggy Knight•Derek Tidball

BETHANY HOUSE PUBLISHERS

MINNEAPOLIS, MINNESOTA 55438
A Division of Bethany Fellowship, Inc.

To each student of the London Bible College, England, who under the instruction of its faculty is being fashioned into a "workman who does not need to be ashamed and who correctly handles the word of truth."

Originally published in Great Britain by Scripture Union under the title **The Bible in Outline**.

Published by Bethany House Publishers
A Division of Bethany Fellowship, Inc.
11300 Hampshire Avenue South
Bloomington, Minnesota 55438

Printed in the United States of America

Library of Congress Cataloging-in-Publication Data

Balchin, John F., 1937–
    The compact survey of the Bible.
      1. Bible—Outlines, syllabi, etc. I. Title.
BS592.B35   1987   220.6'1   87–15124
ISBN 0–87123–964–7

CONTENTS

CONTENTS

New Testament

INTRODUCTION

Christians should need little reminding of the centrality of the Bible in their lives. But though we recognise the importance of the Bible in theory, we have often failed to give any adequate practical demonstration of that conviction. If we are to be the people God intends us to be and fulfil his purposes for us, we must not only take seriously the word he speaks to us in Scripture, but must also allow it to permeate every aspect of our lives.

THE IMPORTANCE OF THE BIBLE. We recognise that our **beliefs** are to be determined by the message of the Bible, but do not always see that some of the things we believe to be biblical are in fact not true to Scripture. We are, after all, people of our time and are affected by current ideas and attitudes. Whenever we come to Scripture we bring these with us, and they cloud our understanding. We are also fallen people and our understanding will therefore never be perfect. The systems of belief we construct may correspond closely with the message of Scripture, but they can never correspond exactly and we can never afford to relax our efforts to revise our thinking in the light of Scripture.

Our **behaviour** must be moulded by Scripture. The rights and wrongs of many things are quite clear, but there are areas which Christians have always debated. Total pacifists and advocates of just war, for example, both find support for their attitudes in Scripture. Particularly on those matters where the Bible is silent, careful thought is needed to arrive at the truth.

Our **worship** should be centred on Scripture. The great emphasis of the Reformers on the Ministry of the Word ensured that in most Protestant traditions preaching stood at the heart of public worship. In later years, the sermon took such a central place that little genuine worship – addressing God with praise, thanksgiving, and expressions of our love – took place. More recently, these elements have been recovered, but with that recovery has come the danger that we become self-indulgent, merely doing those things which we enjoy. In extreme cases, our view of God becomes so distorted that we can hardly be said to be worshipping the God of the Bible.

INTERPRETING THE BIBLE. In each of those three areas – belief, behaviour and worship – one of the greatest dangers is being too selective in our use of Scripture. Nearly all heresies, aberrations and cults have developed from over-emphasising certain sections of Scripture and ignoring others. Even evangelical Christians have too often quoted certain 'proof-texts' and assumed that nothing more was needed. Awkward passages have either been ignored or interpreted to fit our systems. There is, of course, great value in memorising a selection of verses on which we can draw in the struggle with temptation, when sharing our faith or to give depth and meaning to individual and corporate worship. But ultimately the best safeguard against developing one-sided interpretations, wrong behaviour patterns or self-centred worship is to come to terms with the overall message of Scripture. Detailed knowledge of, and over familiarity with, one or two trees is in this case no adequate substitute for an understanding of the whole wood. God has given us Scripture in its totality and it is the whole Scripture that carries his message – we cannot fully understand what he is saying unless we study the message of the whole Bible.

There is an obvious diversity in Scripture; there are different authors, different styles, different literary types, different emphases. But this diversity is always directed to one end and controlled by one hand; there is a unity in Scripture which results from the inspiration of God. Just as the composer of a symphony will use different instruments with their individual characteristics, and changes of tempo, of volume and of key to create his desired effect, so the Spirit of God takes the different authors and styles and uses them to create the rich pattern through which he speaks to men and women. For many years, the major approach to biblical interpretation was to look at the author, the individual book, and the particular section in great depth. In some cases, this resulted in lengthy discussions of the way in which the book was composed, and, in extreme instances, a search for different original sources. More recently there has been an emphasis on interpreting Scripture as it stands and seeing each passage in the context of others around it. We need to go further and see each in the context of the overall message of Scripture.

Any correct understanding of Scripture, therefore, requires both detailed examination and a broad view. The detailed examination demands, in the first place, some knowledge of the background. We can only see the distinctive place and true significance of Amos and Hebrews if we know that the books are addressed to different situations. Questions about when the book was written, who wrote it and to whom, are not simply matters of obscure academic interest. Answers to such ques-

INTRODUCTION

tions are vital if we are to grasp the message. We shall understand better why Amos spoke as he did if we know something of the social conditions in Israel during the eighth century BC. We shall not feel the full force of the warnings in Hebrews until we have begun to comprehend the pressures faced by first-century Jewish Christians.

The detailed approach also demands some understanding of different types of literature and styles of writing. To approach Revelation in exactly the same way as Romans will only result in misunderstandings. To treat Psalms like Mark's Gospel will diminish the impact of both. We shall also need an awareness of the idioms and figures of speech employed by the writers of the Hebrew and Greek.

THE BROAD VIEW. Armed with knowledge like this we are in a position to establish what the writer intended to convey to his original audience. At this point our broad view comes into play. We can begin to see how this relates to the overall purpose and message of the writer. Paul's statement '. . . the living God who is the Saviour of all men . . .' (1 Timothy 4:9) could be taken as an indication that no one will be lost. A reading of the rest of 1 Timothy makes it clear that this is completely contrary to Paul's purpose. We then take our interpretation and relate it to the teaching of Scripture as a whole. In this way, our overall understanding develops. Where necessary we must be prepared to modify our existing convictions. Always we must allow the Scripture to challenge our thinking, moulding it in the way that God intends.

This is, in many ways, the heart of the matter. We do not come to the Bible merely to increase our knowledge nor do we approach it simply as an object of academic study. We come to the Bible above all else to hear God speak to us. When God addresses us we listen and take note. Our engagement with Scripture is one in which we are called to respond. It is not we who analyse Scripture, but Scripture which analyses us. The word of God in Scripture, like any other word of God, 'penetrates . . . it judges the thoughts and attitudes of the heart' (Hebrews 4:12). If our encounter with Scripture is not a life-changing experience, something is wrong with our attitude or our response.

THE MESSAGE FOR TODAY. At this point, another element enters the picture. If the truth of Scripture is to become part of our world view, we must also engage with our society, its ideas, ideals, fears and aspirations. Too often we have been guilty of allowing Scripture to address the concerns of a previous generation or a different culture. The people who expressed their feelings

11

about the efforts of Western missionaries in the words,'. . . But you scratch where we do not itch' captured the situation, Scripture is given not only that we may be 'wise for salvation', but also that we 'may be thoroughly equipped for every good work' (2 Timothy 3:15,17). We must first of all hear what God would say to us and then we must hear what God would say through us to our contemporaries. In this sense, every Christian has a prophetic role, bringing the message of God faithfully and creatively to bear on the world in which he lives.

It is not enough, therefore, to come armed with the right techniques and tools, important though these are. We approach the Bible in humility, recognising our need. We come with the clear expectation that the Spirit who first inspired Scripture will bring the message home to us in lively and relevant ways, and praying to that end. We come obediently so that when we hear the voice of God we are prepared to take appropriate action.

We come from the experience of our lives in this world. We do not leave behind our daily concerns or those of our associates when we come to the Bible; we bring them with us so that God may address them. We do not come in ignorance of the problems of our society; we come burdened by them so that we might hear what God has to say about them.

THE EFFECT OF THE BIBLE. In Scripture God speaks not only to our minds, but to the whole of our personalities. Our emotions will be touched. We shall experience conviction and remorse, we shall find joy and delight in the warmth of God's love, we shall be excited at the realisation of what God has done, is doing and will do for us. Our spirits will be lifted, and we shall respond in worship and praise. As we hear God expressing his love for us we shall find ourselves more and more freely expressing ours for him. Our relationship with him will deepen and we shall find that we know him in new and more intimate ways.

Our wills will be challenged. Behaviour patterns will change; attitudes will be modified. We shall be called to different forms of Christian service and witness. We shall find that through the word the Spirit transforms us into the people God intends – that we become by our very presence in society the salt which preserves, cleanses, and flavours.

Our encounter with Scripture is thus challenging, stimulating and exciting, but never to be taken lightly. A regular contact with Scripture is an essential to any development in the Christian life and should be part of every Christian's programme.

THE BIBLE IN OUTLINE. The intention of *The Bible in Outline* is to give an understanding of the broader view. Each book of the Bible

INTRODUCTION

is analysed in such a way that the overall pattern of the writer's thought emerges. For each book there are five sections: introduction, outline, message, application and key themes.

The introduction fills in the important background details and shows the context in which the book was written. It has been deliberately kept brief and simple while giving all the information necessary to a proper understanding.

The outline shows how the writer's thought develops and indicates the major divisions. Here we can see how different parts of the book relate to one another and how they fit together.

The message draws together the various strands in the writer's thinking. It shows what the author was saying to his original readers and how that message has a relevance and significance in every age.

The application highlights areas where we should look for the teaching to have some effect in our individual lives, in church life or in society.

The key themes underline some of the most important strands in the book's teaching and raise questions for further study and discussion, allowing each reader to formulate a personal response.

The Bible in Outline does not attempt to look at the detailed interpretation of individual passages. Rather it enables us to see the overall pattern and purpose, to see at a glance the general thrust of each book of the Bible. As such it forms a valuable complement to the more detailed commentaries, and many students will find the overview invaluable before they commence more detailed study.

Individuals will find its broader perspective a useful supplement to a regular, systematic programme of Bible reading such as that offered by Scripture Union's Bible Reading Notes. The outline may give the opportunity for a quick read through a whole book. The application and key themes will suggest areas for further thought.

Group leaders or those preparing talks will find the outlines an aid to planning, especially if they are thinking of a series of studies. The key themes suggest areas which either groups or individuals could usefully explore.

Whatever use is made of the book, it is the aim and prayer of authors and publisher that it will give an enhanced understanding of Scripture which results in a deepened relationship with God and a more effective Christian life.

All Scripture is God-breathed and is useful for teaching, rebuking, correcting and training in righteousness, so that the man of God may be thoroughly equipped for every good work.
2 TIMOTHY 3:16,17

Do your best to present yourself to God as one approved, a workman who does not need to be ashamed and who correctly handles the word of truth.
2 TIMOTHY 2:15

THE OLD TESTAMENT

GENESIS

Everything starts here

THE IMPORTANCE OF GENESIS. The rest of the Bible would make very little sense but for the book of Genesis. It answers the 'big' questions, such as why are we here and where did we come from? Genesis speaks of the beginning of the world, of man and society, of families and of nations, of sin and salvation. In particular, it speaks of the start of the Hebrew race.

THE STYLE OF GENESIS.

1. Genesis teaches truth by telling stories rather than by setting out the lessons in a more formal way.

2. The stories are very human. There is no attempt at any 'cover-up'. Even the greatest heroes are painted 'warts and all'.

3. All the stories are majestically and movingly told. By any standards Genesis is brilliantly written.

THE AUTHOR OF GENESIS. Genesis is anonymous, but the New Testament implies that it was written by Moses and this belief was unquestioned by the church until recent times.

We do not know how the book was written, but it is reasonable to see Moses as an editor who put together a great number of stories and facts, some of which would have already been in wide circulation before his time.

THE VALUE OF GENESIS. Many suppose that modern science and history have undermined the value of Genesis. We can however read Genesis with confidence in its reliability for two reasons:

1. For every scientific or historical argument which questions the accuracy of Genesis there is more than one in support of it.

2. Much of the debate is not about truth itself so much as modern ways of approaching truth. Whether or not Genesis is truth as we would express it in a way which is fashionable today, it remains truth. Above all it is truth made known by God about himself, ourselves and the world in which we live.

Outline

1 THE STORY OF MANKIND
1:1–11:30

1:1–2:3 The creation of the world
2:4–25 The creation of man and woman
3:1–24 The fall of man
4:1–26 The story of Cain and Abel
5:1–32 Potted histories – Adam to Noah
6:1–9:28 The story of Noah
10:1–32 The family of Noah
11:1–9 The tower of Babel
11:10–30 Potted histories – Shem to Abram

2 THE STORY OF ABRAHAM
11:31–25:18

11:31–12:9 Abraham starts his journey
12:10–20 Abraham faces famine and Egypt
13:1–18 Abraham separates from Lot
14:1–24 Abraham rescues Lot
15:1–21 Abraham meets with God
16:1–16 Abraham has a son – his way
17:1–27 Abraham meets with God again
18:1–19:38 Abraham receives heavenly visitors
20:1–18 Abraham lies to Abimelech
21:1–7 Abraham has a son – God's way
21:8–34 Abraham faces problems
22:1–24 Abraham faces a severe test
23:1–20 Abraham buries his wife
24:1–67 Abraham plans for the future
25:1–18 Abraham in his final days

3 THE STORY OF ISAAC
25:19–27:40

25:19–34 Isaac has sons
26:1–35 Isaac has problems
27:1–40 Isaac is deceived

4 THE STORY OF JACOB
27:41–37:1

27:41–28:9 Jacob leaves home in a hurry
28:10–22 Jacob meets God at Bethel
29:1–31:55 Jacob serves Laban for years
32:1–33:20 Jacob goes home at last
34:1–31 Jacob has trouble with Shechem
35:1–21 Jacob meets God at Bethel again
35:22–37:1 Jacob's family

5 THE STORY OF JOSEPH
37:2–50:26

37:2–11 Joseph and his childhood dreams
37:12–36 Joseph and his unkind brothers
38:1–30 Judah and Tamar
39:1–40:23 Joseph's undeserved imprisonment
41:1–57 Joseph and his unexpected release
42:1–45:28 Joseph and his needy brothers
46:1–50:3 Joseph and his aged father
50:4–26 Joseph and his final years

Message

It is not always easy to pin-point the teaching of Genesis in particular verses and those given below are merely examples.

1. What Genesis teaches about God
☐ He is eternal and has life in himself. 1:1
☐ He is the creator and life-giver. 1:1–2:9
☐ He is personal and desires a relationship with man. 1:26–2:25; 3:8; 15:1–16
☐ He is holy and will judge sinful men. 3:8–24; 6:5–8; 11:1–9; 18:16–19:29
☐ He is merciful even in judgement. 3:21; 4:15; 6:8; 18:32
☐ He is patient in dealing with his followers, as the story of Abraham and of Jacob demonstrates.
☐ He is sovereign over every power. 18:14; 26:12–16; 50:20

2. What Genesis teaches about man
☐ He is born in the image of God, and so has worth and creative ability. 1:27–30

☐ He is self-willed, and goes his own sinful way without God. 3:1–7
☐ His sin is deeply ingrained in his make-up, as even Abraham shows. 20:1–18
☐ He needs fellowship with his maker, as the life of Abraham teaches.
☐ He is capable of being remade by God, as the life of Jacob shows.
☐ He is under the providential care of God, as the life of Joseph demonstrates.

3. What Genesis teaches about society
☐ Man was created as a social being, not as an isolated individual. 2:18
☐ Examples abound of the difficulties man faces living with his fellow men.
☐ The basic unit in the structure of society is marriage. 2:24
☐ Law and government are also needed to help man live in a fallen world.

Application

The message of Genesis applies to three areas of relationship:

1. To our life with God
☐ Obey him. It is always best to do it God's way.
☐ Believe him. It's right, even when it seems unreasonable to do so.
☐ Trust him. He really does care for you.
☐ Talk with him. He must be asked about problems and decisions.

☐ Let him work. He can change even a twisted life into a life of beauty.

2. To our family life
☐ Be honest with each other.
☐ Don't have favourites.
☐ Watch out for jealousy.
☐ Be faithful, even in difficult times.
☐ Live by God's rules, not your own.

GENESIS

3. To our life in the world
☐ Develop and use the world's resources responsibly.
☐ Remember all men have the same Creator and are made in his image.

☐ Note that God is concerned with international affairs, not just personal, spiritual issues.
☐ Live a life of honesty, and so be a good witness.

Key themes

1. Election
Abel, Noah, Abraham, Jacob and Joseph are all called by God and chosen for their place in the history of God's people. Sometimes, as in the case of Jacob, the choice flies in the face of traditional ways of doing things.
Read again the story of their calls and write down what you can learn about the way God elects people.

2. Salvation
As soon as man committed sin, God made it plain that he was concerned to rescue him. 3:15; 4:4; 22:8 may all refer to the work Christ was one day to do.
What other teaching about salvation do you find in this book?

3. Work
Even before the fall man had a task to do in the world (1:28). Man was made to work. After the fall it became less enjoyable (3:17–19). What does this have to teach about work in today's world?

4. Rest
The idea of one day in seven being a rest day comes from these earliest chapters of the

Bible (2:2, 3). It is not just one of the ten commandments but a basic instruction of our Maker.
What has this to say to our own society?

5. Satan
Read again the story of the fall (3:1–7), and see what it teaches about Satan and his technique.

6. Death
Death is threatened (3:3), overcome (5:24) and often encountered (eg. 49:1–50:3). What can we learn from this?

7. Morality
Throughout the book there is a concern for moral living. What are the chief features of morality outlined here?

8. Marriage
What does 2:18–25 have to teach us about the purpose of marriage?

9. Worship
What does Genesis teach us about how we should worship God (eg. 4:1–7; 28:10–22)?

EXODUS

The birth of a nation

WHY EXODUS? Exodus was the title used for the 'second book of Moses' in the Greek version of the Old Testament and it means 'the way out'. In fact the description of the actual 'exodus' is confined to only part of the book.

WHAT IS IT ABOUT? The book of Exodus divides itself into three main parts.

1. The story of Moses: how his life was preserved as a baby; how he was brought up in Pharaoh's palace; how he was called by God at the burning bush; how he challenged Pharaoh to release his people from slavery and how eventually he led his people in triumph through the Red Sea and into the wilderness of Sinai.

2. The next part of the book is largely taken up with God's dealings with Moses on Mount Sinai, the giving of the ten commandments and other laws.

3. The final section is mainly concerned with three things: the building of the chest (called the ark of testimony) in which the stone tablets bearing the commandments were to be kept; the tabernacle (or tent) in which the ark was to be housed, and details regarding worship.

WHAT IS ITS VALUE TO US TODAY? The dominant note in the book is that of deliverance from slavery – redemption. It provides many illustrations which help us to understand our own redemption through the Lord Jesus Christ. The Passover lamb (12:1-11) is a clear foreshadowing of the Lamb of God who bore away the sin of the world (John 1:29). Christ is referred to as 'our Passover lamb' by Paul (1 Cor. 5:7), whilst Peter speaks of him as being like 'a lamb without blemish or defect' (1 Pet. 1:19).

In the last part of the book we are reminded that a redeemed people is called upon to be a worshipping people.

God teaches his people by using visual aids. The tabernacle was to symbolise God's presence among his people. It is significant that Christ is said to have 'tabernacled' (Greek) among us (John 1:14). So the book of Exodus is an example of how the Old Testament throws light on the New. When we study Exodus we see God's way of delivering men from bondage and his subsequent purposes for them, and this story is applicable to every man who recognises his need to be redeemed.

Outline

EXODUS

Message

1. Redemption from slavery.
Exodus brings us to the beginnings of Israel's existence as a nation. 1:1–12:36

The dominant note is that of deliverance or redemption. In the early chapters we are told of how the people were prepared for deliverance and how God raised up, in the person of Moses, a deliverer. Later the people were led out from Egypt and subsequently at Sinai constituted as a nation. 12:37–19:25

The remainder of the book is taken up with matters relating to Israel's continuance as a people in covenant relationship with God. 20:1–40:38

2. Redemption from sin.
The book of Exodus could be regarded as being in three parts.

☐ The people's need of deliverance is seen as they suffered under Egyptian oppression. This may be seen as a picture of men's slavery to sin from which they desperately need to be delivered.

☐ The place of deliverance is described. There is never any doubt that in the end it will succeed but in the meantime there are many frustrations. It culminates in the sacrifice of the Passover lamb. The blood on the lintels of the doors of the Israelites was a guarantee of their safety. For the Christian, Christ is the Passover lamb whose blood assures forgiveness of sin and new life.

☐ After redemption comes consecration. God was going to enter into a covenant with his people who were to be his special witnesses in the world. As God's redeemed people they were called upon to be obedient to him. The ten commandments represent the moral law of God. It was necessary also that they should keep in close touch with God by regular worship and so they were given instructions as to how they were to proceed. The tabernacle was the place where they met with God and were assured of his presence.

Application

In the book of Exodus we learn a great deal about the nature of God.

1. God is sovereign.
He controls history and he overrules all things to his glory.

2. God is concerned for his people.
He overrules events with the ultimate well-being of his people in mind.

3. God provides for his people.
The daily manna and the quails were proof enough that the Lord does provide for the needs of his children.

4. God is holy.
All through the book this fact is brought home to Moses and to the Israelites generally. We should bow in awe before him.

5. God expects obedience from his people.
The ten commandments represent God's basic requirements from men and women, and he looks for obedience in thought, word and deed.

EXODUS

6. God guides his people.
God guided his people in the wilderness by means of the cloud and the fire – now he guides by his Spirit indwelling his people.

7. God looks for man's worship.
In Moses' day elaborate instructions were given as to how God was to be worshipped.

All these served to remind the worshipper of God's holiness and majesty. Worship is no less important today, and, although we are no longer required to follow the elaborate ritual set out in the Old Testament, we need to remember it is the same holy God whom we worship.

Key themes

1. Liberty
Exodus opens with a picture of the Israelites writhing under the yoke of slavery. Read Exodus 1:11–14. Their deliverance was not easily achieved, but when it did take place it was complete. The Passover lamb will always be seen by Christians as a picture of the Lamb of God and a reminder that we, too, have been released from the peril and bondage of sin.

Look up the New Testament references to Jesus as the Lamb of God: John 1: 29,36; Acts 8:32–35; 1 Corinthians 5:7; 1 Peter 1:18,19, and trace the usage through the book of Revelation. What value do you put on your freedom from slavery to sin?

2. Law
The freed slaves were reminded that God expects obedience from his people. The ten commandments are remarkable for the fact that they constitute a moral code suited to all men at all times. They are not dated. Those who accept Christ as Saviour need to remember they must also serve him as Lord. He said, 'If you love me, you will obey what I command' (John 14:15). Ultimately obedience is to influence attitudes and motives as well as actions. Check Jesus' words in Matthew 5:21–48.

3. Worship
After Israel had been set free they were soon instructed as to how they were to worship God. The tabernacle was a visual reminder of the presence of God among his people, and Israel discovered the nature of divine holiness and that sinful men cannot lightly come before him. The brazen altar was the place of sacrifice and this was the only way of approach into God's presence. The clothing of the priest was carefully prescribed since he was the one who represented man to God. Every detail served to emphasise the holiness of God. We who have become a royal priesthood through becoming God's children are reminded that God is still holy and that this is to be reflected in our worship.

Check out in Exodus the use of the words 'holy' and 'holiness', noting how they refer to both God and his people. What effects should these facts about holiness have on our attitudes, worship and life-style?

LEVITICUS

Rules for life and worship

WHY LEVITICUS? Much of the contents concern Levitical priests, but the repeated phrase 'Speak to the Israelites . . .' shows that it was also meant for everyone. It must be seen as part of the Pentateuch, the first five books of the Bible. Exodus tells how God delivered Israel from Egypt and made a covenant with them. Leviticus explains how the life and the worship of the covenant people is to be organised.

WHO WROTE IT? No author is named in Leviticus. Much of the material was given to Moses by God at Sinai, but we cannot tell when or by whom it was finally brought together and written down.

WHAT IS IT ABOUT? The book mainly consists of laws and regulations, but there is a framework of stories and illustrations showing that these laws fit into real history. It falls naturally into two parts, the great chapter on the Day of Atonement coming in the middle. The first part is about getting right with God – rules on sacrifice and cleansing. The last part is about living as God's people.

LAW. Many of the laws in Leviticus concern ritual and ceremonial, but there are also laws about hygiene and laws about moral behaviour, similar to the ten commandments. No distinction is made between different kinds of law; all reflect God's purpose for Israel and all are to be obeyed. In the New Testament the sacrifice of Christ brings complete cleansing, so the laws on sacrifice and ceremonial cleansing no longer apply. However, they are very helpful in explaining what Christ's death did for us.

SACRIFICE. There are six sacrifices described in Leviticus, falling into three types.

    1. GIFT OFFERING: the aim is to glorify God and to dedicate oneself to him.

☐ Burnt offering: the whole animal is burnt.

☐ Cereal offering: this covers all non-animal gifts.

    2. FELLOWSHIP OFFERINGS: The aim is to keep communion with God.

☐ Peace offering: part is burnt: the rest is eaten in a fellowship meal.

    3. CLEANSING OFFERINGS: The aim is to remove sin and renew relationship with God.

☐ Sin offering: for sins against God.

☐ Guilt offering: where compensation must be paid.

☐ Consecration offering: on behalf of the priests.

Outline

LEVITICUS

Message

1. God is present with his people.
1:1–6:7; 18:1–22:16
- [ ] In worship: all sacrifices and ceremonies take place 'before the Lord'.
- [ ] In everyday life: God is always there, and everything must be done in the light of his presence.

2. God is holy, so his people must be holy.
11:44,45; 19:2; 20:7,8,24–26
The character of the people must reflect the character of God. Holiness as far as the people are concerned, means removing all uncleanness, offering sacrifices and keeping the law.

3. Sin must be dealt with.
1:1–7:38; 11:1–15:33
Because God is holy, he cannot be in contact with anything sinful or unclean. Therefore, if man is to have a relationship with God he must first be cleansed from all kinds of impurity.

4. Atonement involves sacrifice.
1:4; 14:29–31; 16:1–34
Sin is always serious; its removal is not an easy thing. If man is to be cleansed and put right with God then a sacrifice must be offered. This sacrifice 'makes atonement'; it delivers the sinner from the death that he deserves. However, Leviticus makes it clear that it is not the sacrifice as such which gives forgiveness and cleansing; these are the gift of God.

5. God cares about the whole of life.
18:1–22:16
Leviticus doesn't deal only with worship. There are rules about food and drink, illness, clothes, houses, crops, relationships, and working conditions. Every part of life should be lived in a way that reflects God's character.

Application

1. God's blueprint for a holy people.
The laws God gave to Israel tell us about his character and his will and provide principles which still apply.
- [ ] God must be obeyed (17:2).
- [ ] God alone is to be worshipped and served (17:3–9; 20:1–5).
- [ ] Family life must be guarded (18:6–19:2; 20:10–21).
- [ ] The poor must be provided for (19:9,10).
- [ ] Justice is vital in all business transactions (19:11–22,33–37).
- [ ] Everything magical or occult must be avoided (19:26–31; 20:6,27).
- [ ] God's provision must be recognised and remembered (23:1–44).
- [ ] Nobody is to build up great wealth at the expense of others (25:8–55).

2. The meaning of sacrifice and atonement.
Leviticus shows the means God provides to combat sin and helps us understand New Testament teaching about sacrifice and substitution. Chapter 16, on the Day of Atonement, brings out these points.
- [ ] God is holy and can't tolerate sin.
- [ ] Sin separates man from God.
- [ ] If fellowship is to be regained, sin must be removed.

LEVITICUS

- For this to happen, blood must be shed. Sin costs life.
- The daily sacrifices are not enough.
- Even the Day of Atonement needs to be repeated each year.
- Priests, Temple and people – all need cleansing.

- Sacrifice can undo sin's effects.
- Fellowship with God is renewed, if only temporarily.
- The Day of Atonement is a gift from God, a privilege not a right.

Key themes

1. Holiness.

That God is holy is taken for granted in Leviticus and provides the basis for all the laws (11:44, 45; 19:2–4; 20:7,8,24–26). Look up these references. What can we learn from their contexts about the meaning of holiness?

2. Justice.

God's holiness and God's justice go hand in hand. God deals justly with his people and they must deal justly with each other.

The regulations given in chapter 19 show how justice was to be applied in Israel. Make a list of the ways we can apply these principles in the modern world.

3. Covenant.

Because Israel were the people with whom God had made his covenant (his special agreement), it was important that they lived in the pattern he had set. To keep these laws was not optional for Israel, and Leviticus was thus the first book of the Bible studied by Jewish children.

Read chapter 26 and note the eight references to covenant found there. How does this chapter show that relationship with God brings with it responsibilities?

4. Thankfulness.

It was important for Israel to realise that everything they had was given to them by God, including the laws and sacrifices which made it possible for them to renew their relationship with him after they had broken it by sinning. Chapter 23 describes the regular festivals when Israel could show gratitude to God. What other opportunities for offering thankfulness to God are described in Leviticus?

NUMBERS

The people in the wilderness

WHAT IS IT ABOUT? The name of this book in the Hebrew Bible means 'in the wilderness' and that title covers all the events of the book. The title 'Numbers' is used because it records two 'numberings' of the people, in the second year after they left Egypt (chapter 1) and in the fortieth year (chapter 26). Most of the book, however, tells of the experiences of the Israelites during the forty years they were in the desert before they entered the Promised Land.

In many ways Numbers makes sad reading since many of Israel's sufferings were a direct outcome of faithlessness and disobedience. One could say that Numbers is a record of human failure set against divine faithfulness.

WHAT IS THE OVERALL IMPRESSION? One of the features of the book is that it does not attempt to give us a full or strictly continuous narrative. Comparatively little detail is given about those years in the wilderness, but certain events are highlighted and described at some length. The overall impression is left that God is in control in spite of Israel's idolatry and immorality. The book is partly historical and partly legislative.

WHO ARE THE CHIEF CHARACTERS MENTIONED? Obviously Moses figures largely in the book – his concern for Hobab (10:29-32); his prayer at Taberah (11:10-15); his reaction to criticism (12); his lack of faith (13); his concern for God's honour (14:13-19); his exclusion from the Promised Land (20:2-13). Aaron also comes into the picture especially in connection with the rebellion of Korah (16). Miriam, Moses' sister, is another character in the book. Chapter 12 describes how she was punished for her jealousy. Others mentioned include Joshua and Caleb, the two spies who dared to believe God and who were the only men of their generation allowed to enter Canaan. Also recorded is the story of Balaam and Balak (chapters 22-24).

WHAT ABOUT THE DIFFICULTIES? Critics of the Bible have raised a number of queries about the historical and statistical accuracy of the book. Most, if not all, of these are met if we realise that Hebrew writers did not always adhere to a strictly chronological order of events. They were more concerned about their meaning and significance.

Outline

1 THE ORGANISATION
OF ISRAEL
1:1–10:36

1:1–54 The census commanded by God
2:1–4:49 The arrangement of the camp
5:1–6:27 The purity of the camp
7:1–9:14 Worship in the camp
9:15–10:36 Guidance for the camp

2 EXPERIENCES ON THE
JOURNEY
11:1–25:18

11:1–35 Trouble in the camp
12:1–16 Murmuring against Moses
13:1–33 Exploration of Canaan
14:1–45 Rebellion in the camp
15:1–41 Further regulations
16:1–17:13 Revolt against the spiritual
leadership
18:1–19:22 Laws and principles
20:1–21:35 Events on the journey
22:1–24:25 The story of Balaam
25:1–18 Sin and retribution

3 LOOKING FORWARD TO THE
PROMISED LAND
26:1–33:49

26:1–65 The second census
27:1–11 Zelophehad's daughters
27:12–23 Joshua to succeed Moses
28:1–30:16 Laws and principles
31:1–54 The judgement on Midian
32:1–42 Settlement of the Reubenites and
Gadites
33:1–49 The journey reviewed

4 PREPARATIONS FOR
ENTRANCE
INTO CANAAN
33:50–36:13

NUMBERS

Message

1. Good intentions.
1:1–10:10
The opening chapters describe Israel's situation in the wilderness of Sinai and include references to the taking of the census, the choosing of the Levites and their consecration, the setting apart of the Nazarites and an account of the offerings at the dedication of the tabernacle. The underlying emphasis is on the holiness and faithfulness of God.

2. Grumbling and rebellion.
10:11–20:29
Here we trace the journey of the children of Israel after they left Mount Sinai and reached Kadesh Barnea. This section of the book makes sad reading. It is the story of repeated murmurings against God and of punishments which followed. Here is a recurring warning against unbelief.

3. Failures and triumphs.
21:1–36:13
In this third part of the book the picture brightens. The predominant note is that of victory, although there are still failures to record. We find Joshua appointed as Moses' successor, and preparations made to enter the Promised Land. As well as a continued emphasis on the divine holiness, we learn from Numbers that God is a God of order. In the same way he gave clear instructions to his people as to how they were to conduct their lives and also their worship. Under the new covenant, it is equally important that 'everything should be done in a fitting and orderly way' (1 Corinthians 14:40).

Application

1. We are saved to serve.
In Exodus we have the story of Israel being released from bondage; in Numbers the accent lies on service. Only a saved man can truly worship and serve the living God.

2. God is a God of order.
The book contains many laws and principles which serve to remind us that in serving God 'everything should be done in a fitting and orderly way' (1 Corinthians 14:40).

3. There are sins to which God's people are especially prone.
☐ The sin of unbelief. Israel's failure to enter in was due to unbelief.
☐ The sin of rebelliousness. In Numbers there are several accounts of rebellions. We are all too prone to give way to a rebellious spirit and to turn against God's appointed leaders.
☐ The sin of jealousy. Both Aaron and Miriam brought upon themselves God's displeasure. Beware of jealousy.

4. God honours faith.
Caleb and Joshua stand out as men of faith and they were the only two allowed to enter the Promised Land. It is tragically easy to become obsessed with the difficulties but faith laughs at the impossible.

NUMBERS

Key themes

1. Divine provision.
We have several illustrations in Numbers of the ways in which God provides for his people. For example, 20:1–11; 21:1–9; 27:1–11 (see 36:1–12); 27:12–23; 35:1–5; 35:6–28. Think of the ways in which God provides for his people today.

2. Divine displeasure.
One of the sadder aspects of Numbers is the fact that God was frequently angry with his people. See 11:1–3; 11:33; 12:1–16; 14:20–23; 14:36–38; 16:31–35; 25:1–3. How do God's people grieve him now?

3. Divine orderliness.
God is a God of order and discipline. See chapters 1,2,3,4,26,32 for his numbering of the people, the arrangement of the camp and the settlement of the tribes. See also 7:1–19:14; chapters 15,18,19,28,29 for the ordering of worship.

4. Divine guidance.
It is noteworthy that, in spite of their persistent backsliding, God still led his people all through their wanderings, with the cloud and fire (9:15–23). God still guides his people: in what ways does he do so?

DEUTERONOMY

A challenge to the people of God

THE NAME. The Hebrew name for the book of Deuteronomy takes up
the opening line, 'these are the words'. Our name comes from a
Greek word meaning 'second-law' which is a slight mis-
translation of the phrase 'a copy of this law' (17:18).

THE STRUCTURE OF THE BOOK. In Deuteronomy we have a repetition and restressing of the covenant made between God and
Israel at Sinai. The form in which it is presented is related to the
regular pattern of covenant treaties in the ancient Near East
which consisted of a historical background, a list of obligations,
a statement of blessings and curses, and arrangements for
keeping and reading the covenant documents. In
Deuteronomy this pattern is presented by means of three
speeches given by Moses to the people just before he died,
reminding them of what it meant to be the people of God.

THE AUTHOR AND DATE OF WRITING. There is no reason to doubt
that the bulk of the material came directly from Moses himself.

The suggestion that the book was produced entirely during
the reforms of Hezekiah or Josiah, or even after the exile cannot
be supported, as there is nothing in the book which relates to
the Davidic tradition or to the Temple as such, both of which
were very important later on. In fact the pattern of life
described fits the very early background of the period before
the monarchy. However, it does appear that there has been
some editing and working over, so that it is very difficult to date
the final production. The covenant pictures and principles of
Exodus are sometimes expressed rather differently in
Deuteronomy, perhaps to meet a different situation; but if they
were adapted for a later age it does not mean that they are not
thoroughly grounded in Mosaic material.

WHY WAS IT WRITTEN? The original purpose of Moses' speeches
was to confirm Israel as the people of God before he handed
over the leadership to Joshua and the people went out to
conquer Canaan. The book as a whole teaches the content and
meaning of Israel's religion, challenges her to respond to its
demands, and encourages her to commit herself afresh to
God's service. It describes the 'good life' lived in fellowship
with God and enjoying his blessings, and contrasts this with the
awful results of neglecting the covenant. It could almost be
described as a 'constitution' for Israel, but it is very much a call
to the people rather than a handbook for the leaders.

Outline

DEUTERONOMY

Message

1. The God of the covenant.
God is at the centre of the message of Deuteronomy. It is because he is who he is that the covenant can exist at all.
- [ ] He is one, the unique God. 4:35; 6:4
- [ ] He is just and righteous. 16:18; 32:4
- [ ] He is the sovereign ruler. 10:17
- [ ] He is jealous and cannot tolerate rivals. 5:9; 6:15
- [ ] He is gracious and generous. 6:24; 28:1-14
- [ ] He is a Father to Israel. 1:31; 32:6

2. The obligations of the covenant.
If Israel is to be in relationship with God, she must acknowledge his sovereignty, and become a holy people, worthy of a holy God. This means accepting his demands.
- [ ] Absolute obedience in all areas. 8:1,11; 11:1
- [ ] Whole-hearted and unswerving love. 6:5
- [ ] Complete trust in God alone. 6:13; 13:1-18
- [ ] Continual remembrance of God – what he is, what he has done, and what he expects from his people.11:18-20
- [ ] Education of children. 4:9; 11:19

3. Benefits of keeping the covenant.
- [ ] Prosperity for the nation including defeat of enemies. 7:22; 28:1,7,13
- [ ] Prosperity for the land – including fertility for crops and animals and favourable weather conditions. 28:3,5,11,12
- [ ] Prosperity for families – they will have lots of healthy children. 28:4,11; 7:14
- [ ] Prosperity for individuals – including good health and long life. 5:16; 7:15

4. Results of breaking the covenant.
- [ ] Disaster for the nation. They will suffer many defeats and in the end be wiped out. 28:20,25; 4:26
- [ ] Disaster for the land. There will be terrible droughts and crops and animals will die. 28:22-24; 28:38-40
- [ ] Disaster for the people. There will be dreadful epidemics, families will be broken up and security non-existent. 28:21,22,28,32,41

Relationship with God is never to be entered into lightly. The lists of blessings and curses emphasise the seriousness of commitment to God. Deuteronomy makes it quite clear that God does have the power to bring about these blessings and curses.

Application

Deuteronomy teaches us about:

1. Our relationship with God.
- [ ] It must be personal. Belonging to a nation or a family that follows God is not enough. Each individual must have a first-hand and up-to-date experience of God.
- [ ] It must be living. The covenant is much more than a legal contract. God wants fellowship with his people and love from them, with the obedience that springs from love.
- [ ] It must be all-embracing. God wants us to follow him, not just on one day a week or in certain situations, but all the time – he cares about what we do in every area of our lives.

DEUTERONOMY

2. Our worship of God.
☐ It must be pure and not tainted or spoiled by taking over any of the ideas and customs of the surrounding people.

☐ It must be in agreement with the patterns God lays down.
☐ It must be heartfelt and not just a matter of following set forms. It must be joyous.

Key themes

1. God's power.
God is seen not only as the Lord of the covenant and sovereign over Israel, but also as the God of history, sovereign over the world, controlling both nations and nature. He has the power to carry out his promises.

Make a list of the ways in which chapters 4 and 30 show God's power being exercised.

2. God's faithfulness.
One of the things that enabled Israel to see the covenant as the basis of their national life was their knowledge of God's total dependability.

Read chapter 32 and note all the different ways in which God is described.

3. Love.
The basic principle of the covenant was love. It was God's love that started the covenant

and made possible its continuation. The first demand on man is that he should love God. Without love a relationship with God cannot exist.

Look up 4:37; 5:10; 6:5; 7:9,13; 10:12–19; 11:1,13,22; 13:3; 19:9; 23:5; 30:16,20.

4. Commitment.
What God wants from his people is a total commitment, an undivided allegiance, a whole-hearted devotion. This involves following God's will for every sphere of life, as it is set out in the covenant rules.

Look up 5:1–21; 6:4–9; 10:12–22. These verses can be seen as summing up the whole law.

JOSHUA

Take possession of the land

HOW THE BOOK WAS WRITTEN. Joshua is the hero rather than the author of the book. Both tradition and the book itself (24:26) credit him with much of the material. Some of it came from an eye-witness, but a later editor must have put it together in the form we now have (4:8,9; 7:26; 8:28; 24:29,30).

JOSHUA. Joshua had been a young man when the Exodus from Egypt took place and had later become Moses' personal assistant. He proved to be a very reliable and loyal right-hand man. His minority report, with Caleb, of their espionage in Canaan also showed him to be a man of faith and courage. He was a natural successor to Moses and took over from him at the age of seventy. Joshua settled the tribes in Canaan and died at the age of 110.

THE PURPOSE OF THE BOOK. The book of Joshua is first and foremost a historical account of how God kept his promise to bring his people into the Promised Land. Its theme is to be found in 1:11: 'Take possesson of the land the Lord your God is giving you...'

THE CONQUEST OF CANAAN. Possessing the land was no easy task. Joshua was leading a tribal people against well-secured city states. After capturing the key cities of Jericho and Ai, Joshua engaged in longer campaigns in the central, southern and northern regions of Canaan. Although he met with remarkable success he had not finished his task when he began to settle the tribes in their own territories (13:1).

HOW TO UNDERSTAND JOSHUA. Although Joshua is a history book, it has much to say to today's Christian. Hebrews 4:1–11 shows that it is meant to be a means of encouragement to Christians, so that they do not miss out on all that God means them to have. Although Joshua is speaking of military battles and geographic territory, we can apply the principles by which God worked there to the spiritual battles we face and the spiritual territory we have yet to possess.

Outline

 ENTERING THE PROMISED LAND
1:1–5:12

1:1–18 Joshua and the people are prepared
2:1–24 The spies are sent out
3:1–17 The river Jordan is crossed
4:1–24 A memorial is erected
5:1–12 The ceremonies which followed

2 CONQUERING THE PROMISED LAND
5:13–12:24

5:13–15 Joshua meets his commander
6:1–27 The campaign at Jericho
7:1–8:29 The campaign at Ai
8:30–35 The covenanting ceremony
9:1–10:43 Campaigns in the centre and south
11:1–15 The northern campaign
11:16–12:24 A summary of successes

 SETTLING THE PROMISED LAND
13:1–22:34

13:1–7 The unfinished task
13:8–33 Land for Reuben, Gad and Manasseh
14:1–15 Land for Caleb
15:1–63 Land for Judah
16:1–17:18 Land for Manasseh and Ephraim
18:1–19:51 Land for the other tribes
20:1–9 Cities of refuge
21:1–45 Cities for Levites
22:1–34 The East-Jordan tribes go home

4 LEAVING THE PROMISED LAND
23:1–24:33

23:1–16 Joshua's farewell address
24:1–28 Joshua's second farewell
24:29–33 Joshua bows out

JOSHUA

Message

1. What Joshua teaches about God.
- [ ] The promise of God. Joshua teaches that God keeps his promises. God had promised the land to Moses (Exodus 6:4) and promised that Joshua would lead his people into it (Deuteronomy 3:27,28). Joshua is the outworking of Deuteronomy 11:22-25. (See Psalm 18:30, Joshua 23:14.)
- [ ] The will of God. Joshua emphasises that God wanted his people to take full possession of the land. Strangely, it is the people themselves who sometimes seem reluctant to do so. Hebrews 4:1-11 gives the New Testament application of this lesson. 13:1; 18:3
- [ ] The goodness of God. Joshua describes the generosity of God in that he gave this land to the people and gave them victory in their battles. The people still had to fight, but the outcome was already determined. What gifts God generously gives to his people! 1:2; 6:16; 10:8 (See 1 Corinthians 3:21-23.)
- [ ] The power of God. Joshua illustrates that God is more powerful than armies and cities; that he is in control of natural happenings; that he is greater than his people's disobedience, or other people's trickery; he can also overcome his people's lack of zeal. 3:7-17; 10:12

2. What Joshua teaches the people of God.
They need to be:
- [ ] A people with an aim. We must possess the land God gives to us fully. 1:2-11
- [ ] A people of obedience. Obedience must be complete. 1:7,8
- [ ] A people of faith. Their trust in God must be proved by taking an active step in obedience to his command. 3:15; 6:16,20
- [ ] A people without compromise. No sin is permitted, and no compromise with the enemy. Holiness is demanded. 7:1-26; 13:13; 16:10; 17:13; 23:11-13
- [ ] A people who persevere. They must not give up easily, but must serve the one Lord loyally to the end. 17:14-18

Application

In the light of Joshua Christians should ask themselves:

- [ ] How much progress am I making in my Christian life?
- [ ] What are the spiritual enemies which hinder my progress?
- [ ] How much do I obey what God's Word teaches me in my daily life?
- [ ] Do I take God at his word and believe him, even when it would seem foolish to do so?
- [ ] At what points am I tempted to compromise my Christian faith?
- [ ] Am I as keen to follow God now as I always was?
- [ ] In listing my priorities in life where would I place holiness?

JOSHUA

☐ How much do I prayerfully read my Bible?
☐ Am I content with the place God has allotted me in life?

☐ If I were to give my testimony of God as Joshua did, what would I say about him?

Key themes

1. Explore this doctrine.
Joshua touches on the theme of salvation.

Joshua's name means 'saviour'. Some people find other similarities between him and Jesus. What might they be?

What can we learn about salvation from Rahab? (See Hebrews 11:30,31.)

The cities of refuge (20:1–9) provide a picture of salvation. List other illustrations or examples of salvation which are found in the book of Joshua.

2. Obey this instruction.
Look carefully at God's command to Joshua (1:8), and find out why God's Word is so important: how it is to be studied; what is the purpose and what is the result of studying it.

3. Follow this man.
Joshua is an attractive leader of his people and ends his life full of gratitude for the goodness of God (23:14). List the lessons you can learn from Joshua's character and example.

4. Avoid these mistakes.
Joshua is an honest book and records the failures of God's people as well as their successes (7:1–26; 9:1–27; 17:14–18). What do they have to teach the church today?

5. Explain these ceremonies.
Joshua records memorial stones being set up (4:1-24); circumcision (5:2–9); the Passover meal (5:10); a covenant ceremony (8:30–35) and the building of an altar (22:10–34). Work out what the equivalent of these ceremonies might be today.

6. Consider the supernatural.
God is shown to be God of the supernatural (3:7–17; 6:20; 10:12). What place has the miraculous in the modern secular world?

JUDGES

The sin-cycle

THE BOOK. Judges is important. It provides the link between Joshua, who led Israel into Canaan, and Saul, David and the other kings of Israel. During the period of the judges, Israel gradually learned to act together as a nation, rather than as twelve separate tribes.

ITS AUTHOR. We do not know who wrote this book. It was probably put together from the records of the period at a much later time. Three times it states that 'in those days Israel had no king' (17:6; 18:1; 21:25), suggesting that the book was put together at some time after the monarchy began.

WHO WERE THE JUDGES? The title is rather misleading, for the twelve 'judges' were not merely concerned with legal matters; they were princes, inspired by the Holy Spirit to give a charismatic kind of leadership in times of need.

There were twelve judges and it is interesting that Jephthah refers to God as 'the Lord, the Judge' (11:27), using the same title as is given to the twelve judges. They recognised that they led by divine will, not merely by human choice.

THE SIN-CYCLE. The book consists of an introduction (1:1–2:5), and an appendix (17:1–21:25), with the rest devoted to the stories of the twelve judges and the six periods of oppression.

A cycle of events becomes apparent:

1. All is going well for the people. There is no particular need of God. So he is left out, and gods of pagan neighbours take his place.

2. Oppression. God abandons them to their own ways. Let them try to manage alone! Moab and Ammon, the Philistines and the Midianites all in turn attack Israel.

3. Repentance. Israel admits her mistake, turns to God, asks for forgiveness. Each time God is willing to forgive and restore.

4. Deliverance. A judge appears who delivers his people. Each time it is made clear that it is God who saves, through the judge.

5. All is going well for the people . . . the sin-cycle starts again.

Outline

Message

1. Seven years of oppression.
Note the drastic conditions to which Israel was brought, living like cave-men in the mountains, before they were ready to ask God for help. 6:1–6

2. A thankless task.
The judges had the glory of being deliverers and received the thanks of God's people. This unnamed prophet had the unpleasant task of bringing God's message of judgement. But he did the job God gave him. 6:7–10

3. God appears to Gideon.
When God saves it must be seen to be God saving, not man (see Deuteronomy 7:6–11), and so God chooses a nobody, Gideon, someone he can use who will not take any credit for himself. 6:11–24

4. A crucial decision.
Gideon has yet to declare himself. He is made to take an irrevocable step: he challenges Baal and he takes his stand for God. Note his father's argument when the people want to punish Gideon for breaking down Baal's altar: 'If Baal is really a god, he can defend himself when someone breaks down his altar'! But he couldn't because he wasn't God. 6:25–32

5. Putting out a fleece.
But Gideon had his doubts, understandably.

See how patient God was with him, and his need for encouragement. 6:33–40

6. Midian defeated.
Their army looked like a swarm of locusts (7:12). Gideon had only 32,000 men. This was still a sizeable army for Israel. Cut back to 10,000 when the fearful lot went home. Cut back to 300 when those who relaxed their vigilance were sent home. But 300 plus God were enough.
7:1–25

7. More problems for Gideon.
The Ephraimites wanted to be in on the victory (although they might not have been so keen before the fight began). Note Gideon's restrained response under real provocation. And the people of Succoth didn't help Gideon. They wanted to be sure of the result before backing either side. So Gideon managed without them. But they missed the thrill of being on the winning side. 8:1–21

8. Gideon becomes a problem.
Tragedy: victory turns the head. Or was it gold that turned his head; gold that took the place of God? 8:22–27

9. Gideon's death.
The people return to the worship of Baal. 8:28–35.

Application

1. The weakness of unaided man.
The book of Judges covers a period of about

400 years. In this comparatively short period twelve deliverers had to be found to rescue

JUDGES

the Israelites from the consequences of their own behaviour. They could not have been ignorant of history. They must have known what had always happened when they abandoned God. Yet again and again they went the same route, the route of rebellion.

'All that we learn from history is that we learn nothing from history.' Spiritually, at least, this seems to be true. Man without God is helpless. The Christian without the Spirit of God cannot cope. The book of Judges gives us an unmistakable object lesson, showing us our need of a Saviour.

2. The undeserved grace of God.
The second great lesson of Judges is that God is always and unconditionally ready to

forgive and to rescue the repentant (Isaiah 65:1–3). But this second lesson is a reminder that we are expected to show others the same kind of grace. More than this; if we don't forgive others, we cannot expect to be forgiven (Matthew 6:15).

3. Leaders need humility.
The third great teaching of Judges is that it is God who judges and God who delivers, not man. It is easy for those who are leaders to imagine that God needs them, or the church needs them; that they are indispensable. Notice how God picks Gideon, least important of his family and out of the least important of the clans. God plus a nobody means power!

Key themes

1. The danger of syncretism.
Syncretism is mixing things up; the good and the bad, God's things and man's things.

When the Israelites went into Canaan they found many religions to choose from. The Canaanites' gods seemed to help them to grow crops and fight battles. But their worship was grossly immoral.

The Canaanites remained and worked for the Israelites (1:28,30,33,35). But Canaanite religion gradually weakened Israel, and took them away from God. Note our Lord's words; you can't serve God and Mammon (Matthew 6:24). Study the Bible teaching on separation (eg. 1 Corinthians 5; 2 Corinthians 6:14–18; 1 John 2:15–17).

2. The crucial decision.
The Christian is converted **from** one way of life **to** another. Very often the point of conversion involves a crisis. We know that there will be no going back. It might mean doing something new, say going to church. It

might mean giving away my money. For Gideon it meant pulling down an idol.

It is impossible just to try out Christianity to see if it works. Just as Gideon cut off his way of retreat and put himself entirely into God's hand, so do we, when we come to Christ.

Study some of the crisis decisions of the Bible. Note the magicians who burned their magic books (Acts 19:19); Ruth, who stayed with her mother-in-law. (Ruth 1:1–18); and Rahab who decided to shelter Joshua's spies (Joshua 2:1–21; 6:22–25). What crisis decisions can you think of for people who become Christians today?

3. Repentance.
That was the one condition of deliverance for Israel. But what is repentance? Use a concordance to study this vital theme in the Bible. Here are some Scriptures to get you started: Matthew 21:28–32; Luke 15:3–7, 17–20; 2 Samuel 12:7–17; Psalm 51:1–10; Acts 8:20–22; 2 Corinthians 7:9–11.

RUTH

Loyalty rewarded

BACKGROUND. Ruth has been described as the book of human loyalty. No one knows who wrote it. It relates to the period of the Judges and gives us insight into the domestic life of Israel at that time. The story itself covers a period of about ten years.

PURPOSE. Ruth is basically the tale of the friendship of Ruth with her mother-in-law, Naomi. It is of special interest because it reminds us that King David was a descendant of Ruth and her husband, Boaz. Furthermore, on the human side Jesus could trace his ancestry back through Ruth (Matthew 1:5). Thus the book tells us that the messianic family from which over a thousand years later the Messiah was born included someone who was not a Jew.

SPECIAL FEATURES. Ruth gives us a glimpse of marriage customs at that time. It was the duty of the next of kin of a widow who had children to take the deceased husband's place. This responsibility normally fell to the dead man's brother (Deuteronomy 25:5–10). Ruth's husband, Mahlon, had died without leaving any children. Boaz was not her brother-in-law, but he is described as a relative of Naomi (2:1). Ruth had to show Boaz that she was interested in the possibility of marriage, and this she did (3:1–18).

Boaz recognised he was a relative of Ruth, but pointed out that there was a nearer relation than he. Only if the nearest relative declined was it possible for Boaz to take his place. In chapter four we are told of the process by which Ruth eventually became wife to Boaz. There was the further complication: whoever married Ruth would be required to redeem a portion of land which Naomi was selling on her behalf. The nearest relative was not prepared to do this (4:6), and accordingly waived his rights (4:7,8). The way was now clear for Boaz to marry Ruth.

Outline

RUTH

Message

God is concerned for the everyday lives of each of his people. This is seen in God's overruling in the case of human relationships:

1. In Ruth's loyalty to Naomi in her bereavement. 1:1–22
When Elimelech, Naomi's husband, died, her daughters-in-law stood by her, and Ruth actually returned to Bethlehem with her, since she was not prepared to see her mother-in-law left to a lonely old age.

2. In Ruth's first contact with Boaz. 2:1–23
Boaz's kindness to Ruth went far beyond the law's demands. Daughter-in-law and mother-in-law rejoiced together in the Lord's goodness.

3. In Boaz's response to Ruth. 3:1–18
Once more we see the goodness of the Lord in that, strictly speaking, Boaz was not Elimelech's closest relative, yet he looked with favour on Ruth and was prepared to become her 'kinsman-redeemer'.

4. In the marriage relationship. 4:1–22
Boaz married Ruth and she presented Naomi with a grandson, who was to become the grandfather of King David, the founder of the royal line of Israel.

Application

1. Use your common sense.
Naomi was genuinely solicitous for the well-being of her daughter-in-law. She gave Ruth wise counsel, and Ruth willingly accepted the advice she was given. Godly living calls for sanctified common sense, and provides opportunities for helping one another in practical ways.

2. Keep to the rules.
Boaz was very happy to marry Ruth but he was concerned that justice should be seen to be done. He would not proceed until the nearest relative had publicly renounced his claims. God is a God of order and it is wise not to try to circumvent correct procedures.

3. Remember God overrules in our lives.
In due course Ruth was able to bring encouragement to Naomi, in presenting her with a grandchild. That child in turn had a son whom he named Jesse, and Jesse had eight sons the youngest of whom was David! God was working out his purpose in Ruth's circumstances even though she was not aware of it.

RUTH

Key themes

1. Human need.
The Bible is never romantic when describing human need. Here we have a realistic picture of the desperate plight of two widows who in those days had no means of support. In Moab, Naomi's situation was even worse, as she was also a foreigner. God can enter the poorest of social conditions and work out his purposes through them. What is the significance of Christ's reference to the poor in Luke 4:18?

2. Loyalty.
Ruth's commitment to her mother-in-law is an outstanding expression of love and loyalty. God honours such faithfulness. Orpah disappears off the pages of Scripture. Ruth is numbered among the ancestors of the Messiah. In what ways does modern society fail to maintain biblical standards of responsibility to the family? How is this affecting relationships in Christian families?

3. God's overruling.
Trace the way in which God's purpose works itself out throughout the book even when those involved were not aware of the fact. What grounds have we for believing that God is similarly at work in our circumstances today? (See Romans 8:28,29)

1 SAMUEL

How Israel got a king

A TALE OF THREE PEOPLE. 1 and 2 Samuel were originally one book. However, whereas the second volume deals solely with King David, the first has to do with three characters whose lives overlapped – Samuel, Saul and David. The account is not complete; whoever put it together used more than one source. This does not matter as long as we remember that for the ancient authors what the event **meant** was more important than its exact timing. This is more than bald history; it is the story of God's dealings with his people. At the same time the accounts are certainly truthful. Even national heroes like David appear as being rather mixed up and very human.

'WE WANT A KING'. The book of Judges concludes by telling us that anarchy prevailed in Israel in those days because 'Israel had no king' (Judges 21:25). Although Samuel, the last judge, was popular, his influence was local and limited. The people needed a national leader. However, their request for a king was not just a criticism of Samuel's leadership; it showed how human their expectations were. Only God, in fact, could lead them to victory; their defeats were not because they lacked a king, but because they had forgotten the covenant (10:18,19; 12:6–15). They were already adopting pagan worship.

The idea of kingship was not wrong in itself, but they wanted a king like the pagan nations around them. Samuel warned them that kings have great potential for good – and for evil – as they would learn.

THE PHILISTINES. Because they never eliminated them when they settled in Canaan, Israel's neighbours were a constant threat to their security. We read about the Amorites, the Amalekites and the Ammonites, but most about the Philistines. These latter lived in five cities on the coastal plain – Ashdod, Gath, Ekron, Gaza, and Ashkelon – and had a stranglehold on Israel (13:19–21). Saul and Jonathan started a revolt, but it was King David who finally dealt with the Philistines, and with the others, once and for all.

Outline

1 ELI AND
SAMUEL
1:1–7:17

1:1–2:11 Hannah's answered prayer
2:12–3:21 Judgement for Eli's family
4:1–6:21 The ark lost and restored
7:1–17 Ebenezer: God has helped us

2 SAMUEL AND
SAUL
8:1–15:35

8:1–22 Israel asks for a king
9:1–11:15 Saul chosen and confirmed
12:1–25 Samuel hands over
13:1–15:35 Saul fails to measure up

3 SAUL AND
DAVID
16:1–31:13

16:1–23 David chosen: Saul rejected
17:1–18:30 David triumphs: Saul is jealous
19:1–26:25 God's man on the run
27:1–12 David's duplicity
28:1–25 Saul's desperation
29:1–30:31 David defeats the Amalekites
31:1–13 Saul kills himself

1 SAMUEL

Message

1. Samuel, the servant of the Lord.
- [ ] Samuel was an answer to prayer, and his godly mother's dedication gave him the best start to life. This may have meant that he was to live as a Nazirite, although usually this meant a temporary rather than a life-long vow. 1:10, 11,27,28; 2:26; Numbers 6:1–21
- [ ] In days when God's voice was not being heard in Israel, Samuel stood out as being one to whom God appeared and who had the gift of a seer – that is, he could see what others could not. 3:1–10,19–21; 9:9
- [ ] Samuel comes across as a man of God and of great personal integrity. He was certainly not in it for what he could get out of it, like his sons. His reaction to Saul's steady decline shows that he put God first. 9:6; 12:3–5; 15:11,35

2. Saul, the king who went wrong.
- [ ] Saul was a man who began well and with great promise. Anointed as a sign that God had chosen him for the task, he was modest, large-hearted, and spiritually gifted, acting with great decision in time of crisis. 10:1,10,22; 11:6,12,13
- [ ] However, we can follow his gradual deterioration as he began to take matters into his own hands, make rash vows and disobey God's commands. His son Jonathan shamed him by his simple nobility. Saul, by contrast, became jealous, bitter and depressed, wasting his time and energy hunting down David.
- [ ] Desperate for guidance, he stooped to spiritualism, which earlier he had banned, and at last became one of the Bible's rare suicides. 13:8–14; 14:24; 15:9–29; 16:14; 18:8–12; 28:6,7; 31:4

3. David, the Lord's choice.
- [ ] As God's replacement for Saul, David was a man whose heart was right and whose faith was great. No wonder Jonathan found him such an attractive friend. Specially gifted by the Spirit for his work, he was able to mould a rabble into an effective fighting force or take on a giant single-handed. He waited for God to avenge him, regularly asking for guidance and trusting him for deliverance. A great leader, he was to become Israel's greatest king. 16:7,13,18; 17:26,34–37,45–51; 18:1–4; 22:5–15; 23:2,4,9–12; 24:12; 30:6–8, 23–25
- [ ] Even David is drawn in very human terms. He could get angry and be tempted into rash action, and he could deceive. God's dealings with him as with us were in grace. 25:32–34; 27:10–12

Application

1. God answers prayer.
Whether it is an individual praying about her personal distress, or leaders interceding for their people, this book tells us that God answers earnest prayer. Prayer is seen as a ministry which we can exercise on behalf of others. In answer to prayer God grants and does what is humanly impossible.

2. God looks after his own.
In spite of the people's disobedience, God is committed to work out his saving purpose

and to defend his honour. He can do this without any human help at all, if necessary. At other times he gives his people leaders who will take them to victory.

When we are in God's will, success does not depend on human strengths or ability. He can take the weakest and use them for his glory if they trust him.

3. We must be right with God.

God chooses and uses those whose hearts are right with him. He gifts, empowers and blesses those who serve him. He is equally prepared to judge and confound those who disobey him. So a good start is no guarantee of future success. We need to keep right with him, obedient and trusting, if we want to see his continued blessing.

Key themes

1. Prayer and praise.

There is a good deal in this book about prayer and praise. In particular, we see God's man seeking his guidance when it comes to making important decisions. See 1:10–18; 2:1–10; 7:5,6,12; 8:6,21; 12:18,19,23; 15:11; 22:15; 23:2–4,9–12; 30:7,8.

2. Rules for service.

There are some basic conditions for spiritual progress which cannot be ignored if we are to know God's blessing. See 2:30; 7:3,4; 12:14,15,20–25; 15:22,23,26; 16:7; 26:23. Constrast the superstition of the Israelites who thought they could manipulate God into acting for them (4:1–11). Note that they had a reputation but no power.

3. Spiritual gifts.

As in the book of Judges we see God specially gifting those who would serve him. When God's Spirit came on them, they were able to do what they could not naturally do before. See 10:6,7,9–13; 11:6; 16:13. (Compare 19:23,24 where the Lord seems to be restraining but not recommissioning Saul.) At the same time we have evidence that this need not be permanent, nor did it mean that thereafter they lived holy lives. There is no replacement for a continuous relationship with God.

2 SAMUEL

The house of David

DAVID'S LINE. 2 Samuel has sometimes been regarded as the Court Chronicles of David. We are told about his successes, his failures and sins, and in particular, the treachery and domestic strife he had to endure.

However, embedded in this story is a promise which found its fulfilment in Christ. David was not just God's choice for that time; he was to head up a line which would lead to the Messiah himself.

DAVID'S ENEMIES. David's great gift was that of military commander. He attracted 'mighty men' whose exploits became legends in their own time.

Once on the throne of all Israel, he consolidated his kingdom by dealing with his unruly neighbours in a series of campaigns (8:1–14; 10:1–19; 11:1; 12:26–31). This secured his territory against raids, and gave him control of a larger area than ever before.

DAVID'S ADMINISTRATION. Occasionally we are told who held office in David's government (8:15–18; 20:23–26). Absalom's ability to fire the people's discontent (15:1–6) suggests that David was not the most efficient administrator. Although David could inspire intense loyalty, the fact that Absalom could stir up civil war means that, probably, as the king got older, he lost his grip on things somewhat. It has been suggested that the census he took was so wrong because it might have been connected with plans for forced labour (24:1–10), something his son Solomon was to exploit cruelly.

DAVID'S DOMESTIC PROBLEMS. Polygamy was not forbidden in the Old Testament, but the story of David's home life shows its perils. In those days, many wives and concubines, and a large family, were seen as a status symbol. However, it involved real dangers. Every son was a potential heir to the throne, and if headstrong, a threat to his father.

Added to this, David does not come across as the best of parents. He failed to discipline his children as he ought, and suffered as a consequence.

Outline

1 SAD NEWS ABOUT SAUL
1:1–27

1:1–16 An unexpected reward
1:17–27 How the mighty have fallen!

2 DAVID OVER JUDAH
2:1–4:12

2:1–7 A welcome at Hebron
2:8–32 A bitter encounter
3:1–39 Joab gets revenge
4:1–12 Tragic death of a weak king

3 THE KINGDOM CONSOLIDATED
5:1–9:13

5:1–5 King over all Israel
5:6–16 David takes Jerusalem
5:17–25 Reckoning for the Philistines
6:1–23 Bringing up the ark
7:1–29 God's love for David
8:1–14 Victories all round
8:15–18 How the country was run
9:1–13 David's magnanimity

4 VICTORY AND SORE DEFEAT
10:1–12:31

10:1–19 Teaching the Ammonites a lesson
11:1–27 David defeats himself
12:1–31 Moment of truth for a king

5 CIVIL WAR
13:1–20:26

13:1–39 Amnon's stupidity and Absalom's revenge
14:1–15:12 Prelude to disaster
15:13–16:14 David forced to flee
16:15–17:29 Delaying tactics
18:1–19:43 Absalom slain; David restored
20:1–26 Sheba's rebellion

6 ABOUT GIBEONITES AND PHILISTINES
21:1–22

7 DAVID'S TESTIMONY
22:1–23:7

22:1–51 The Lord is my rock
23:1–7 What kingship should mean

8 DAVID'S MIGHTY MEN
23:8–39

9 DAVID COUNTS HIS PEOPLE
24:1–25

2 SAMUEL

Message

1. David's faith.
☐ David is described as a man whose men would protect and follow him to their deaths if necessary. He was absolutely impartial in his judgements, and very careful to do what was right in all circumstances. He was ready to punish those who deserved it, and to reward those who earned it. Yet he could equally feel for others and share their grief. 1:11–27; 3:36; 4:9–12; 15:21; 18:3; 23:13–17

In his dealings with Mephibosheth, who as Saul's son was a possible rival, and who would simply have been eliminated in any other regime, his behaviour reflects something of God's gracious dealings with us. 9:1–13

☐ David simply believed God and trusted him: that was the reason for the success he had. We find him regularly praying and seeking God's guidance. Equally we see him publicly expressing his praise and joy in God without a care of what other people thought about him. He was a grateful man who could speak and sing God's praises, freely acknowledging that he was what he was by God's grace. 2:1; 5:19,23–25; 6:14–23; 15:31; 21:1; 22:1–51

☐ He was a man who could accept his reverses in a spirit of humble submission. Even when he was in the wrong, he was quick to repent and put things right with God, taking God's discipline without grumbling. 12:13,15–23; 15:25,26; 16:10–12; 24:10,14,24

2. David's faults.
☐ In spite of his impartiality, David found it hard to discipline others at times. He allowed Joab quite literally to get away with murder. He tolerated Amnon's rape of his sister, and was soft with Absalom to the point of stupidity. 3:28,29; 13:21, 23–39; 18:4,5,32,33; 19:1–4
☐ He gave in to temptation, misusing his privileges as any pagan monarch might have done in those days. What is more, in trying to cover up his adultery with Bathsheba, he compounded his sin with murder. 11:1–27
☐ He neglected his duties and let things slide, thus opening himself to severe criticism. 15:1–4

Application

1. God prospers and protects.
Those who trust in God and seek to live in his will can leave their affairs with him. He is prepared to guide, to be a refuge in times of trouble, and to lead his people 'into a spacious place'. His purposes may seem a long time in coming to fruition, but he has pledged himself to see us through.

2. We are all prone to temptation.
Human nature is the same now as it was then. Satan tempts us through what we see and feel, but this does not mean that we have to give in. We have to remember our duty to God and obey him, rather than yield to our selfish inclinations.

2 SAMUEL

3. What about our families?
It is no good succeeding in our public lives if our domestic affairs do not honour God. The very first place where we must prove him is in our homes and in our family relationships. Real love means discipline and obedience. In this way parents are real fathers and mothers to their children, and children true sons and daughters.

4. Getting right with God.
When we sin and become aware of our stupidity, it is no good trying to cover our tracks. The only thing we can do is to admit our guilt and ask for forgiveness, accepting whatever discipline God might send. In this respect we also need to remember that earlier successes and victories are no guarantee against future failures. Age also is no proof against trials. In fact, it might even bring new temptations.

Key themes

1. Son of David.
God's agreement with David, which we call 'the Davidic covenant', was that all future true kings of Israel would come from his family (7:11–16; 23:5). It was for this reason that the Jews in Jesus' day were looking for a Messiah – that is, an 'anointed one' – who would fulfil all the ideals of kingship as David's descendant. See how this works out in the New Testament: Matthew 1:1,17; Luke 1:32,33,69; Mark 10:47,48; Matthew 9:27; 15:22; 21:9; Mark 11:10; Matthew 22:41–45; Acts 13:22,23; Romans 1:3; Revelation 3:7; 5:5; 22:16.

2. David's Lord.
David owed everything he had to God whose character shines through these chapters in a variety of ways. Note especially the different expressions of his holiness (6:6,7; 12:1–14; 24:1), and work through those passages which tell us most about him (7:5–29; 22:1–23:7). List out the ways in which God is described, and how we must therefore respond to him.

3. Treachery.
There is a great deal about human deceitfulness and wickedness in this book. Note how David's men, family and subjects all failed him, displaying human nature at its worst. Perhaps it was because David did not know at times who he could trust, that he cultivated such a faith in God who is absolutely trustworthy (7:28; 22:1–3, 26,31,32,47).

1 KINGS

The kingdom united and divided

THE BOOK. 1 Kings is the first half of what was originally a single book giving an account of the life of Israel during the four centuries from the death of David to the deportation of the people to Babylon. It tells us how a strong and united nation was divided into two; how the larger northern kingdom of Israel continually turned its back on God and was eventually wiped out; how Judah also failed to keep the covenant and how she, too, was overtaken by disaster, coming to a head with the destruction of Jerusalem and the mass deportation to Babylon. 1 Kings covers the first 120 years of the story.

WHO WROTE IT? The book was probably written by a prophet or a group of prophets writing in Babylon during the exile, sometime around 550 BC. Material was drawn from many different sources, such as official government records or collections of stories about the prophets, and then brought together in such a way as to emphasise the points the author wanted to make.

HIS PURPOSE. In 1 and 2 Kings the writer is not trying to give a complete history of the whole period. He spends a good deal of time telling us about events and people he sees as important, such as Solomon or Elijah, but skips very quickly over others. Kings is concerned only with the significance that events have for the development of the spiritual life of the people.

HIS POINT OF VIEW. The concern of the author is to show how important it was that God's people keep God's covenant. Men and nations are both judged according to how closely they seek to follow God's will. If they love God and keep his laws, he will bless them; if they turn away from him, then disaster will follow. In many cases the attitude of the king is seen as summing up the attitude of the nation as a whole; in one sense the king is presented as a representative of the people.

HIS METHOD. The story of the two nations of Israel and Judah is easy to follow if we realise the system used. We are kept up to date by being told about each country in turn. A description of the events in the life of a king in Israel, for example, is followed by the story of all the kings of Judah who came to the throne during his reign, and so on.

Outline

1 KINGS

Message

1. God is the powerful Lord of history.
☐ Rehoboam tried to leave God out of the reckoning and that can never be done. It was God's judgement and not the people's revolt that really caused him to lose ten tribes. Even before Solomon died Jeroboam had been appointed by God to rule Israel. 11:26–12:24
☐ Ahab had seen a demonstration of God's power when Baal's prophets were defeated on Mount Carmel. In spite of this, in the Syrian war, Ahab tried to avoid God's purposes by going in disguise; but he died just as God had said. 18:1–46; 22:5–40

2. It is only work for God that counts.
☐ Solomon was rich, wise and powerful, and for many years he loved and served God, but that didn't mean he could then do what he liked. When he sinned, God punished him just like anyone else. 3:1–11:43
☐ Omri was very successful. He gave Israel a new capital and put her on the commercial map, but Kings only comments that he sinned against God. 16:15–28

3. God can be trusted.
☐ God gave Jeroboam a kingdom, but he didn't trust God to stop the people defecting back to Judah. Instead, he broke God's law and built a golden image. He learned that God does keep promises – to bless and to punish! 12:25–14:20
☐ When God gives a job he also gives the means to get it done. He provided for Elijah all through the drought and showed him how to fight the worship of Baal. 17:1–18:46

4. God doesn't easily write people off.
☐ To disobey God and to receive his punishment does not mean that we can no longer serve him. The Judeans learned this after the kingdom was split. God had punished them but he was still their God and still spoke his word to them. 12:1–24
☐ None of Israel's first seven kings served God, but God did not yet give up on Israel. He still wanted their worship, and on Mount Carmel gave them another unmistakable demonstration of his power. 18:1–46

Application

1 Kings teaches us:

1. About God's servant.
Elijah shows us some of the characteristics of a good servant of God.
☐ He listened to God's word (17:1,2,8).
☐ He waited for God's timing (18:1).
☐ He acted courageously (18:7–40).
☐ He explained himself clearly (18:21).
☐ He had total confidence in God (18:30–38).
☐ He kept faithfully to God's word (18:36).
☐ He persevered (18:41–45).

2. About God's service.
☐ God doesn't always use the tools we expect – he chose a foreign widow to help Elijah (17:8–16).
☐ To help God's servants is to serve God, and God rewards service (17:17–24; 18:3–15).

1 KINGS

☐ God restores his servants when they fall (19:4–8).
☐ One finished task does not mean a useless future (19:14–18).

3. About the Temple.
☐ It was built because of God's promise (8:15–21).

☐ It was a place for worship (8:22–26).
☐ It could never limit God (8:27).
☐ It was a place for prayer (8:28–40).
☐ It was to be open for people from all countries (8:41–43).

Key themes

1. The sovereignty of God.
This theme is brought out throughout the book, as it tells how God is involved in history.

Read 8:14–61; 19:9–18; 20:1–30. What do these passages tell us about God and his sovereignty?

2. Righteousness.
God expects his people to be obedient and loyal. After the land was divided, 1 Kings describes the reigns of eight kings of Israel and four kings of Judah.

Make a list of these kings. How many served the Lord? On what basis does the writer of Kings make his judgement of them?

3. Weakness.
☐ 1 Kings never tries to present us with an idealised picture of God's servants. We see their faults as well as their good points, for God accepted them and used them just as they were.

Look up 1:1–3:1; 11:1–13; 19:1–21. What weaknesses can you see in David, Solomon and Elijah?
☐ Read the story of Ahab in 18:1–22:40. We are told in 21:27–29 that he repented, and that because of this God lightened his punishment. Why do you think 1 Kings describes Ahab as evil, rather than just weak?

2 KINGS

Reforms and rebellions

THE BOOK. 2 Kings takes up the story of the nations of Israel and Judah just before the death of Elijah, and carries it through until Israel was destroyed and Judah exiled to Babylon. The overlap of the story of Elijah into 2 Kings reminds us that this is simply the second half of the single book of Kings. There is no real reason behind the point of division of 1 and 2 Kings, but as the two parts are about the same length, perhaps they fitted easily on two scrolls. Some of the information we find in Kings is also found in Chronicles, although the author of Chronicles writes from a rather different point of view and is interested only in the southern kingdom of Judah.

WHY IT WAS WRITTEN. 2 Kings covers about 270 years, more than twice the period dealt with in 1 Kings, but nevertheless half the space is given to the lifetime of one man, Elisha. Again, those who had significance for the spiritual life of the nation, such as Hezekiah and Josiah, are mentioned in some detail, whereas others, in spite of their long and prosperous reigns, are given only a brief note. The Jews recognised that the purpose of all the so-called historical books was really religious, and they put them in a category known as 'the former prophets'.

THE PROPHETS. Many of the writing prophets (known in the Hebrew Scriptures as 'the latter prophets') had their ministry during the time covered by 2 Kings, and their books give us much information about the extent of the corruption in both nations. However we learn very little from Kings about their work or their influence. We are told that Hezekiah went to see Isaiah but Amos, Hosea, Micah and Jeremiah are not mentioned at all. The concern of the writer of Kings is more with the way in which kings and people responded to God's message rather than with how and from whom they received that message.

THE KINGS. It is difficult to make a list of all the kings and their reigns because part years are always counted as whole years and where, as sometimes happened, a son ruled for a while as regent alongside his father, then that time is counted in the reigns of both.

Confusion can sometimes arise, too, over the names of the kings. There was a King Jehoram and a King Jehoash in both Israel and Judah, and as both these names are sometimes used in shortened forms, as Joram and Joash, we have to be careful to distinguish between them.

Outline

1 ELIJAH'S WORK ENDS – ELISHA'S BEGINS
1:1–3:27

1:1–18 Ahaziah sends to Baal-Zebub
2:1–12 Elijah is taken up to heaven
2:13–18 The prophets look for Elijah
2:19–22 Elisha purifies Jericho's water
2:23–25 Youths mock Elisha
3:1–27 Moab rebels

2 ELISHA – THE PEOPLE'S FRIEND
4:1–6:7

4:1–7 The poor prophet's widow
4:8–37 The wealthy woman and her son
4:38–44 The hungry prophets
5:1–27 Naaman, the Syrian commander
6:1–7 The man who lost an axe

3 ELISHA – THE PROPHET
6:8–8:29

6:8–23 Elisha outwits the Syrians
6:24–7:2 Samaria under siege
7:3–20 Four lepers bring good news
8:1–6 The wealthy woman is helped again
8:7–29 Kings of Syria, Israel and Judah

4 JEHU – THE FIERCE CHARIOTEER
9:1–10:36

9:1–13 Jehu is anointed king
9:14–10:17 Ahab's family is wiped out
10:18–28 Jehu destroys the Baal-worshippers
10:29–36 Jehu's enthusiasm wanes

5 INTRIGUE IN JUDAH
11:1–12:21

11:1–3 Wicked Athaliah takes control
11:4–21 Jehoiada outwits Athaliah

12:1–16 Joash repairs the Temple
12:17–21 Joash is killed

6 WAR AND PEACE
13:1–17:41

13:1–13 Israel and Syria at war
13:14–21 The death of Elisha
13:22–25 Syria is defeated by Israel
14:1–22 Amaziah of Judah – a good king
14:23–29 Jeroboam II of Israel
15:1–7 Azariah of Judah – a long reign
15:8–31 Five wicked kings of Israel
15:32–16:20 Jotham and Ahaz of Judah
17:1–41 Israel is conquered by Assyria

7 JUDAH ALONE
18:1–21:26

18:1–12 Hezekiah's reign begins
18:13–37 Jerusalem is besieged
19:1–7 Hezekiah asks Isaiah's advice
19:8–37 Assyria's letter: Hezekiah trusts God
20:1–11 Hezekiah is ill, but recovers
20:12–19 Messengers from Babylon
20:20,21 Hezekiah's death
21:1–26 Manasseh and Amon – evil kings

8 THE LAST CHANCE
22:1–25:30

22:1–7 Josiah repairs the Temple
22:8–20 The book of the law is found
23:1–25 Reforms are carried out
23:26–30 Josiah's death
23:31–37 Jehoahaz and Jehoiakim
24:1–7 Nebuchadnezzar conquers Jerusalem
24:8–25:17 The last king of Judah
25:18–30 Exile to Babylon

2 KINGS

Message

1. God is the powerful Lord of history.
☐ God is concerned for and in control of, not only Israel and Judah, but all the other nations as well. For very different reasons both Naaman and Hazael of Syria recognised the power of the God of Israel. 5:1–27; 8:7–15
☐ The forces of God are very real, and are always present with his people, even if not always visible. 6:15–17

2. It is only work for God that counts.
☐ Jehu started off with a real enthusiasm to serve God and to keep the worship of Israel pure, but his concern for God's service did not outlast his own rise to power. God recognised and rewarded the work Jehu did do, but it was not enough. 9:1–10:36
☐ Azariah was basically a good king, but his good start was spoiled by pride (2 Chronicles 26:16). This later failure meant that no spiritual progress was made during his reign, and therefore Kings skips over him very quickly. 15:1–17

3. God can be trusted.
☐ The rich woman from Shunem served God in a practical way by giving hospitality to Elisha. She wasn't looking for reward (4:13), but in time of crisis she knew that only God could help, and she trusted that he would. 4:18–37; 8:1–6
☐ Hezekiah faced some desperate situations, for the nation and for himself, but he took his problems to God, knowing that he could be trusted to deal with the situation, and in each case, God delivered him. 19:1–37; 20:1–11

4. God doesn't easily write people off.
In spite of their continued sin, God kept on working in Israel. Hardship had not brought them back to him, therefore in the time of Jeroboam II he gave them prosperity. Sadly, their response was not repentance, but even more moral and social corruption. They spurned God's mercy; therefore, in the end, judgement had to come. 14:23–29; 17:7–18

Application

2 Kings teaches us:

1. About God's servants.
God doesn't always choose the same kind of person. Elisha was a very different character from Elijah, but we can learn from him, too, about how to be a leader for God.
☐ He knew how to be a follower (2:1–8).
☐ He didn't mind doing the dirty work (3:11).
☐ He cared equally for rich and poor (4:1–37).
☐ He knew when to keep in the background (5:1–27).
☐ He had complete trust in God (6:15–17).
☐ He had insight into human nature (8:11).
☐ He cared about his people (8:12).
☐ He was not afraid to delegate (9:1–4).

2 KINGS

2. About God's service:

☐ It brings responsibility: God's servants are responsible for showing what God is really like. To take payment for service is not wrong, but Gehazi gave the impression that God's favour could be bought, and this was a very serious offence (5:20–27).

☐ God often works with imperfect people: Jehoahaz and Jehoash were not righteous kings, but they both acknowledged God's power to some extent and God rewarded them for it (13:1–25).

☐ God sometimes blesses the ungodly for the sake of his own people (3:13–15; 8:16–19).

☐ Faith and action must always go together. Any real turning to God must be accompanied by obedience to his word. Josiah knew that this was so (22:11–23:25).

Key themes

1. Response.

God is sovereign but Kings never sees this as implying that the actions or prayers of men do not matter. God does respond to men, and his dealings with them depend on their response to him.

God answered Hezekiah's prayer (19:14–19). Can you find other passages in 2 Kings where God makes a direct response to man's need?

2. Reform.

Hezekiah and Josiah both tried to lead the people back to God (18:1–20:21; 22:1–23:30). Read through these passages. Why do you think their reforms were not successful?

3. Righteousness.

God rewards righteousness and punishes evil. 17:7–18 is a summary of this message of Kings, and acts as a kind of obituary for the nation of Israel.

Judah was brought back from exile, Israel was not. What reasons can you find for this in the book of Kings?

4. Responsibility.

Elijah and Elisha are not the only men of God described in Kings. Look up 11:1–12:21; 22:1–23:30. What can we learn about leadership from the lives of Jehoiada, Joash and Josiah?

1 CHRONICLES

The spiritual history of Israel

WHAT IS 1 CHRONICLES ABOUT? 1 Chronicles is a history book chiefly concerned with King David's reign (1000-961BC).

The opening chapters (1-9) sum up all the earlier history of Israel by listing its families from Adam onwards. It also very briefly mentions Saul's downfall and Solomon's accession. But for the rest David occupies the centre of the stage on his own.

HOW WAS 1 CHRONICLES WRITTEN? 1 Chronicles does not have an author but a compiler, who has skilfully woven together a number of earlier works (see 9:1; 29:29,30) to make a unified history.

Jewish tradition claimed that the Chronicler, as he is called, was Ezra.

The book is part of a four-volume work which includes 2 Chronicles, Ezra and Nehemiah.

Various dates have been suggested as to when it was compiled. If Ezra was the editor, it must have been compiled in the fourth century, BC.

WHY WAS 1 CHRONICLES WRITTEN? The history to be found in 1 Chronicles is written from a particular point of view, not just recording the facts of history, but also spelling out the meaning of what happened. It is history written from God's viewpoint.

It was written when God's people were living in a very secular environment. Their nation had been destroyed by war, and consequently many lost faith. They could neither see God's hand in their affairs nor believe that he was a God who kept his promises. 1 Chronicles explains why their history took the course it did, and why belief was still possible.

IS 1 CHRONICLES RELIABLE? The Chronicler seems to select events from history to prove his argument, with the result that much of the story of Israel is left out and the picture he draws looks somewhat different from that found in Samuel or Kings. Among the omissions are the stories of Elijah and some of the less flattering events in David's life.

Despite this it cannot be said that 1 Chronicles is inaccurate. The Chronicler did not invent his story; he simply used what was there to draw out certain lessons for his own day. History is still written in this way. In fact, it is difficult when writing history not to select the evidence to argue a point. And that is all that the Chronicler does.

Outline

1 CHRONICLES

Message

1 Chronicles is essentially about the relationship of the people of Israel to their God. It emphasises:

1. The need for worship.
It should be:
- [ ] Joyful. The note of thanksgiving is often sounded here. 13:8; 15:16; 16:4–36; 29:22
- [ ] Musical. Music adds both to the enjoyment and the praise. 13:8; 15:16,28; 25:3,6,7
- [ ] Correct. They were not carried away with joy and did not worship God in any way they chose. Their worship was according to God's law. 15:2,12–15; 16:1,40; 23:31; 24:19
- [ ] Pure. Both cleansing and confession are necessary if worship is to be pleasing to God. 15:12–15; 23:28
- [ ] Humble. David's prayers stress how gracious God has been and how undeserved his generosity has been. There is no sense in which David feels he has 'rights' before God. 16:29,30; 17:16–27; 29:10–19

2. The need for obedience.
- [ ] Saul was overthrown because of disobedience. 10:13,14; 1 Samuel 28:3–25
- [ ] Uzzah is killed because of disobedience. 13:9,10; 15:2
- [ ] David is blessed because of his willingness to find out what God wants, and obey. 13:2; 14:10,14; 17:1–27; 22:13

3. The need for trust.
God can be trusted because:
- [ ] His promises come true. 11:2,3; 12:23; 17:26; 27:23
- [ ] He secures the outcome of battles. 14:10–17; 18:13; 19:13
- [ ] He controls the future. 17:9–14

4. The need for service
- [ ] that is the best for God. 13:7; 22:5
- [ ] that is alert to temptation. 21:1
- [ ] that is sacrificial. 21:24
- [ ] that is whole-hearted. 28:9
- [ ] that is willing. 28:9

Application

1. The message for the church.
- [ ] Worship should be:
  - an enjoyable celebration.
  - a musical thanksgiving.
  - a reverent observance.
  - a humble adoration.
- [ ] Service should be:
  - for the right motives.
  - in the right spirit.
  - not conducted casually.
  - the best for God.
- [ ] Buildings should:
  - reflect God's greatness.
  - not limit our vision of God.

2. The message for the Christian.
- [ ] Trust God confidently.
- [ ] Obey God completely.
- [ ] Serve God joyfully.

1 CHRONICLES

3. The message for the unbeliever.
☐ God is at work behind the events of our world.

☐ God is not to be treated lightly.
☐ God's people are not to be ill-treated.

Key themes

1. What we can learn about prayer.
Study the prayers of David (16:8–36; 17:16–27; 29:10–19). In what ways do they provide us with a pattern for our own prayers?

2. What we can learn about service.
It is easy to skip over the long list of names but to do so means missing some important truths. Look at some of the lists (eg. 12:23–37;25:1–8) and note what can be learned about Christian service from the way these men served David.

3. What we can learn about failure.
David's sin in conducting a census shows us that we need always to be alert to temptation. Study the incident (21:1–22:1) and see why David was in the wrong; how David had to suffer the consequences; what David learned, and how he reacted, and how good came out of it in the end.

4. What we can learn about buildings.
Present-day Christianity places great emphasis on buildings. Study God's refusal to allow David to build the Temple (17:3–15) and the preparations David made for the Temple (22:2–19). What dangers are mentioned about buildings, and what principles can be discovered?

5. What we can learn about election.
A major theme of 1 Chronicles is that God chose David and his family to reign over Israel in Jerusalem (16:13; 28:4–6,10; 29:1). Why is this truth emphasised here, and what is the practical purpose of the doctrine of election?

6. What we can learn about giving.
What principles are taught with regard to giving to God's work (29:3–5)? Trace the New Testament teaching (1 Corinthians 16:1,2; 2 Corinthians 8 and 9) and list the additional principles to be found there.

2 CHRONICLES

Lessons about faithfulness

THE CONTENTS OF 2 CHRONICLES. 2 Chronicles takes up the story of God's people where 1 Chronicles leaves off: with the reign of Solomon. It traces the varying fortunes of Judah through nearly four hundred years until the nation finally collapses; its people are exiled and its capital city is destroyed (587 BC). This devastation is not quite the final word. The very last verses of the book point the way forward to a hopeful future when the nation would be restored through an edict of Cyrus (36:23).

WHY THE BOOK WAS WRITTEN. The Chronicler has three reasons for writing:

1. To interpret history. He explains why some kings had peaceful and prosperous reigns whilst others ruled over years of unrest. The secret of success lay in faithfulness to God.

2. To teach lessons. In writing, the Chronicler is not content merely to unravel the past. He wants to call God's people to learn from the mistakes of history, and be faithful to him in the present.

3. To inspire faith. Many Jews felt that God had abandoned them. In explaining the inner reasons for their suffering, the Chronicler is encouraging them to believe again in a great and powerful God.

For detailed comments on the way in which 2 Chronicles was written see the notes on 1 Chronicles.

SPECIAL FEATURES. 1. The Chronicler is loyal to the house of David and shows how, despite every reason not to do so, God is faithful in keeping his promise that David's throne would be secure (eg. 21:7).

2. The northern kingdom of Israel is seen as wrong to have broken away from the throne of David (13:1-12). Throughout the book Israel's actions are seen as evil (eg. 21:6,13). The history of Israel is ignored except where it can be used as a warning against wrong-doing.

3. The events of history are used in a very selective way in order that their full spiritual significance may stand out. The Chronicler neither invents nor twists history; he is not inaccurate. 1 and 2 Kings give a much fuller picture of the story of both Israel and Judah but they do not show the same concern to use history to teach spiritual lessons.

Outline

2 CHRONICLES

Message

1. The importance of the covenant.
The central message of 2 Chronicles is found in 15:2: 'The Lord is with you when you are with him. If you seek him, he will be found by you, but if you forsake him, he will forsake you.'

God's relationship with his people was controlled by an agreement in which God blessed them as long as they obeyed him. This book vividly illustrates the outworking of that principle in the history of Judah. Keeping the covenant leads to prosperity; breaking the covenant leads to ruin.

2. The Lord of the covenant.
- [ ] He is great. 2:6; 6:18
- [ ] He is good. 5:13
- [ ] He is just. 12:6
- [ ] He is powerful. 13:12
- [ ] He prospers those who trust him. 13:18; 17:5,6; 20:20; 25:7−9; 27:6
- [ ] He helps the powerless. 14:11; 20:12, 15−17
- [ ] He is long-suffering. 21:7

3. The law of the covenant.
- [ ] The law spells out what men must do to experience God's full blessing. 6:16; 33:8
- [ ] Ignoring it leads to disaster. 12:1,2
- [ ] Revival leads to spreading the law. 17:9
- [ ] The law concerns human affairs. 19:10
- [ ] The law concerns correct worship. 23:18; 29:15
- [ ] Obedience leads to prosperity. 31:21
- [ ] Because of sin man often needs to repent and renew his commitment to the law. 14:2−5; 17:6; 24:1−14; 29:1−31:21; 34:1−35:27

4. The men of the covenant.
- [ ] They need to keep on obeying right to the end. 16:1−14; 24:17−27; 26:16−23
- [ ] They must beware of the danger of pride. 32:24−31
- [ ] They must keep alert to the voice of God. 19:2,3; 20:35−37; 35:20−26
- [ ] They must bear the consequences of sin. 35:20−25
- [ ] They can respond to the good news of forgiveness. 33:10−20

Application

1. To world governments.
- [ ] God controls the affairs of all nations.
- [ ] God expects obedience from all nations.
- [ ] God uses the destiny of each nation for his own ends.
- [ ] God outshines the wealth of all nations.

2. To Christian believers.
- [ ] As worshippers:
  - Worship centres on God's greatness.
  - Worship requires careful obedience.
  - Worship must be kept pure.
  - Worship implies joyful praise.
  - Worship involves cheerful giving.
- [ ] As workers:
  - Service must be willing.
  - Service must be prompt.
  - Service must be for the Lord.
- [ ] As disciples:
  - We must renew our commitment often.
  - We must be ready to meet temptation daily.
  - We must listen to the voice of God carefully.
  - We must aim for consistent discipleship.

2 CHRONICLES

Key themes

1. Wisdom.
Look at Solomon's request, and note why God was pleased with it and what resulted from it (1:7–17). Is wisdom on our prayer list?

2. The Temple.
List the lessons which can be learned from the way Solomon built the Temple: the things he said to God, and God said to him (2:1–7:22).

3. Spiritual props.
What does the experience of some of the kings (22:3; 24:17–19; 26:5) teach about the blessings and dangers of fellowship with more mature Christians?

4. Suffering.
Suffering may be a messenger from God (16:12; 32:24,25; 33:10–13); the crucial issue is our reaction to suffering. How else might God speak to us today?

5. Change.
The book contains many examples of kings who change for the worse and of one who changes for the better. Who are they? What dangers do those who are unfaithful point out? Does our gospel really allow for dramatic change (33:1–20)?

6. Praise.
Study the rich teaching concerning praising God (5:11–14; 6:14–42; 20:15–30). What does it say to the church today about the reasons and content of our worship?

7. Guidance.
What was wrong with Ahab's method of seeking guidance (18:1–34)? To what extent do we make the same mistakes?

8. Giving.
What are the chief lessons that 2 Chronicles teaches about giving (24:10; 31:2–21)? Search out the New Testament teaching on this subject.

9. Faith.
Write down the areas in your life where you need to practise faith, as Jehoshaphat did (20:20).

EZRA

A nation rises from the dust

THE BACKGROUND. Jerusalem had been destroyed by the Babylonian army in 587 BC, and the people of Judah taken into exile. It was to be almost fifty years before the Babylonian empire was overthrown by the Persians. Their ruler Cyrus adopted a new policy of allowing exiles to return to their homes, giving them every assistance in rebuilding their temples and in restarting their worship. Many Jews had become so comfortable in their exile that they did not wish to return to their native land. Ezra opens with some Jews returning home in about 538 BC. Chapters 1-6 tell the story of those next twenty-two years when, led by Zerubbabel, they faced much discouragement, but eventually finished rebuilding the Temple. Ezra himself is not introduced until 7:1. He led another group of exiles home in about 458 BC. Chapters 7-10 tell of the way in which he rebuilt the people themselves into a people whose lives were pleasing to God. It should be noted that there is a period of almost sixty years of silence between 6:22 and 7:1.

THE BOOK. The book of Ezra is part of a continuous story which runs from the beginning of 1 Chronicles to the end of Nehemiah. Note:

1. Ezra probably did not write the book himself although the second half draws on his diaries.

2. There are sometimes difficulties in working out the various dates. The story of the opposition under Artaxerxes (4:7-24) refers to a much later period than anything else in the first part of the book.

3. Ezra is not just a historical record. The author uses history to teach us how God deals with his people. Those lessons are still relevant.

EZRA. Ezra was a scholar who became Secretary of State for Jewish affairs under Artaxerxes. His life which must have been very impressive at the court is marked by three characteristics: he was devoted to the study of the Scripture (7:10); he displayed a daring trust in God (8:21-23) and he humbly showed solidarity with his people (9:6-15).

Outline

1 THE RETURN UNDER CYRUS 1:1–6:22

Rebuilding the Temple

1:1–11 Cyrus lets the Jews go home
2:1–67 List of exiles who returned
2:68–70 First things first in Jerusalem
3:1–6 The ancient worship is revived
3:7–13 The Temple foundation is laid
4:1–24 The Jews face opposition
5:1–17 The records are searched
6:1–12 The persecution pays a dividend
6:13–22 The Temple is finished

2 THE RETURN UNDER ARTAXERXES 7:1–10:44

Rebuilding the people

7:1–28 Ezra is ordered home
8:1–20 List of exiles who returned
8:21–36 The arrangements Ezra made
9:1–5 Sin exposed
9:6–15 Ezra's prayer of confession
10:1–5 The reformation begins
10:6–15 Straight talk from Ezra
10:16–44 The roll-call of dishonour

Message

1. What Ezra teaches about God.
Ezra speaks of God as the Lord of the heavens and the earth (1:2; 5:11), and yet a God who can be known and trusted by his people.

This God:
- [ ] Keeps his promises. 1:1
- [ ] Achieves his own ends. 1:1,5
- [ ] Maintains absolute holiness. 4:3; 9:15
- [ ] Turns bad into good. 5:3–6:12
- [ ] Takes a hand in people's lives. 7:27,28
- [ ] Protects his people. 8:21–23
- [ ] Answers their prayers. 8:23,31
- [ ] Above all, is good. 3:11

2. What Ezra teaches about worship.
The restoration of worship was the chief priority of the returning exiles. 3:1–6

The people who worshipped were:
- [ ] United. 3:1
- [ ] Joyful. 3:11–13, 6:16
- [ ] Uncompromised. 4:1–3, 6:21
- [ ] Repentant. 6:17
- [ ] Obedient. 3:2, 6:18

3. What Ezra teaches about sin.
- [ ] It needs to be treated seriously. 9:3,4; 10:6
- [ ] It may take the form of subtle compromise. 4:1–3; 9:1–3
- [ ] It demands honest confession without any attempt at self-justification. 9:5–15
- [ ] Its only cure is the mercy of God. 9:13
- [ ] It requires practical steps to get rid of it. 10:7–17

Application

1. For world leaders.
- [ ] God controls world affairs.
- [ ] God will bless those who treat oppressed people with justice.
- [ ] God will honour those who keep their word.

2. For the Christian church.
- [ ] Money should be given to God's work freely and generously.
- [ ] Worship should be offered to God joyfully.
- [ ] Unity in the church is important.
- [ ] Keep your worship pure: do not give up your distinctiveness by compromising with other faiths.

- [ ] A radical change in behaviour – giving up sinful behaviour – may be needed if God is going to bless you.

3. For the individual Christian.
- [ ] Make the worship of God a priority.
- [ ] Don't treat sin casually.
- [ ] Study the Scriptures seriously.
- [ ] Obey the Lord absolutely.
- [ ] Trust in the care of God.
- [ ] Give to God generously.
- [ ] Take practical steps to increase in holiness.

EZRA

Key themes

A number of themes in Ezra invite the Christian to review his own life with God.

1. Christian experience.
Ezra was aware that God was at work in his life and guiding his movements. Note especially the phrase, 'the hand of the Lord his God was on him' (7:6,9,28; 8:22,31). On what occasions have you been aware of God in your life?

2. Christian ambition.
Ezra's passion in life was the word of God (7:10). He studied it; obeyed it and taught it. Study and obedience are meant to go together. See how closely they are related in Psalm 119. In what ways has studying the Bible affected your life?

3. Christian giving.
The use of your material possessions is an indication of your spiritual state. The returning Jews gave spontaneously to God (2:68,69). Think over what you give to God in the light of the teaching in 2 Corinthians 8 and 9, and 1 Corinthians 16:2.

4. Christian purity.
Review your life with a view to discovering the points where you are likely to compromise your faith. What practical steps can you take to ensure you do not compromise?

5. Christian failure.
When you have failed, as the Jews had done, what have you done about it? Some try to forget it, but Ezra (9:1–10:44) teaches that it needs facing; confessing; mourning and putting right. Then true forgiveness can be known.

6. Christian faith.
Ezra was very brave to return to Jerusalem without an armed escort (8:21–23). Why did he do so? To what acts of faith, small or great, has God called you in your Christian life? To what extent does spiritual growth depend on such acts of faith?

NEHEMIAH

Rebuilding the walls

THE HISTORICAL BACKGROUND. After the death of Solomon, the kingdom of Israel was split into two – the northern and southern kingdoms. The capital of the northern kingdom was Samaria, and in 722 BC the Assyrians captured the city and carried off captive many of the people. Something rather similar happened to the southern kingdom, Judah, when Jerusalem was captured by the Babylonians in 586 BC. In 539 BC the Babylonians were themselves conquered by the Persians – and the king of Persia encouraged some of the Jews to return to their own land. About 50,000 did so and started on the task of rebuilding the Temple, but they became discouraged and only the foundation was laid.

The subsequent history is a little complicated but it seems that about sixteen or so years later God sent two prophets, Haggai and Zechariah, to stir up the people. They had settled down in their own houses but neglected to rebuild God's house. As a result work again started on the Temple and this time it was completed.

In 458 BC, another batch of Jews returned to Jerusalem under the leadership of Ezra. Ezra did his best to rally the people and lift their moral and spiritual tone, but he met with much discouragement. Some years afterwards, around 445 BC, God spoke to another man, Nehemiah, and called him to concentrate particularly on building the ruined walls of the city.

Some would place Ezra's return after that of Nehemiah, but the evidence is not conclusive.

WHO WAS NEHEMIAH? As royal cupbearer Nehemiah tasted the wine before passing it to the king, to prove that it was not poisoned. Only the most trustworthy attained this high position in the Persian king's palace. Yet Nehemiah's heart was set on doing the task to which he felt God was calling him. He has been described as a businessman whose whole life was steeped in prayer.

Nehemiah did not forget his own people. He was prepared to forsake the luxury of a royal court and go to Jerusalem to help in the rebuilding of the city. When eventually he did go there he went as civil governor with the authority of the king of Persia.

Outline

1 **THE BAD NEWS ABOUT JERUSALEM** 1:1–4

2 **NEHEMIAH'S PRAYER** 1:5–11

1:5 An appeal to God's covenant faithfulness
1:6,7 Contrition for the nation's sins
1:8–10 Remembrance of God's unfailing grace
1:11 A cry for help in time of need

3 **NEHEMIAH GETS HIS COMMISSION** 2:1–10

2:1–5 He makes his request to the king
2:6–9 The king gives his blessing
2:10 Early signs of opposition

4 **NEHEMIAH IN JERUSALEM** 2:11–20

2:11–16 Nehemiah inspects the walls
2:17–20 Nehemiah seeks co-operation for the task

5 **THE BUILDING OF THE CITY WALLS** 3:1–6:19

3:1–32 The distribution of the work
4:1–23 Opposition to the work
5:1–6:14 Internal dissension
6:15–19 The task completed

6 **EXILES WHO RETURNED WITH ZERUBBABEL** 7:1–73

7 **EZRA READS THE LAW** 8:1–18

8 **THE RENEWAL OF THE COVENANT** 9:1–10:39

9:1–38 Confession of sin
10:1–39 Assent to the covenant

9 **THE PEOPLE INVOLVED** 11:1–12:26

11:1–24 Residents in Jerusalem
11:25–36 List of villages
12:1–26 Priests and Levites

10 **DEDICATION OF THE WALLS AND ADMINISTRATION** 12:27–13:31

12:27–43 Dedication of the walls
12:44–47 The organisation of the Levites
13:1–31 Nehemiah's further reforms

NEHEMIAH

Message

Nehemiah comes across as the ideal worker for God. The key words are prayer and work. He not only prayed and worked himself but he inspired his followers to do the same.

1. Pray in every circumstance of life.
☐ He prayed when he heard of the state of Jerusalem. 1:4–11
☐ He prayed when he faced King Artaxerxes with his request to be allowed to go to Jerusalem. 2:4
☐ He prayed in the face of opposition. 4:4,9

☐ He prayed when false accusations were made. 6:8,9
☐ He prayed when the work was completed. 13:14

2. Prayer and work go hand in hand.
☐ He surveyed the scene beforehand to ascertain what was involved. 2:11–16
☐ He organised the work force so that everyone knew what was expected of them. 3:1–32
☐ He inspired others to work. 2:17,18; 4:6,23
☐ He recognised the sacredness of the work God had given him to do. 6:3

Application

1. Be burdened for your own people.
When Nehemiah received news of the tragic state of affairs in the battered city of Jerusalem he was overwhelmed by it.

2. Be ready for action.
Nehemiah wisely prayed before he took action. He sought guidance first, but having received it he was not slow to get to work.

3. Be prepared for opposition.
The work of God never goes unchallenged. Nehemiah found he had enemies both inside and outside the city, but he proved it is possible to triumph over all opposition.

4. Be aware of the danger of falling back.
Nehemiah called the people together to hear God's Word and they were responsive, but when he returned to the city after an absence of twelve years he found that the people had forgotten God and that a further reformation was necessary.

NEHEMIAH

Key themes

Nehemiah is clearly seen as the ideal worker for God – 'a man of patriotism and courage, fearless, enthusiastic and enterprising, a man of prayer and hard work, and one who feared God and sought his blessing.' His life was marked by a healthy balance between prayer and hard work. Study the references in this book to these two elements. Compare them with a similar study of Paul's life.

1. Patriotism.
Patriotism in itself is not wrong. Paul had a great burden for his own people (Romans 10:1). Christ encouraged his disciples to give 'Ceasar' his rightful place (Matthew 22:21). Nehemiah had a deep concern for his own people (1:3–11). True patriotism is concerned for the state of the nation. How can Christians today influence national attitudes?

2. Prayer.
Nehemiah turned to prayer at all times and under all circumstances (1:4; 2:4; 4:4; 5:19; 6:9,14; 13:14,22,29,31). Consider this alongside Paul's instruction in Philippians 4:6,7. What is the purpose of prayer?

3. Dedication.
Nehemiah took the work God gave him seriously – he was thorough. He was determined to know the exact state of affairs (2:12). He knew the sacredness of his work (6:3). He inspired others to work as well as himself (2:17,18; 4:6,23). List the tasks that need doing in your local church or group, and plan for their completion.

4. Perseverance.
Nehemiah was unmoved by opposition whether from within or without. He met ridicule and scorn by reliance on God (2:19,20). He refused to be distracted from the task in hand (6:2,3). Find information on those who suffer for Christ under hostile regimes, and use it to stimulate regular prayer. Think through your own situation in relation to opposition.

ESTHER

God rules behind the scenes

THE STORY IN BRIEF. Esther, the adopted daughter of her uncle Mordecai, is made queen to the Persian King Xerxes, otherwise known as Ahasuerus. His chief minister, Haman, hates the Jews and plots to exterminate them. His prime target is Mordecai. Esther skillfully gets the king to reverse his decision against the Jews, and Haman is hanged. Mordecai comes to power, and the Jews have something to celebrate.

THE SETTING. The story is set in the Persian capital of Susa during the rule of Xerxes who reigned 486-465 BC.

THE PURPOSE OF THE BOOK. There are three reasons why the book was written:

1. The most specific reason is to explain to the Jews the origin of the Feast of Purim which they celebrate between the 13th and 15th Adar (February-March). See 9:20–32 and 3:7.

2. Another clear reason for the book is to warn people against anti-Semitism. The Jews are God's special people who possess a unique place in history and an amazing power to survive against all odds. Esther is one episode in that intriguing history.

3. The book also demonstrates the power of God to control events and care for his people even when everything seems to be against them.

SPECIAL FEATURES.

1. The book never mentions God once, yet God can be seen everywhere.

2. The book shows a detailed knowledge of the Persian court and customs.

3. It is one of only two books in the Bible named after a woman.

4. Many have questioned the value of the book because of its strong Jewish nationalism and lack of reference to God. But its story and message are not be missed.

Outline

1 QUEEN VASHTI DEPOSED
1:1–22

1:1–9 The king throws a party
1:10–12 The queen refuses to go
1:13–22 The king deposes the queen

2 ESTHER BECOMES QUEEN
2:1–18

2:1–4 The king looks for a new queen
2:5–18 An orphaned Jewess is chosen

3 THE KING'S LIFE SAVED
2:19–23

4 HAMAN THE JEW-HATER
3:1–15

3:1–6 Haman plots to exterminate them
3:7–15 Haman involves the king

5 ESTHER TO THE RESCUE
4:1–5:8

4:1–17 Esther learns of the plot
5:1–8 Esther begins diplomatic moves

6 HAMAN BLOWS HIS TRUMPET
5:9–14

7 THE TABLES TURN
6:1–14

6:1–11 Mordecai rewarded for loyalty
6:12–14 Haman sulks

8 THE TRUTH IS OUT
7:1–8:17

7:1–10 Haman's plot is uncovered and Haman hanged
8:1–17 The king reverses his decree

9 THE JEWS CELEBRATE
9:1–32

9:1–17 The Jews get revenge
9:18–32 The Jews have a feast

10 MORDECAI'S FINAL HONOUR
10:1–3

ESTHER

Message

Esther makes two main points:

1. The providence of God.
The providence of God means that he is in ultimate control of the world. It also refers to his loving care for his people (Romans 8:28). In Esther note:

- [ ] God remembers his people. Many Jews, exiled in Persia, thought that God had forgotten them. They would have felt even more deserted when Haman plotted to destroy them. But God remembered them.
- [ ] God controls events. God placed Esther in a key position at the right time. He even made Xerxes have a sleepless night when necessary (6:1)!
- [ ] God times his moves perfectly. This is clear throughout the story, but note 4:14 particularly.
- [ ] God really is at work. He did not choose to work miraculously here. He simply worked through ordinary human relationships and diplomacy. None the less he really is at work. God is never in the forefront of this story, but his people know that he is there, working out all things for their good.

2. The people of God.
- [ ] God's special people. The story shows the Jews to be God's chosen people (see Deuteronomy 7:7,8). Esther is one more chapter in that relationship.
- [ ] God's secure people. They can rely on God's deliverance; although they know they will be secure only as long as they keep the covenant. See Psalm 81:13–16.
- [ ] God's honest people (2:19–23). The honesty of Mordecai and the brave honesty of Esther are key causes of the Jews' deliverance. God's people must be people of integrity. 7:1–10
- [ ] God's minority people. Although a minority, God's people can achieve amazing successes when he is with them.
- [ ] God's trusting people. In these crises the Jews trusted in God. 4:15,16

Application

Esther teaches us:

- [ ] To have confidence in God, for he cares.
- [ ] To trust in God, because his timing is perfect.
- [ ] To do what is right and leave the rest to God.
- [ ] To be brave, no matter what the cost.
- [ ] To resort to prayer in times of crisis.
- [ ] To care for minority racial groups.
- [ ] To remember God's special place for the Jews.

ESTHER

Key themes

Esther is a book of character studies. Look carefully at the following people:

1. Esther.
She is meek and attractive (2:1–18); dependent on God (4:15–17); brave (4:16); diplomatic (5:1–8; 7:1–6). What else would you say of her?

2. Mordecai.
You can read his character two ways. Either he was a scheming Jew who was motivated by a secular nationalism (see 2:10; 9:2–4), or he was a godly man motivated by his love for God's people (see 2:7,19–23; 4:1–17; 10:3). What do you make of him?

3. Haman.
His downfall was caused by greedy ambition (5:10–12), aided by his wife (5:14), and by her change of mind (6:13). He had a long way to fall (3:1,2). What has Haman to teach the church today about ambition?

JOB

Why do the innocent suffer?

ISRAEL'S WISE MEN. Along with the prophets and the priests, God's people were served by a group called 'the Wise'. These were counsellors and advisers who spent their time deciding on the wisest and most prudent ways to live and to govern. Their studies were always applied to real life. We see this in their books usually called 'the Wisdom Literature' (Job, Proverbs, Ecclesiastes, plus some of the Psalms).

Sometimes they put their advice into short pithy sayings or 'proverbs'. Elsewhere they dealt with the great problems of life, especially the problem of suffering.

WHO WAS JOB? We do not know any more about Job than the description at the beginning of the book. It seems that he was well-known (Ezekiel 14:14,20), but because there are no references to Israel's history, he may have lived very early on before God's people settled in Canaan. Some suggest that the story of his suffering was used by some unknown author as the setting for discussing the problem of suffering.

We do not know when the book was written either. Interest in God's wisdom goes back at least to Solomon's time, and the book could be as early as his reign.

THE PROBLEM. The book deals with the age-old question, 'Why do the innocent suffer?' Job was a good man who suddenly lost everything, which seemed, like much of our suffering, unjust and unfair. His friends' ready-made answer – that God judges the wicked, and therefore Job must be wicked – simply did not fit.

They say it in different ways. Eliphaz is polite and somewhat mystical. Bildad, the traditionalist, argues from what people had thought for years, while Zophar is the brash and blunt contender for God. All three eventually lose patience with Job. In fact, on the third round, Bildad says very little, while Zophar refuses to speak again. Job argues both with them and with God, and in so doing asks questions which were only to be answered in the New Testament. Because Elihu was a young man, he did not command the respect of the others. His arguments are full of youthful confidence but are also somewhat rambling and half-digested. They may have been a later addition to the book.

Outline

 WHY IT ALL HAPPENED
1:1–3:26

1:1–2:10 Satan tests Job
2:11–13 The friends arrive
3:1–26 Job asks 'Why?'

 THE FIRST DEBATE
4:1–14:22

4:1–5:27 Eliphaz states his case
6:1–7:21 Job mourns his lot
8:1–22 Bildad defends tradition
9:1–10:22 Job is bitter
11:1–20 Zophar defends God
12:1–14:22 Job protests his innocence

3 **THE SECOND DEBATE**
15:1–21:34

15:1–35 Eliphaz says he knows better
16:1–17:16 Job feels helpless
18:1–21 Bildad repeats his point
19:1–29 Job reaches out
20:1–29 Zophar agrees with his friends
21:1–34 Job contradicts them

4 **THE THIRD DEBATE**
22:1–31:40

22:1–30 Eliphaz accuses Job
23:1–24:25 Job wants justice
25:1–6 Bildad is exasperated
26:1–27:23 Job agrees and disagrees
28:1–28 In praise of wisdom
29:1–31:40 Job sums up

 ELIHU SPEAKS OUT
32:1–37:24

32:1–22 He is frustrated
33:1–33 Suffering is discipline
34:1–35:16 God can do no wrong
36:1–37:24 God knows what he is doing

6 **GOD REPLIES TO JOB**
38:1–42:6

7 **HOW IT ALL ENDED**
42:7–17

JOB

Message

1. Stripped down to faith.
- Job is an example of a man who trusted God when all was well and who continued to do so when everything went wrong. 1:1,20–22; 2:10
- He would have understood his losses as God's punishment, and yet he had sincerely done everything he could to serve God. God seemed to have abandoned him. 12:4; 13:19; 16:15–17; 23:10–12; 27:2–6
- His friends' accusations and his wife's opposition meant that he was entirely on his own. 2:9; 19:13–20

2. Worthless comforters.
- Job's friends were really no help at all. It would have been better if they had said nothing. 13:4,5; 16:2–3; 19:1–3
- Their main point, that God blesses the godly and judges the wicked, is quite true in a general sense. But it is wrong to apply it without qualification to the whole of life. It did not explain why the innocent sometimes suffered and the ungodly got away with it. 4:7; 5:19–26; 8:5–7,20–22; 11:13–20
- They concluded that as Job was suffering, it must be God judging his sins. Job's claim to innocence only made them more angry. 22:1–30

3. Suffering as discipline.
Elihu's argument that suffering can be the way in which God teaches us lessons has much to be said for it. But that neither Job nor God answered Elihu may tell us that it was not relevant here. 5:17,18; 33:14–30; 36:5–16

4. Job's rashness.
- Job was provoked into saying many rash things by the hardness of his unsympathetic friends. Where he really did go astray, however, was in the way he took on God and wanted to argue it out with him. He seems to be claiming that he knew better than God. 7:11–21; 9:14–35; 13:3,15–28; 23:2–7; 31:35–37
- Like his friends, Job could only think in terms of this life. As it was, his demands for justice actually began to reach out beyond death and to expect future judgement. 10:20–22; 14:7–22; 17:13–16; 19:23–27

5. God's answer.
God did not really explain to Job why he suffered as he did. Instead he gave Job a glimpse of his greatness and his infinite wisdom, seen especially in the wonders of creation. If Job could not grasp the simplest secrets, how could he understand God's purpose in his life? 38:1–42:6

Application

1. Suffering comes to all.
Everybody living in this sinful, fallen world has his share of suffering. We cannot expect a painless or trouble-free existence just because we are God's people.

2. Don't distort the truth.
As a general rule God does bless and prosper those who love him. He also judges the wicked. But it does not follow that he must do it in this life. It is entirely wrong and cruel to

JOB

argue backwards, to say that if someone is suffering it must be because of his sins.

3. Behind the scenes.
We do not know what is happening in spiritual realms which affects our circumstances on earth. What we suffer may represent the spiritual warfare which goes on 'in the heavenly places'.

4. Crisis and growth.
When there is nothing more that we can do

than trust God who knows what he is doing, faith really becomes faith. God sometimes takes away all the props we lean on so that we fall back on him.

5. Too big for us.
Although we can sometimes see God's purpose in our suffering, his ways are so much higher than ours that his full purpose is always beyond us. Many of our explanations are just words. It would be better if we kept silent and trusted God at such times.

Key themes

1. God's character and works.
God is sovereign. Even the devil cannot act without his permission. Both Job and his friends were aware of this, and of the fact that God made the world and keeps it going. The book is full of God's greatness and wisdom. See 5:8–16; 9:2–13; 11:7–9; 12:10,13–25; 25:2–6; 26:5–14; 34:10–15; 35:10,11; 36:22–33; 37:1–24; 38:1–39:30; 40:8–41:34.

2. Man's weakness.
Job's case illustrates our weakness, ignorance, sinfulness and the shortness of our lives. Job's plea for justice really demanded a life beyond this one where God could punish the wicked and right the wrongs of this world. See 4:17–21; 5:7; 7:1–10; 9;2,25,26; 14:1,2,4,7–12; 15:14–16; 25:4–6.

3. Wisdom.
God's wisdom, that is, God's mind, intelligence and purpose are described for us as being naturally beyond our reach

(28:1–28). If we are to be let into some of his secrets, it will not be due to our cleverness. It is only as we submit to him that we begin to understand a little of his ways. Think about the implications of Isaiah 55:8 and 1 Corinthians 1:18–31.

4. Comforting others.
Job's friends give us a good example of how not to do it! Many of the things they said were true in themselves but beside the point and hurtful. Note how Paul set about comforting others. What does this imply about how we should use life's experiences (2 Corinthians 1:3–8)?

5. Job and the New Testament.
Although Job is only named once in the New Testament (James 5:11), the questions he asked can be understood far more clearly from a Christian point of view. For example see Job 9:33, 1 Timothy 2:5; Job 14:14, John 11:25; Job 16:19, Hebrews 9:24; Job 19:25, Hebrews 7:25; Job 23:3, John 14:6.

PSALMS 1

Praise and thanksgiving

HOW THEY CAME TOGETHER. The Psalms are a collection of praises and prayers which came together over a long period in Israel's history, stretching at least from David's time until after the Exile to Babylon. We might even say it is 'a collection of collections', because the 150 psalms are split up into five 'books': 1–41, 42–72, 73–89, 90–106, 107–150.

Although scholars see some differences between these groups, it is certainly not in their subject matter. Unlike our hymn books, the Psalms contain prayers and thanksgivings, petitions and praises with no real order.

Some psalms come more than once. For example, Psalm 14 = Psalm 53; Psalm 60:5–12 = Psalm 108:6–13; Psalm 70 = Psalm 40:13–17. We find some psalms repeated in other books in the Old Testament, where we also find psalms not in the main collections.

In our study we are going to collect together psalms on different subjects, and see what they have to teach us today.

HEBREW POETRY. A good deal of poetry nowadays rhymes, but this was not the case in ancient Israel. They tended to balance one saying with another, sometimes the same thing repeated in a different way, sometimes its opposite. See, for example, Psalm 146:3:

'Do not put your trust in princes,
　in mortal men, who cannot save.'

Or Psalm 11:5:

'The Lord examines the righteous,
　but the wicked and those who
　love violence his soul hates.'

Sometimes the thought is continued into the next verse.

This sort of poetry does not lose very much when it is translated into another language, which means that we can enjoy it today. Some psalm writers began each line or group of lines with the same letter. Psalm 119 works almost through the Hebrew alphabet in this way.

PSALMS AND WORSHIP. A good number of psalms were first of all personal prayers or praises, but many were written for public worship. We have some addressed to the choirmaster or to the Temple singers like 'the sons of Korah'. They were used in Temple worship, especially at the great festivals. Just in the same way that our hymn books contain a wide range of devotion from many different authors in very different places and situations, the Psalms express Israel's worship across the years.

Outline

 PSALMS OF PRAISE AND THANKSGIVING

8 What is man?
24 The King of glory
29 Give God his due!
33 God is over all
46 Our refuge and strength
47 Sing praise to our God
48 God and his city
65 Harvest thanksgiving
67 Our God has blessed us
68 Mercy and majesty
75 God is in control
76 A God to be feared
81 Learn from what God has done
87 Zion, city of our God
93 The Lord on high is mighty
95 Let us worship and bow down
96 The Judge is coming!
97 God loves his own
98 Shout for joy to the Lord

99 The Lord reigns
100 The Lord is good
104 The God who made it all
105 God led his people out
108 (57,60) The One who gives victory
111 God's works are very wonderful
113 Who is like the Lord our God?
114 When the sea turned back
115 Our God does what he wants
117 Praise him, everybody!
122 The Holy City
133 When brothers are united
134 Come, bless the Lord
135 Our Lord is above all gods
136 His love endures for ever
145 Faithful to all his promises
146 What a God to have!
147 He heals the broken-hearted
148 His name alone is exalted
149 God takes pleasure in his people
150 Let everything praise the Lord!

Message

1. God should be worshipped.

☐ **Because of who he is:** God is the great and powerful king whose authority is worldwide in scope. He gets his own way and nothing can withstand his purposes. Compared with him, all other gods are nothing. 24:7–10; 29:1–11; 47:8,9; 93:1–4; 99:1,2; 113:1–6; 135:5,6; 145:10–13

He is holy and righteous in his dealings with men and women. Because of this he judges men and women, and no one can avoid his judgement. 33:4,5; 75:7; 76:7–9; 96:10–13; 97:6; 99:3–5; 105:7

He is loving and caring to all. He is especially concerned for the weak and helpless, and of course, for his own people, Israel. At the same time, he is good to all, and men and women can always depend on his love. 33:18,19,22; 68:5,6; 100:5; 108:4; 113:7–9; 117:1,2; 136:1–26; 145:8,9; 146:5–9

☐ **Because of what he has made:** God has created the world and everything in it. He did this in great power, but with great ease. All things owe their existence to him. 24:1,2; 33:6–9; 65:5–8; 95:1–5; 135: 5–7; 136:4–9; 147:4,5

But he not only made everything, he has also supplied their every need. He keeps the world going by his power. 65:9–13; 67:6,7; 104:1–35; 111:5; 146:5–7; 147:8,9

Included in this, of course, is man himself, so small and helpless, and yet the crown of God's creation. 8:3–9; 95:6,7; 100:3

☐ **Because of what he has done:** He made Israel his own people by rescuing them from Egypt and then leading them through the desert to the promised land of Canaan. He drove out their enemies before them. 68:7–18; 81:1–10; 99:6–8; 105:1–45; 114:1–8; 135:8–12; 136:10–25

He continues to give his people victory over those who threaten them. 33:10–19; 46:6–11; 76:1–12

2. Praise leads on:

☐ **To confidence:** If God is so great and loving, and if he has helped his people in the past, he can and will save them in their present needs whatever they may be. 24:3–5; 29:11; 33:18–22; 46:1–11; 97:10–12; 108:7–13; 115:9–15

☐ **To prayer:** This is the way in which God's people naturally express their trust in him. They turn their needs into prayers. 67:1,2; 68:28; 106:4,5; 108:6,12,13; 122:6–9

☐ **To commitment:** Praising God with words is not enough; we must praise him with lives given over to his service. We must fulfil the promises we have made to him. 65:1,2; 76:11; 81:8–10; 95:7–11

Application

1. God is wonderfully great.

We cannot begin to measure his power and his might. The world and all its detail, including the affairs of men and nations, are all under his control. Everything we have and everything we are come from him. Because of this:

☐ We feel a sense of littleness and insignificance when we think of him.

☐ We owe him our praise, worship and thanksgiving, both by lip and life.

2. God is concerned.
He loves what he has made, and provides for it in every way. In his great power he chose a people for himself, freed them, and gave them an inheritance. Because of this:
☐ We know that we can trust him to supply our needs.
☐ We can expect him to act on behalf of his own.

3. God is good.
Despite his awesome greatness, he willingly gives generously. He wants our best and is committed to our welfare. Because of this:
☐ We worship him with joy and delight and not just out of duty.
☐ We find deep satisfaction as we give him something of the praise and glory which are his due.

Key themes

1. Worship.
Again and again we are invited to join in worshipping God, that is, in giving him something of the praise and adoration which he deserves. What do the following sample verses tell us about true worship? 24:3,4; 29:1,2; 33:1–3; 47:1,6,7; 75:1,9; 95:1,2,6; 96:1–3; 98:1,4–6; 99:5,9; 100:4; 105:4; 147:1; 150:1–6.

2. God's people.
These are the ones who are doing the worshipping. God chose them to be his very own, and promised to protect them. Because of the cross, all who trust in Jesus Christ can now claim this privilege. See 33:12; 47:4; 48:14; 105:7–15; 135:4. Here and there we get a glimpse of all nations worshipping God: 68:29, 31–33; 113:1–4; 117:1; 148:7–12.

3. Zion and the Temple.
Jerusalem and God's Temple were the centre of Israel's worship, and God's people would come on pilgrimage to praise him there. 24:3; 46:4,5; 48:1–3,8,9,11–14; 87:1–7; 122:1–9; 147:12–14. Because Christ is everywhere by his Spirit, our worship is not confined to one place or building, but we can capture something of their joy as we meet to worship God.

It is not surprising that in the New Testament Zion, the Holy City, becomes a picture of heaven. See Hebrews 12:22–24; Revelation 21:1–22:5.

In times of trouble

OUR HUMAN LOT. The psalmists were not exempt from human suffering in all its varied forms. Whether it was the king trying to rule his country, facing enemies or intrigue, or the individual going through it, their miseries and their prayers are recorded for us. At times they speak on behalf of the whole nation; at others they pour out their lonely complaints to the only One who seemed to listen.

Although sometimes their suffering was simply because of their sins, on other occasions it seemed dreadfully unfair. God had promised to bless and prosper those who loved and obeyed him. So why did the reverse happen when they suffered and the wicked prospered?

Another problem arose when they were sick or when their lives were threatened. Very seldom does the Old Testament speak about an after-life where God rights the wrongs of this one. Life in Sheol – the place of the dead – was less than real life, and far from attractive. So rewards or punishments had to happen here and now. You can imagine how they felt when it did not work out that way.

CRIES FOR VENGEANCE? In spite of all this, the psalmists are confident that because God is just, he will judge sinners and vindicate his people. It is here that we face the difficulty of what they often prayed for their enemies. There was no love or forgiveness. Nothing could be too bad for those who opposed the righteous, which is hardly Christian. We also find it difficult to take what seems to be their sheer self-righteousness on which they based their pleas to God. How are we to understand this from a Christian point of view? Firstly, we need to note that they were not boasting of their righteousness like the Pharisees in the Gospels. As far as they knew how, they had been faithful to God, and they could not understand why they were suffering. Remember, they had no idea of God's future judgements, and in the cruel and bloodthirsty age in which they lived, God's reckoning could only be seen to take that form.

Secondly, we must remember that by opposing God's people, their enemies were really defying God. In the New Testament we may be told to love our enemies, but we are also assured that God will judge sinners. The fact that sin deserves punishment is never overlooked.

THE INNOCENT SUFFERING. The whole idea of suffering without deserving it, and looking to God for vindication looks forward to the supreme case of Jesus Christ. It is no mistake that many of these psalms written in times of suffering were remembered when his story was told.

Outline

 PSALMS IN TIMES OF TROUBLE

3 God is all I need
4 Put your trust in him
5 Lead me, Lord
6 I am so weary
7 God is just
10 Why do the wicked prosper?
11 God knows what goes on
12 God has promised to help
13 I have trusted in your love
14 (53) Everyone seems godless
17 Lord, show that I am in the right
22 Why has God left me?
25 The Lord is good and upright
28 God has heard my prayer
31 My times are in your hands
35 Deal with my enemies, Lord
38 Lord, I'm sick and sinful
39 I'm not here for long
42 Why am I so depressed?
43 I **will** praise God again!
44 Why don't you hear us, Lord?
51 Have mercy on me!
54 God is my helper
55 My friend has turned against me
56 I trust in God
57 In the shadow of his wings
58 Men are wicked; God is just

59 God is my strength
60 Lord, we need your help
61 The rock that is higher
62 My soul finds rest
64 God will judge the wicked
69 Save me – I am sinking!
71 God will see me through
73 Why do the innocent suffer?
74 Why have you deserted us?
77 Has God forgotten?
79 The groaning of the prisoners
80 Restore your people, Lord
83 Our enemies are your enemies
85 Revive us again
86 Teach me your way
88 Save me from death
90 Only seventy years
94 The all-knowing God
102 I change; he never does
109 Dealing with the treacherous
120 I want peace
123 We look to you, Lord
129 We have suffered enough
130 Out of the depths
137 How can we sing?
140 You are my God
141 Keep me true
142 Release me from prison
143 Unfailing love in the morning

Message

1. All kinds of trouble.
By far the most frequent problem the psalmists bring to God is the opposition of their enemies. This sometimes means the nation's enemies; other kings and peoples threatening God's people. Often they are personal enemies who in their ambition, jealousy and hatred want to get rid of the psalmist. 12:1–4; 14:1–4; 17:10–12; 22:12–16; 55:9–14; 64:1–6; 74:3–8; 79:1–4; 83:1–8; 94:4–7; 109:1–5; 137:7; 140:1–5

On some occasions the writers know that their troubles are due to their sins, and that these must be put right if they are going to be able to expect God's blessing. 25:6,7,11; 38:4,18; 51:1–19; 69:5; 130:3,4

One of the reasons why these particular psalms have been such a help to many is that they do not hold back in describing depression, sickness and personal misery. 25:16–18; 38:1–22; 42:1–11; 69:1–3; 109:22–25

2. Troubles become prayers.
☐ **For justice,** especially that God may be seen to be on the side of good people, that he might vindicate his own. 7:3–9; 17:1–5; 35:11–17,22–26; 94:1–3; 140:12,13
☐ **For victory,** that the enemy might know that God is fighting for his people. 3:7,8; 35:1–3; 60:1–5
☐ **For guidance,** so that the psalmist might know God's will in perplexing times. 5:8; 25:4,5; 86:11; 143:8,10
☐ **For healing,** especially in view of the shortness of our time here. 6:1–7; 31:9–13
☐ **For protection,** that God might prove to be the psalmist's security. 11:1; 31:1–5; 61:1–4; 142:5
☐ **For forgiveness,** so that nothing might stand between God and his servant. 25:11,18; 51:1,2,7,9,10; 79:8,9
☐ **For national restoration,** that others may see and know that the Lord has a special agreement with his people, Israel. 14:7; 25:22; 51:18,19; 79:1–13; 80:1–19; 85:1–13

3. God will answer.
☐ He is that kind of God: someone who loves and stands by his own; someone who gives strength to the weak and who delivers the helpless. 17:7–9; 51:1; 62:5–8; 85:7–13; 109:21,26; 143:1
☐ He has done so before; we can be sure that he will do so again. 22:3–5; 77:13–20
☐ Because they were so confident, prayers which began with a tale of woe often ended with praise to the One they knew would step in and save them. 7:17; 13:5,6; 28:6,7; 56:10–13; 69:30–36; 109:30,31

PSALMS 2

Application

1. Troubles come to all.
God's people are not exempt from troubles of various kinds. Trusting God is no guarantee of an easy life. In fact, in this fallen world, the innocent often suffer and the godless come out on top.

2. Tell God about it.
We can be honest and open with God when we share our hurts, disappointments and sorrows with him. He hears and understands even if no one else does.

3. God has promised.
God is committed to helping his own. He is both loving and faithful to his covenant, his special agreement with his people.

4. It will work out.
Although God may not seem to answer our prayers, he is just and one day he will judge the wicked and show that those who trust him are in the right.

5. God's opportunities.
Times of trouble become times of trusting and proving God in new and deeper ways. When everything is going well, we tend to trust ourselves.

6. Praising God in trouble.
Because God is who he is, those who trust him can praise him even when things go wrong. Although we may change, he never does.

Key themes

1. Unanswered prayer.
One problem which keeps cropping up in these psalms is the fact that God does not always seem to hear or answer our prayers. At these times we may be tempted to doubt his power or his love. Look up the following verses and see how the psalmists dealt with this: 10:1–18; 13:1–6; 22:1–5; 42:1–11; 73:1–20; 77:1–20.

2. This life is short.
In their troubles, especially when their lives were being threatened, the psalmists remind us that we are not here for long. Even though we have been shown more clearly than they were that this life is not everything there is, it is a timely reminder that we ought to take the opportunities while we can. See 39:4–6,12,13; 88:3–12; 90:3–12; 102:3–11,23–28.

3. Consolation in God.
In a changing world, with fickle friends and frightening circumstances, these psalms remind us repeatedly that God is always the same. We can run to him and hide behind him when we feel threatened or lonely or in despair. See 17:15; 38:9; 39:7; 73:21–28; 94:18,19.

PSALMS 3

About testimony, good living and the king

THE GOOD LIFE. Repeatedly in the psalms we are reminded of the privilege of belonging to God and of living for him. Sometimes it is in the form of testimony, when the psalmist has proved God's goodness and wants to pass it on to others. In other psalms we are told how to live lives which please and honour God. Here the psalmist draws on his accumulated practical wisdom in order to teach others the ways of God.

PSALMS WITH TITLES. Many of the psalms have a title like 'a psalm of David', or 'for the director of music'. These may give us some clue as to when they were written and why.

Over seventy are credited to David; several connected with events in his life. This probably means that David wrote them, although the words could mean 'for David' or even 'for the king', as the king came from David's family. Others appear to be part of various collections used by the Temple choirs.

THE KING AND THE NATION. Our selection of psalms about the king is a little artificial because a good number of others also come from the king. In fact, because the king represented the nation, he often spoke for all the people and not just for himself.

God made a special arrangement, or covenant, with David and his successors (see 2 Samuel 7:1–29). They reigned on his behalf over the people. They were required to be merciful and just, while for his part, God promised to stand by them in their troubles and to prosper their reigns.

THE COMING KING. All Israel's kings, including David, failed to live up to the high ideal of what they should have been. Some were better than others; some practically abandoned God and went over to idols. This was one of the reasons why God eventually punished the whole nation by taking them from their land. However, through it all the hope began to grow that one day the ideal King would come. Because kings were anointed with oil, this coming King came to be known as 'the anointed one' (in Hebrew, 'Messiah': in Greek, 'Christ'). By New Testament times, with the land occupied by alien Roman armies, the people were eagerly looking for him. This is why they welcomed Jesus as 'Son of David' (Matthew 21:9). Jesus, of course, became King in a rather different way from what they expected. After his resurrection, his followers began to see that many of the kingly psalms referred to him, and that especially at his return, he would fulfil these ancient ideals as God's King.

Outline

Message

1. Good living.
The truly good man lives that way because he knows that God is good, and that he wants that kind of behaviour. 15:2–5; 19:14; 101:2–6. He deliberately resolves to keep God's law. The fear of the Lord, that sense that he is living out his life in God's sight, controls what he does. 1:2; 19:1–11; 37:31; 112:1; 119:1–176; 128:1. He also knows that God will judge the actions of men and women. 1:5; 50:6; 82:1,8 1:5; 50:6; 82:1,8

Living a good life means just as deliberately avoiding what is evil. This may involve not mixing with people who disregard God's law. Instead, the godly man finds his friends among those who put God first. 1:1; 26:4,5; 37:8,27; 101:3–8

2. Testimony.
The fact that God is good and faithful comes home in a personal way to those who trust him. When they turn to him in times of distress, he hears and answers their prayers. The result is praise and thanksgiving. 30:1,4; 34:1–3; 40:1,2; 103:1–3; 107:1–43; 118:1–4

When God answers prayer like this, it leads to telling others of what he has done, so that they might prove him too. 9:1,11; 40:9,10; 66:16–19; 107:2,3. What is more, it makes the psalmist commit himself in fresh obedience, looking to God for further answers to prayer. Testimony spills over into petition. 40:6–8; 116:12–19; 27:7–12; 40:11–17; 126:4,5

3. The king.
The special thing about Israel's king was that, as one of David's line, he was appointed by God to the task. Both people and king relied on God's pledge that David's family would reign for ever. Because of this, the king was seen as God's adopted son. 2:1–11; 18:50; 72:17; 89:1–4,19–37; 132:1–5,10–12,17,18

It was extremely important that the king should not misuse his privileges. His job was to rule justly and fairly over God's people, as well as to lead them out into battle against their enemies. 18:20–26; 45:7; 72:1–4,7,12–14; 89:14,30–32

The king who measured up to these demands had nothing to fear. God promised to fight on his behalf, to give him a good long reign, and to prosper him in all he did. God made faithful kings great, and the king's greatness and fame in turn brought honour to God. 2:4–9; 18:1–50; 21:1–13; 110:1,2,5–7

Application

1. God's king reigns.
The ideal descriptions of the king in these psalms, which were never fulfilled in Israel's history, speak to us of Jesus Christ. Because he is God's Son, risen from the dead and seated at God's right hand, he qualifies as the One who will reign for ever and whose kingdom is over all.

He is already on the throne, but one day he will return in majesty to establish his righteous rule on earth. In that day all these pictures of the king's glory will be seen to be real and true.

2. God wants obedience.

If God's Son is sovereign, we must submit to his rule here and now. This means taking God's Word seriously and putting it into practice in our daily living. This may mean that we will have to cut out some things that we are doing. It will certainly mean bringing our lives into line with God's will for us.

However, because of what we know of God's goodness to those who honour him, this is no hard duty but rather a delight and joy.

3. God is our refuge.

As we obey God we will also begin to discover his power in our lives. We will learn how to run to him in times of trouble and danger. We will see that he can answer our prayers and meet our needs. This is truth that deserves to be told, so that others might come to know him in this way too. Personal recommendation is the most powerful witness.

Key themes

1. God's blessings.

There is much in these psalms about what God can do for those who trust him. He gives them refuge, victory, vindication, guidance, joy, life, strength and forgiveness. See how these themes come out in the following selection of verses: 1:3; 9:3,4,9,10; 16:7,8; 18:16–18,29–36,50; 27:11; 32:1–5; 34:4–10,15–22; 37:3–6,23–26; 46:1–11; 52:8,9; 66:5–12; 91:1–16; 103:1–5,8–18; 112:1–10; 118:5–7; 128:1–6; 144:1,2.

2. The king's universal reign.

God's king will reign over the whole of his creation (2:8–11; 72:8–11,17; 89:27). This will certainly be true when Christ returns, but what bearing has this on our worldwide preaching of the good news here and now?

3. Promise and fulfilment.

When the New Testament writers wanted to describe the majesty of the Lord Jesus Christ they often used the book of Psalms, probably because Jesus himself had pointed that way. See Psalm 2 in Acts 4:25,26; 13:33; Hebrews 1:5; 5:5; Revelation 2:26,27; 19:15. Psalm 18:49 in Romans 15:9. Psalm 45:6,7 in Hebrews 1:8,9. Psalm 89 in Acts 2:30; Revelation 1:5. Psalm 110 in Mark 12:36; 14:62; 16:19; Acts 2:34,35; 1 Corinthians 15:25; Ephesians 1:20–22; Colossians 3:1; Hebrews 1:3,13; 5:6; 8:1; 10:12,13; 12:2. Psalm 132 in Acts 2:30.

PROVERBS

Get wise!

THE BOOK OF WISDOM. Proverbs is the work of several authors, three of whom are identified by name – Solomon, Agur and Lemuel. At least one section of the book is anonymous. The bulk of the book is taken up with the proverbs of Solomon (ch. 10:1–22:16; 25:1–29:27). He is credited with having written 3,000 Proverbs and 1,005 songs (1 Kings 4:31,32). The book consists of down-to-earth observations which no doubt Solomon and others had gathered from many different sources, supplementing them with their own experiences of life. The purpose of the book is clearly stated at the outset (1:2–6).

A recurring emphasis in the book is 'the fear of the Lord'.

WHAT IS A PROVERB? Proverbial teaching represents one of the world's most ancient forms of instruction. Here are clear crisp sentences, capable of being easily memorised and passed on from generation to generation. Solomon was a man of many parts. He was not only a king but a philosopher with remarkable powers of intuition and discernment, and also a scientist of no mean ability. Sadly, in his private life, he did not always live up to the wisdom he knew.

GOD'S WISDOM. In Proverbs, wisdom is represented as dwelling with God from all eternity. It is personified so that, at times, 'wisdom' can be seen as representing Christ (Proverbs 8:23–31; see John 1:2; Hebrews 1:2; Colossians 2:3). It is pointed out that wisdom is available to every man. The wise are those who heed God's commands while the foolish ignore them. Wisdom is all-important in the business of living (4:7).

STRUCTURE. Many attempts have been made to analyse the book of Proverbs. Some commentators have pointed out the three divisions represented by the use of the phrase 'the proverbs of Solomon' (1:1; 10:1; 25:1). It is further suggested that proverbs with pronouns in the second person were proverbs **for** Solomon taught by his teachers, while those pronouns in the third person were proverbs **by** Solomon himself. It is, however, very difficult to be sure.

Outline

1 **INTRODUCTION**
1:1–7

1:1 The title
1:2–6 The purpose of the book
1:7 The secret

2 **FACETS OF WISDOM**
1:8–9:18

1:8–19 Wisdom in the choice of friends
1:20–33 The challenge of wisdom
2:1–22 The protection wisdom provides
3:1–35 The prosperity wisdom brings
4:1–27 Wisdom throughout life
5:1–23 Wisdom about marriage
6:1–35 Warnings against folly and adultery
7:1–27 Warnings against loose women
8:1–36 The appeal of wisdom
9:1–18 The feast of wisdom and the feast of folly

3 **PROVERBS OF SOLOMON**
10:1–22:16

4 **SAYINGS OF WISE MEN**
22:17–24:34

5 **MORE PROVERBS OF SOLOMON**
25:1–29:27

6 **WORDS OF AGUR**
30:1–33

7 **WORDS OF KING LEMUEL**
31:1–9

8 **THE IDEAL WIFE PORTRAYED**
31:10–31

PROVERBS

Message

The message of Proverbs cannot be summarised in the way that is possible with most other Bible books. It is best to look at different subjects which are dealt with here and there throughout the book. The following lessons seem to be clearly taught:

☐ Wisdom is the ultimate goal which we should seek. 1:20–33; 2:1–22; 3:1–35; 4:1–27; 8:1–36; 22:17–24:34
☐ The way of the fool – the man who ignores God's will – is the way of disaster. 1:7; 12:16,23; 14:9; 15:20; 17:24; 18:2,6,7; 28:26

☐ Laziness inevitably leads to shame. 6:6,9: 19:15; 13:4; 15:19; 19:24; 20:4; 21:25; 22:13; 24:30; 26:13,16
☐ True friends are to be highly prized. 17:17; 18:24; 27:6,17
☐ Words are no substitute for deeds. 26:20–28
☐ Stability in society stems from a healthy family life. 10:1; 13:1,24; 17:21,25; 19:13,18,27; 20:11; 22:6,15; 23:13–16, 19–28; 28:7,24; 29:15,17; 30:11,17
☐ A godly life is blessed by God, whereas an evil life results in shame and death. 3:25; 5:4; 11:29; 14:12

Application

1. Don't be a fool!
The subject of wisdom and folly runs right through the book. Wisdom means living by God's standards, folly is ignoring God and living for self. The outcome of a wise man's life is blessedness but a foolish man's life ends in death and destruction.

2. Watch your words.
Proverbs has much to say about the use of speech. Words have great potential for good or ill. The wise man is in control of his tongue and avoids idle gossip or flattery.

3. Take family life seriously.
The stability of a nation is determined by the quality of family life in that nation. Parents have responsibilities toward their children. Adultery is sin.

4. Work hard.
'All hard work brings a profit' (14:23). Proverbs gives many warnings against the perils of laziness. There is nothing to be said in favour of slackness.

PROVERBS

Key themes

1. Work.
Key passage: 6:6–11. The slacker exaggerates his difficulties and becomes immobilised (22:13; 26:13,14; 21:25,26).

Note the effects of slackness (10:4,5; 12:24; 13:4; 19:15).

The diligent man acquires wealth as he buys up opportunities (10:4,5). He is given responsibility (12:27) and he prospers. (Compare Matthew 25:24–30; John 9:4; Galatians 6:9,10; Ephesians 5:16.)

2. The use of the tongue.
Key passages: 10:11,13,18–21,31,32. Wise men are careful in the words they use, whereas the foolish lack discretion, and cause hurt and harm. (See also 6:16,18,19; 10:11,19; 11:13; 12:18; 14:23; 15:1; 16:28; 17:9,22; 18:6–8; 20:19; 24:2; 25:11,15,23; 26:20,22; 29:11; 31:26. Compare Matthew 7:1–5; 12:34–36; 15:11,17,18; James 3:5–8.)

3. Friendship.
Key chapter: 18. A few close friends are better than many acquaintances. Friendship has to be won; it calls for a kindly disposition (3:29; 25:8,9,21,22; 24:17,19; 11:12; 14:21; 21:10; 12:26).

A good friend is loyal and unfailing (14:20; 19:4,6,7; 17:17). He is also candid (27:6; 29:5). He is both reassuring and challenging (17:9,17). True friendship calls for both wisdom and sensitivity (25:17; 27:14; 26:18,19). Even so, human friendship is always at risk (2:17; 16:28; 17:9).

4. Wealth and poverty.
Key chapter: 19. Wealth has distinct advantages. It gives a sense of security (10:15; 18:11). It opens various doors (18:16). It attracts many friends (14:20; 19:4,6). At the same time it tends to make a man hard (18:23) and give him unwarranted power (22:7). It breeds self-confidence (30:8,9). However, worldly wealth is impermanent (23:4,5; 27:24). Riches are of no avail when it comes to the Judgement Day (11:4), whereas an empty purse helps a man to trust in God and keep straight (15:16; 28:6). A poor man may have great wealth (13:7; compare Matthew 6:19–24; 2 Corinthians 6:10).

ECCLESIASTES

What is life all about?

WHAT IT'S ALL ABOUT? Anyone reading Ecclesiastes for the first time will be struck by the strange mixture of faith and fatalism in the book. At times the author seems to be resigned to all the frustration and futility of life; at others he appears to be telling us to enjoy ourselves while we can; and all the way through there are plenty of hints that God knows what is going on, that we must trust and serve him, and that one day we will answer to him.

Some have felt that these different points of view are the work of several authors, each trying to improve on the others, and not just one. They see the book as contradicting itself and a good deal of other biblical teaching as well. But we do not need to come to this conclusion if we understand it as a sort of Old Testament tract for worldly people.

It is as though the author were saying, 'Come on then. Let's see what a life without God is really like. What have you got if you only live for the things of this world? Life is futile and meaningless, frustrating and miserable. But God can make a difference!'

WHO WROTE IT AND WHEN? The author tells us that he was a son of David (1:1), and king in Jerusalem. Some think this must mean Solomon, although his name does not occur in the book. Certainly, his lifestyle and interest in wisdom seem to be reflected here, and these are the sort of conclusions we would have expected him to come to after his long and often worldly life.

One of the difficulties with this view is that he speaks of his predecessors in Jerusalem (2:9) and, of course, there had only been one. Another is that the language in which the book is written is from a much later time than Solomon. So if it is his work, it was brought up to date later on. Or it might be, as some suggest, a study based on Solomon's sayings.

This all makes the actual date very difficult to determine. If it was by Solomon and towards the end of his life, it could have been written as early as around 940 BC. If the work of another, it might be as late as 200 BC.

THE PREACHER. The author actually calls himself Koheleth, a word which could mean a preacher, teacher, debater or even the leader of an assembly (1:1). He had the good of others in mind when he set out to discuss the issues of life and death (12:9–12). Because of this we also can draw on his experience and advice as we read the book today.

Outline

1 **LIFE IS POINTLESS**
1:1–2:26

1:1–11 Everything is futile
1:12–18 Knowledge does not help
2:1–11 Pleasure leads nowhere
2:12–16 Everybody has to die
2:17–23 Achievement means nothing
2:24–26 Only God gives contentment

2 **THE WAY GOD MADE IT**
3:1–22

3:1–8 Everything in its time
3:9–15 Man in his place
3:16–22 God makes the difference

3 **POVERTY, RICHES AND GOD**
4:1–6:6

4:1–8 Man's lot is miserable
4:9–12 Consolation in fellowship
4:13–16 The perils of privilege
5:1–7 Keeping God in view
5:8–6:6 Coping with possessions

4 **MAKING THE BEST OF IT**
6:7–7:29

6:7–12 What's the use?
7:1–22 Some wise advice
7:23–29 Wisdom and human perversity

5 **ANSWERING TO MAN AND TO GOD**
8:1–17

8:1–8 Keeping the king's command
8:9–15 Good living is best
8:16,17 But there's too much to know

6 **LIFE AND HOW TO LIVE IT**
9:1–12:14

9:1–10 Life is short
9:11–18 Life seems unjust
10:1–11:8 More wise advice
11:9–12:8 Serve God while you may
12:9–14 Summing up

ECCLESIASTES

Message

1. Life without God is meaningless.
When we stop to look at life it seems to be going nowhere. Things happen and go on happening with seemingly no purpose at all. 1:1–11; 3:15; 6:10,11; 11:8; 12:8

Nothing we can do provides us with a satisfying answer. All our thinking leads us nowhere. All our pleasure leaves us unsatisfied. All our prosperity and achievement come to nothing. 1:8,12–18; 2:1–11; 4:7,8; 5:10

What is more, life seems to be unjust. Good men suffer; wicked men prosper. There do not seem to be any rewards or punishments whatever we do or however we live. 4:1–8; 5:13–17; 6:2; 7:15; 8:9,10,14; 9:11,12; 10:5–7

This can make a person very cynical, hating this life and even wishing that he had never been born. 2:17–23; 5:16,17; 6:3–6

2. Man needs a divine dimension.
All this should show us that we need God in our lives. For all this drab and doleful description of life, God is always just in the background.
- ☐ **He is sovereign.** In sharp contrast to us, he does what he wants and he knows where he is going. Because of this we ought to revere and worship him. 3:14; 7:13,14; 9:1

- ☐ **He is judge,** watching over the affairs of men and one day calling them to account. Because we will have to answer to him then, we should live daily in the light of this. 3:15–17; 8:12,13; 12:14
- ☐ **He is our maker,** giving us all that we need. We should serve him as early as we can and while we can. 11:5; 12:1

3. Accepting what God gives.
We should learn to take and enjoy God's good gifts, getting on with the business of living this life, even though we cannot understand God's purposes.

This means that we can be content with our lot and be happy with a simple lifestyle. It matters little whether we are rich or poor. 2:24–26; 3:1–8,12,13,22; 4:6; 5:12; 8:15; 9:7–10; 11:7–10

One of God's particular blessings is that of fellowship. When we can share the difficulties of life it makes them easier to bear. 4:9–12

Although the total meaning of life may be hidden from us, this kind of living in simple dependence on God is real wisdom. 2:12–14; 4:13; 7:11,12,19; 8:1; 9:13–18

Application

1. Up to date.
This book has a curiously modern ring about it. Today many people are attempting to live their lives without God, and are finding that the whole of their existence is purposeless. As in the days of the Preacher, they try every way to give meaning to their lives, but often end up by asking, 'Who am I?' 'What am I doing here?' 'Where am I going?'

2. So much pain.
The problem of evil in the world and

ECCLESIASTES

especially the suffering of the innocent are still the same. Life seems so unfair, and by ourselves we have no answer.

3. We need God.
So then, only God can satisfy the deep spiritual appetites which he has put within us. This does not mean that we will know all the answers, but we can trust him and we can enjoy his good gifts in our place and time.

4. Judgement is coming.
We also need to remember that we only live once, and that one day he will call us to judgement. Because of this we ought to be taking every opportunity he gives us here and now to serve him and to live for him. Only in this way will we get an insight into the meaning of life.

Key themes

1. Man.
Strangely enough, through all this questioning, we come to an important insight into the way God made us. The very fact that we get worried about these things, that we need a purpose in life, witnesses to a dignity in man as God created him (3:10,11). It also tells us of his woeful, natural ignorance of spiritual things (7:23,24; 8:16,17; 11:5,6). What is worse, it shows us that we are not what God intended us to be (7:20,27-29).

2. Mortality.
The book steadily reminds us of a fact that we would like to forget, that we are all going to die one day. This ought to sharpen us up when it comes to using our present opportunities. See 2:14-16; 3:18-21; 5:15,16; 6:12; 8:7,8; 9:2-6; 12:1-7.

3. Fearing God.
As often in the Old Testament, our proper response to God is described as fearing him,

that is, acknowledging him to be God, and living our lives in that attitude. It means that we will worship him and seek to please him in all we do. It includes the idea that he sees all that we do and that one day we will answer to him. See 5:1-7; 7:18,26; 8:2,12,13; 12:1,13.

4. Wisdom.
This book is one of those which dwells on the idea of wisdom. This wisdom really belongs to God alone, but he gives it to men and women (2:26). Lest we should think that this all sounds highly intellectual, we also have examples of how practical wisdom was understood to be (8:2-6; 10:1-11:6).
In fact, the Preacher's final warning is that life is not a matter of knowing, but doing (12:12-14).

THE SONG OF SONGS

A love story

TITLE. The name Song of Songs is a literal translation of the Hebrew title. It is the Hebrew way of saying the best or the greatest song.

AUTHOR. There are seven references to Solomon in the Song, and traditionally he has been looked on as the author. The first verse could mean that it was a song written by Solomon, but it could also mean that it was 'for' or 'about' Solomon. Apart from Solomon's name, no historical background is given, so it is impossible to be really certain about the author or the date. However, there is nothing in the book which prevents it being dated in the time of Solomon.

CONTENT. The Song of Songs is basically love poetry. It is a celebration of and an exulting in the love between a man and a woman. The language is very powerful and expressive; there is an outspoken and unashamed appreciation of physical attraction. There is no mention of God in the Song and many have assumed that the book must have been included in the Bible because it was really meant to be a picture of God's love for man. However, the Song itself contains no indication that the reader is meant to look for a hidden meaning.

STRUCTURE. Most scholars would see a unity in the book; and certainly the repetition of words, phrases and ideas do indicate common authorship. It is not always easy to identify the different characters, or to know who is speaking when. Apart from the two lovers, there seems to be a group of friends standing by on some occasions, and the daughters of Jerusalem are mentioned as a group, as are the citizens of Jerusalem.

SETTING. The poems are set mainly in the country, apparently in the spring, although this could of course simply be part of the poetry. The writer is certainly well-versed in country lore: he mentions twenty-one varieties of plants and fifteen species of animals.

Outline

 THE CHARACTERS ARE INTRODUCED
1:1–2:7

1:1–7 The beloved declares her love
1:8–11 The lover responds
1:12–14 She compares him to perfume
1:15–2:2 Mutual appreciation
2:3–7 She rejoices in his company

 THE LOVER COMES
2:8–3:5

2:8–13 The beloved waits to welcome him
2:14,15 He searches for her
2:16–3:5 A dream of searching and finding

 WEDDING CELEBRATIONS
3:6–5:1

3:6–11 Solomon's procession
4:1–15 The lover praises his bride

4:16 The beloved's invitation
5:1 The lover's response

 THE LOVERS DESCRIBE ONE ANOTHER
5:2–7:9

5:2–8 An unexpected visit
5:9 The friends' challenge
5:10–16 The beloved describes her loved one
6:1 Her friends help her look for him
6:2,3 He is in his garden
6:4–7:9 The lover describes his beloved

5 **REJOICING IN LOVE**
7:10–8:14

7:10–8:4 The two belong together
8:5 Friends notice their togetherness
8:6,7 Love is priceless
8:8,9 The little sister
8:10–12 Confidence in being loved
8:13–14 Final declarations

THE SONG OF SONGS

Message

There are two distinct ways of interpreting the Song of Songs:

1. Face-value interpretations.

☐ **Drama:** the whole song is seen as a dramatic telling of the story either of the love between Solomon and a Shulamite girl, or of Solomon's attempt to win the Shulamite girl who in fact remains true to her shepherd lover. The problem with this view is that the plot is very difficult to trace, and that the drama was virtually unknown among the Hebrews.

☐ **Wedding song:** some have seen parallels with songs used in Syrian wedding feasts where the bride and groom are acclaimed as king and queen. However, the Shulamite is never called queen, and there is no evidence that the same marriage customs applied in ancient Israel.

☐ **Love poems:** the book is seen as a collection of love songs, not tied to a specific occasion like a wedding, although apparently linked together, and glorying in the love between a particular man and woman.

2. The hidden meaning.

☐ **Allegory:** here the surface story is considered to be irrelevant, but each character and each picture is assumed to represent something completely different. Jewish scholars have seen in it a description of God's love for Israel, and Christian scholars, of Christ's love for the church. The problem is that the particular interpretations chosen cannot be applied consistently throughout the story, and some very far-fetched pictures have been proposed. However, this kind of interpretation is probably the only ground on which many in the past considered the Song worthy of inclusion in the canon of Scripture. Certainly both God's love for man and Christ's love for the church are elsewhere in the Bible compared with the love between husband and wife.

☐ **Type:** this is when the basic literal sense is accepted but it is assumed that there is also another spiritual meaning which must be brought out.

Application

1. Human sexual love is God's glorious gift to man.

The love between a man and a woman is God-given, a good and joyful part of creation. It is designed to be fully appreciated and enjoyed by both men and women. We learn from elsewhere in the Bible that this must be within the bounds that God has also laid down, but the Song of Songs concentrates simply on rejoicing in the fact of this loving and passionate relationship. It is a relationship that goes beyond but most definitely includes the physical expression of love. It is important to realise that there is no clash between sex and holiness. There is no place in Scripture for the view of some early church fathers that sex was in itself something faintly sinful and definitely to be avoided. The inclusion of the Song in the Bible makes it clear that the physical aspect of marriage is something beautiful, pure and precious.

THE SONG OF SONGS

2. Pointing to the love of God.
Although unlike other biblical allegories, the Song of Songs does not provide its own clues to a hidden meaning, its descriptions of love do remind us of a love that is purer and greater than man's love.
- [ ] God's love for us is real and deep.
- [ ] He has committed himself to us.
- [ ] He loves us just as we are.
- [ ] He considers us to be of great value.
- [ ] We can have complete confidence in his love.
- [ ] He longs for our love in return.
- [ ] He wants us to express our love for him.

Key themes

Consider these themes in the light of contemporary secular and Christian attitudes. How do they serve as a guide for marriage relationships today?

1. The joy of love.
'How delightful is your love, my sister, my bride! How much more pleasing is your love than wine' (4:10). See also 1:2,4; 7:6.

2. The strength of love.
'Place me like a seal over your heart, like a seal over your arm; for love is as strong as death' (8:6).

3. The commitment of love.
'I am my lover's and my lover is mine' (6:3). See also 2:16; 7:10.

4. The value of love.
'If one were to give all the wealth of his house for love, it would be utterly scorned' (8:7).

5. Love is not to be treated lightly.
'Daughters of Jerusalem, I charge you: Do not arouse or awaken love until it so desires' (8:4). See also 2:7; 3:5.

ISAIAH 1

Salvation and judgement

HIS MESSAGE. 'Isaiah' means 'The Lord is Salvation' and he is the prophet of salvation. Yet salvation and judgement always go together in the Bible: if you won't be saved, then you must be judged. So Isaiah combines these two themes: judgement (1–35) and salvation (40–66). These main divisions are linked by a historical section about King Hezekiah (36–39).

DATE. Isaiah's visions came to him during the reigns of four kings: Uzziah, Jotham, Ahaz and Hezekiah (1:1). Uzziah died in 740 BC (see 6:1), and Hezekiah in 687 BC, so these visions spread over half a century.

PROPHECY. Isaiah was a prophet, not merely a preacher, and the book is prophecy, not just history. Isaiah had visions, not just insight.

Prophecy assumes that there is a God who knows the future and who reveals parts of his plan to prophets.

BACKGROUND. When Isaiah began his work, Israel was in the final stages of collapse. In 722 BC the northern kingdom, with its ten tribes, was captured by Assyria (2 Kings 17).

But the southern kingdom, Judah, was heading for a similar fate. They were corrupt socially, politically and in their religious faith.

The northern kingdom had been judged and had disappeared. But Judah was different. She must be judged, but because of God's eternal covenant she would also be saved. One day, out of Judah there would come the Servant of the Lord, the Saviour, to redeem not just Judah but the whole world.

AUTHORSHIP AND UNITY. The author is named in 1:1 as Isaiah. However, it is sometimes suggested that the three main divisions (1–35, 36–39, 40–46) are by different authors. A reason given includes an apparent difference in style between 1–35 and the rest, the appearance of the names Bel and Nebo, Babylonian gods, and even the name of Cyrus, conqueror of the Babylonian empire, and Isaiah's talk about a return from exile long before the exile itself.

But the book itself emphasises God's ability to reveal the future (eg. 41:21–27; 42:8,9; 44:6–8; 48:3). There is no manuscript evidence that two or more books of Isaiah exist and no trace of other authors. The New Testament quotes from all parts of the book and simply refers to 'Isaiah'.

Outline

 JUDGEMENT
1:1–5:30

1:1–31 Condemnation: Judah the rebel
2:1–22 The Day of the Lord: future
judgement
3:1–26 Jerusalem and Judah: present
judgement
4:1–6 The Day of the Lord: the branch
5:1–30 Judah: a useless fruitless vineyard

 A VISION AND A
COMMISSION
6:1–13

 IMMANUEL
7:1–12:6

7:1–25 The sign of Immanuel
8:1–22 The sign of Isaiah's own son
9:1–7 The sign of the Prince of Peace
9:8–10:19 Judgement: Israel and Assyria
10:20–34 A remnant will survive
11:1–16 A root, a branch and a banner
12:1–6 A song of salvation

 WOES TO THE
NATIONS
13:1–24:23

13:1–14:23 Against Babylon I
14:24–27 Against Assyria
14:28–32 Against Philistia
15:1–16:14 Against Moab
17:1–14 Against Damascus
18:1–7 Against 'Cush' (Ethiopia?)
19:1–20:6 Against Egypt and 'Cush'
21:1–10 Against Babylon II

21:11–12 Against Edom
21:13–17 Against Arabia
22:1–25 Against Jerusalem
23:1–18 Against Tyre
24:1–23 A warning

 SONGS OF
SALVATION
25:1–27:13

 WOES TO THE PEOPLE
OF GOD
28:1–31:9

28:1–29 A warning to the northern
kingdom
29:1–24 A warning to the southern kingdom
30:1–33 A warning to the obstinate
31:1–9 A warning to political opportunists

7 **THE KINGDOM BRINGS**
JUDGEMENT
32:1–35:10

32:1–8 The king and the kingdom
32:9–20 Judgement, justice and
righteousness
33:1–24 The exalted king
34:1–17 Judgement and the nations
35:1–10 The kingdom of joy

8 **A HISTORICAL**
CONTRIBUTION
36:1–39:8

36:1–22 Sennacherib's threats
37:1–20 Hezekiah's response
37:21–38 Sennacherib dealt with
38:9–20 A song from Hezekiah
39:1–8 The messengers from Babylon

Message

1. Holiness.
- [ ] God is 'The Holy One of Israel'. 1:4; 5:19; 5:24; 10:20; 12:6; 17:7; 29:19
- [ ] Isaiah's call comes from the God who is holy. 6:3
- [ ] God calls to Isaiah from the 'Holy of holies' or 'the most holy place', in the Temple. 6:1–4
- [ ] Although Judah must be judged, a holy remnant will be saved. 6:13
- [ ] Mount Zion, on which Jerusalem was built, is to be a holy mountain. 11:9; 27:13
- [ ] To be holy means to be different, to be 'set apart', which is the translation of the Hebrew word for 'holy' in this verse. 23:18
- [ ] The 'way' walked by God's people is the way of holiness. One of the early labels given to Christianity was, 'The Way' (Acts 9:2; 19:9,23; 22:4; 24:22). 35:8

2. Righteousness.
- [ ] Justice and righteousness belong together. The man who is 'religiously righteous' will be 'socially just'. 1:21
- [ ] Faith and righteousness also belong together: **faith** in God leads on to being **right** with God, which leads on to being **just**, fair, with people. 1:26
- [ ] The Bible teaches that **in the long run** it is well with the righteous. 3:10; 26:2

- [ ] Righteousness is the characteristic of God's judgement: God is not influenced by a man's wealth or position. 11:3,4
- [ ] Righteousness cannot be 'learned' by people who are doing wrong. A man's good environment will not make him a good man. 26:10
- [ ] The reign of the Messiah will be a reign of righteousness. 32:1

3. Judgement.
Isaiah considers this in two ways:
- [ ] Human judgement. We ought to be fair, open, honest in every case where judgement is involved. 1:17,21,26; 5:20–23; 10:1–4; 33:13–16
- [ ] God's judgement. This we cannot escape. It is God's way of setting the account straight, of making sense of life's injustices. 1:24–28; 2:6–21; 3:13–15; 5:18–30; 11:1–5; 28:16–29; 33:2–6

4. The Day of the Lord.
The Day of the Lord is closely connected with the idea of judgement. But the Day is also the time when everything is put right: peace reigns. These two aspects of the Day are always in mind in Isaiah. 2:6–22; 13:9–22; 22:5–14; 24:1–23; 2:1–5; 4:2–6; 11:1–16; 12:1–6; 14:1–8; 25:1–9

Application

Judgement and the love of God.
The first part of Isaiah's prophecy is concerned with judgement and this is a regularly recurring theme in the Bible. There is Cain in Genesis 4, the flood in Genesis 7, Sodom and Gomorrah in Genesis 19. There

is the judgement of Egypt in Exodus 12 and the judgement of the Israelites in Exodus 32.

In the New Testament we have the account of Ananias and Sapphira in Acts 5 and of Herod in Acts 12. Elymas the magician is dealt with in Acts 13. And, of course, there is the great judgement scene in Revelation 20. Jesus told the story of the rich man being tormented in hell (Luke 16).

And yet many people, and even some Christians, find it hard to accept the idea of judgement. Isaiah makes clear two aspects of judgement: present and future, temporary and eternal. Chapter 2 focuses on the final judgement with a reminder of that Day, the Day of the Lord.

Most of us have an idea of justice. We often complain, 'It's not fair'. It's judgement that makes it fair. Obviously things don't work out fairly **now**. If life is going to make sense at all, it must make sense after this life is over.

Christ died to deliver us from that judgement. If anyone is condemned then, it will be because they have refused God's way out.

But Christians should know that there is also present judgement. Isaiah 3 warned Judah of present judgement, of the exile, of captivity. The Christian must be aware of the reality of present judgement (Hebrews 12:1–29).

Key themes

1. God (chapter 6).
Chapter 6 records a vision given to Isaiah to show him clearly who God is and what he does.
- ☐ **The vision** (1–4): What are the characteristics of God as shown here?
- ☐ **The response** (5–7): What is the significance of the 'live coal' and where did it come from (Exodus 30:1–10)?
- ☐ **The request** (8): 'Whom shall I send?' God sends, and invites volunteers. What is the first requirement for the missionary (see also John 20:21–23)?
- ☐ **The reality** (9–13): The messenger is not guaranteed immense success but he is guaranteed **some** success (see also Isaiah 55:11). Follow up the New Testament references to verse 9: Matthew 13:1–17; John 12:23–43; Acts 28:23–28; Romans 11:1–8.

2. Interpreting prophecy (chapter 7).
Prophecies were usually spoken to certain people at a particular time. In interpreting a prophecy we must ask two questions:
– What did these words mean to them?
– What do these words mean to us?

Usually prophecies refer **both** to the events of the prophet's own time **and** to the future. This is the case with Isaiah 7:14. Read carefully 7:1–25; 2 Kings 15:27–16:9; 2 Chronicles 28:1–21.

The first fulfilment of the prophecy came when a young woman had a baby and before he was old enough to choose his own food, the besieging armies of Israel and Syria inexplicably retreated.

The second fulfilment came when a virgin gave birth to Jesus. Read Matthew 1:18–23.

3. The vineyard (chapter 5).
The people of God, the Jews, prided themselves on being God's vine. In New Testament times a huge golden vine decorated the outside wall of the Temple. Study chapter 5. What did the owner of the vineyard do in it? Since this is a parable, how would you interpret these actions? If we are today God's 'vineyard', what does he do in us? Why did the owner of the vineyard do all this work? What does God expect from his people today? Read Matthew 21:33–46; 20:1–16. What do these passages add to our understanding of Isaiah's illustration?

ISAIAH 2

Salvation and the Servant

This section of Isaiah has as its theme **salvation**. The Lord's messenger brings comfort to God's people.

Judgement (1–39) cannot be eliminated from any writing that deals with salvation, but these chapters, 40–66, deal with a God who is ready to save at all costs.

FOR WHOM WAS THIS WRITTEN? Isaiah's message was first of all for the people of Judah in captivity in Babylon. This captivity is the consequence of Isaiah part one, 'Judgement'. But now Isaiah is given the fresh word, the word of salvation. The people in Babylon must not give up: God will come to them and they will be saved. But of course these chapters are written for us, too. Babylon was a real city, but it frequently stands in the Bible as an illustration of Satan's kingdom. The Jews were in captivity to sin, and so are we; they needed to be saved, and so do we. It was written for them. It was written for us.

THE SERVANT OF THE LORD. Four passages from Isaiah have been called the Servant Songs: 42:1–4; 49:1–6; 50:4–9; 52:13–53:12. However, the word 'servant' and the idea of the Servant of the Lord appear right through 41:8–53:12, and, in fact, the word 'servant' occurs fairly regularly throughout Isaiah.

God's servant is presented in three ways as:
1. All the descendants of Abraham.
2. Just the faithful descendants of Abraham.
3. An unnamed individual, identified in the New Testament as Jesus.

Notice especially 49:1–6; 52:13–53:12. Both of these 'songs' picture a servant who is **not** Israel, but an individual.

THE HUMILITY OF GOD. Chapters 63–65 are a remarkable witness to God's humility. In chapter 63 Isaiah looks back historically to see what God did for his people in the past. In chapter 64 Isaiah appeals to God to show that he still has the same power. He even appears to question God's justice: 'Do not be angry beyond measure, O Lord; do not remember our sins for ever' (64:9).

In chapter 65:1–5 is God's answer. He showed himself to people who did not ask for him; he was found by people who were not looking for him; he replied to people who were not speaking to him; he offered grace to blatant sinners.

Outline

OVERTURE
40:1–11

THE INCOMPARABLE GOD
40:12–48:22

40:12–31 God: and the absurdity of idolatry I
41:1–24 God: the helper of Israel
41:25–29 God: Lord of future events
42:1–9 The Servant of the Lord I
42:10–17 A song of praise to God
42:18–25 The blind and deaf servant
43:1–13 God: the redeemer of Israel
43:14–28 The thankless servant
44:1–5 God: Lord and giver of life
44:6–23 God: and the absurdity of idolatry II
44:24–45:7 The unwitting servant, Cyrus
45:8–13 God: the master potter
45:14–25 God: the supreme Lord
46:1–13 God: and the absurdity of idolatry III
47:1–15 A lament for Babylon
48:1–22 Stubborn Israel, patient God

SUFFERING AND SALVATION
49:1–55:13

49:1–6 The Servant of the Lord II
49:7–26 Salvation: Israel restored
50:1–3 Israel: separated but never divorced
50:4–11 The Servant of the Lord III
51:1–16 Salvation and righteousness
51:17–23 Salvation and wrath
52:1–12 Salvation and redemption
52:13–53:12 The Servant of the Lord IV
54:1–17 Salvation: a glimpse of glory
55:1–13 Salvation: an invitation to the thirsty

REKINDLING THE CONSCIENCE
56:1–59:21

56:1–8 Why leave out the foreigner?
56:9–57:13 Why not exclude Israel?
57:14–21 A call for repentance
58:1–14 A call for genuine fasting
59:1–21 Sin, salvation and the Spirit

SALVATION IN SIGHT!
60:1–63:6

60:1–22 A vision of the new Jerusalem
61:1–11 A vision of jubilee
62:1–12 A vision of the Saviour
63:1–6 Salvation and judgement

6 **THE HUMILITY OF GOD**
63:7–65:16

63:7–10 Reminiscence: what God was
63:11–64:12 Remonstrance: where is he now?
65:1–16 Response: I have always been here

7 **A NEW HEAVEN AND A NEW EARTH**
65:17–66:24

Message

1. Comfort is offered to God's people.
☐ God speaks to Isaiah: a new task is given: 'Comfort my people'. 40:1,2
☐ Two heralds speak: they prepare the way. 40:3,6
☐ Isaiah speaks. His is the despairing voice of the human preacher. But 'the word of our God stands for ever'. 40:6–8
☐ A third herald speaks and demands that good news be announced **now**. **He** can see God coming! 40:9–11

2. Faith is faith in one unique God.
☐ God's people and God's service. But it's not enough to be comforted. God's people must decide for the one God or for the idols. 44:1–23
☐ Israel the chosen. He must become 'Israel-the-upright' ('Jeshurun', v.2, means 'The upright one'). 44:1–5
☐ Israel's God: King, Redeemer, Lord Almighty, First, Last, Unique, Rock. 44:6–8
☐ The alternative: idols that cannot reward even their makers! 44:9–20
☐ The hour of decision: 'Return to me.' The past can be forgiven, swept away like clouds. 44:21–23

3. Faith is faith in God's mighty acts.
☐ The suffering servant. The God who is revealed to us in the Bible cannot merely forgive sin. Sin must be paid for, by the sinner or by the Saviour. The Christian church has always taken this passage to refer to Christ. 52:13–53:12
☐ Suffering and glory. This passage begins with glory; the Servant will, one day, be highly exalted (Philippians 2:1–11). But suffering comes first. As it was for the Servant, so it often is for God's servants today. 52:13–15
☐ Suffering. No easy childhood for the Servant (like a root out of dry ground), no easy life, no easy death. But all of it was on our account: **our** infirmities, **our** sorrows, **our** transgressions, **our** iniquities. 53:1–9
☐ An explanation. This suffering of the Servant was no accident, not a miscarriage of justice: 'it was the Lord's will to crush him' 53:10–11
☐ Glory. So God the Father welcomes back his Servant who 'divides out the spoils' and we are back to the beginning of this final Servant Song: 'He will be raised and lifted up and highly exalted'. 52:13; 53:12

Application

The character of God.
Isaiah is a missionary book. God has chosen a people to be his witnesses. But witness to God must come from those who are rightly related to him, living the kind of lives that God demands. 'Righteousness' is the word often used by Isaiah to describe what God demands of his witnesses.

It is the character of God that demands this righteousness from his people. God is 'holy', different, and so his people must be different, too.

A problem is posed because we are not righteous. We don't do what is right. Two possibilities follow. If we can do nothing to produce the righteousness God demands, and if God does nothing to make us righteous, then punishment is inevitable. And that is bad news, because our 'righteous acts' are like 'filthy rags' so far as God is concerned (Isaiah 64:6).

The character of God is lit up again at this point by the news that God does deal with our problem. The Servant of the Lord comes and he suffers for **our** transgressions, **our** iniquities (53:5).

So Isaiah strikes home with his picture of a holy God who makes impossible demands of righteousness on us, and then himself makes a way of salvation available to us. And that is the sheer **grace** of God.

One thing more must be said. God is also unique: 'With whom will you compare me?' (40:18–25; 44:7; 46:5,9). A vital word for today is this word from God:

'I, even I, am the Lord, and apart from me there is no saviour' (43:11).

Key themes

1. The Servant of the Lord.

Work through the entire passage (40–66) and note every reference to 'my servant'. Now divide these references into three groups: those which refer to 'Jacob' or 'Israel', those which refer to just a faithful part of Jacob or Israel, and those which are obviously references to an individual.

The meaning of the servant teaching of Isaiah has been illustrated by means of a triangle with all Israel at the bottom, the faithful remnant in the middle, and the Messiah at the peak. How might this be applied to the church? Study the great New Testament 'Servant' passages such as John 13: 1–20; Mark 10:32–45 and Matthew 10:24–42.

2. The uniqueness of God.

Right through chapters 40–49 we find references to God's uniqueness. He is unique:
☐ as creator of the universe;
☐ as life-giver to man;
☐ as the One who plans the future;
☐ the God of covenant and call;
☐ the only Saviour and Redeemer.
Identify all those passages which go under each of these headings.

3. The foolishness of idolatry.

There are three main passages which deal with this theme:
☐ 40:18–24, the idol that cannot move. Chained down or weighed down, lacking the crudest indicator of life, which is movement.
☐ 44:9–20, the idol that cannot reward. Ironsmith and carpenter sweat at their task, but the idol they make cannot reward even them!
☐ 46:1–7, the idol that is a burden. When an empire fell its idols were hauled off to captivity along with the people. A burden to be carried! Note God's comment: but I have always carried **you**.

These three are not the only passages which deal with idolatry. Find the others. What is Isaiah's teaching about idols? How does this apply to other religions? See Acts 19:21–41 and Ephesians 2:11–16.

4. The sovereignty of God.

It is easy to forget that God is Lord of a pagan king like Cyrus just as he is Lord of the church. Note the various references to Cyrus, (44:28; 45:1; 41:25; 46:11) and see the fulfilment of prophecy in 2 Chronicles 36 and Ezra 1. But why bother to find God's will for my life? See Romans 12:1,2.

JEREMIAH 1

The futility of formality

THE PROBLEM OF THE PROPHECY. Jeremiah is difficult to read straight through. It is long, and there seems to be no pattern to the book. It is not arranged chronologically.

AN EXPLANATION. First, there is no reason why any book should be presented in neat, chronological order. This book is not meant to be a history book, although it contains history. It is a **prophetic** book, so history takes second place.

Second, chapter 36 explains that we have a re-write of the original book. King Jehoiakim read the original scroll and burned it.

Speaking very generally, chapters 1–20 come mostly from Josiah's reign and the rest is from the reigns of Jehoiakim, Jehoiachin and Zedekiah. Also, the first part is mainly prophecy plus some biography and history, but the second part is biography and history plus some prophecy.

THE LIFE AND TIMES OF JEREMIAH. Jeremiah was a prophet for more than forty years: from the thirteenth year of King Josiah, 627 BC, until the destruction of Jerusalem and the beginning of the Exile in 587/6 BC. He grew up during the rule of the apostate King Manasseh, and saw some encouragement during Josiah's reforms, but no real national repentance.

At the beginning of this period Assyria and Egypt were the two great powers. Assyria was eclipsed by Babylonia in 612 BC, and Egypt similarly disposed of at Carchemish in 605 BC. From then on Jeremiah consistently urged Judah to submit to Babylon, to accept the consequence of their sins, the Exile. He knew that the Exile would end in a dramatic demonstration of God's pardon and restoration.

PESSIMIST OR OPTIMIST? Jeremiah is often called 'the Prophet of Doom'. But he was also 'the Prophet of Invincible Hope'. Punishment for sin was inevitable but beyond it Jeremiah saw God always waiting to forgive.

He blasts away at three particular sins:
- ☐ idolatry: 7:30–8:3; 19:1–15;
- ☐ immorality: 5:1–9;
- ☐ lying prophecy: 7:3–11; 14:11–16; 23:9–40.

The great lesson of Jeremiah is that it is not enough to **know** our sins or even to regret them. Repentance is what God demands.

Outline

1 THE BOOK OF JUDGEMENT
1–25

2 INTRODUCTION
1:1–19
Jeremiah's call and commission

3 PROLOGUE TO JUDGEMENT
2:1–6:30
2:1–3:5 The indictment
3:6–4:4 An appeal for repentance
4:5–31 A warning: judgement from Babylon
5:1–31 A fruitless search for the godly
6:1–30 The warning renewed: judgement from Babylon

4 SPEECH FOR THE PROSECUTION
7:1–10:25
7:1–29 The externals of religion
7:30–8:3 Judgement of idolatry I
8:4–22 The stubbornness of the sinner
9:1–26 A chapter of tears
10:1–16 Judgement of idolatry II
10:17–22 A warning of imminent destruction
10:23–25 The prayer of a man of God I

5 SENTENCE ANTICIPATED
11:1–13:27
11:1–17 Covenant and curse
11:18–23 The plot against the man of God I
12:1–17 An objection anticipated: Why do the wicked flourish?
13:1–14 A buried belt and ruined wineskins
13:15–27 The threat of exile

6 SHADOW OF DOOM
14:1–20:18
14:1–15:21 Drought, famine and war
16:1–21 When God goes away
17:1–11 The fate of the man of the world
17:12–18 The prayer of a man of God II
17:19–27 The importance of the sabbath
18:1–12 At the house of the potter
18:13–17 The potter's accusation
18:18–23 The plot against the man of God II
19:1–15 The sign of the clay pot
20:1–6 Jeremiah in the stocks
20:7–18 Complaint of the man of God

7 LIFE AND DEATH
21:1–24:10
21:1–14 When life means death and death means life
22:1–30 Condemnation for kings
23:1–8 The Righteous Branch: the offer of mercy
23:9–40 The lying prophets
24:1–10 Two baskets of figs

8 CONCLUSION
25:1–38
25:1–14 Seventy years of exile
25:15–38 The wrath of God

Message

7:1–29
These verses provide a clear summary of Jeremiah's message. Five stages can be seen; through the prophet, God
- [ ] Demands and describes true repentance
- [ ] Disabuses the people of their absurd sense of security
- [ ] Itemises their sins
- [ ] Explains the true content of the Law
- [ ] Warns of the inevitability of judgement. .

1. Where it all happened.
Jeremiah was a preacher, not a writer. He had to speak out in public. The gate of the Lord's house was probably the gate between the inner and outer courts, where the worshippers inside and the marketeers outside could all hear. 7:1,2a

2. Jeremiah begins with the appeal!
'Reform your ways and your actions.' Repentance is not merely a matter of 'saying you're sorry', but of doing things differently.
 Note the idiotic complacency of the people: 'This is the Temple of the Lord', so because we have **it** we must have God, too. The real presence of God with us is proved by our behaviour, not by our owning religious symbols such as crosses and Bibles and churches. 7:2b–8

3. Safe to sin.
That's what the people thought: we have the Temple so we can act as we please. Theft, murder, adultery, lying, even idolatry . . . and then off to church for a touch of religion. 7:9–11

4. Shiloh.
When Israel entered Canaan, the Tent of Meeting was set up at Shiloh, and Shiloh remained their centre of worship through the time of the Judges. But Psalm 78:56–64 shows that Shiloh was destroyed when the people rebelled, and the Jews must now realise that the Temple building can't deliver them, either. 7:12–15

5. Family sin.
The whole family joined in the worship of Ishtar, the goddess of war and of love. Note that just as good things are catching so are bad things. 7:16–20; 2 Timothy 1:4,5

6. Obedience, the proof of faith.
The essence of godly behaviour is not sacrifice but a humble, obedient and holy life style. 7:21–29

Application

1. The success syndrome.
Christians are often misled into expecting that if they lead good lives they will be prosperous, socially looked up to and respected, and generally happy. It sometimes happens. The book of Jeremiah is a reminder that it is not always so. The man who can always be depended on to speak the truth may be a real embarrassment.

JEREMIAH 1

2. The externals of religion.
A Hindu once commented to a Christian missionary, 'I can never forgive you for presenting Christianity as another religion.' Christianity is not just a religion, with rules to follow, fasts and festivals, prayers to be said. It is a way of life. It **is** life, the whole of life. That was where the Jews of Jeremiah's day failed miserably. They all had 'religion'. They all believed in god . . . some sort of god. Chapter 7 warns of the futility of the **externals** of religion. The little letter of James has much to say on this subject.

3. The unforgivable sin.
Can we go too far? Is it possible to provoke God too long? To leave repentance too late? Chapter 16 suggests that it is possible, that we may provoke God so far that he leaves us. These are some of the most solemn words in the whole Bible:

'I have withdrawn my blessing, my love and my pity from this people' (16:5).

Notice the New Testament limitation on forgiveness (Matthew 12:22–37).

Key themes

1. Sin.
The people had the wrong idea of sin. Sin was a religious term and it had come to mean the neglect of religious duties. So God was concerned only with what happened on one day of the week, but it was none of his business what went on on the other six days!

Go through these chapters and list all that Jeremiah identifies as the sins of the people. What is the common denominator? Look at John 16:5–11. How is sin defined there?

Why should we expect that belief in Jesus will alter a person's behaviour?

2. Idolatry: sin and symbols.
It is strange that we always want something to **look at** when we worship. So the world's religions usually provide something, like the enormous statues of the Buddha all over Asia.

But notice how biblical symbols have also been turned into idols. Study the story of the bronze snake (Numbers 21:4–9; 2 Kings 18:1–4). Study the history of the Ark of the Covenant (Exodus 25:10–22; 1 Samuel 4:1–11).

Notice God's specific ban on any kind of image for worship (Exodus 20:4–6,22,23).

How does all this bear on Christianity? Is there any danger in the use of a cross in worship?

3. Preaching through pictures.
Jeremiah uses many illustrations in his preaching to ensure that the people remember what he has said. He speaks about marriage, divorce and prostitution. He speaks of tents and vines. He pictures battles and chariots and childbirth, birds in cages, camels in the deserts.

Make a collection of these illustrations. Compare them with the kind of picture language used by our Lord. Why are they so similar? What kind of picture language would we expect a modern Jeremiah to use?

4. The potter (chapter 18).
Trace this theme through the Bible. (See especially Psalm 2:1–9; Isaiah 45:9,10; 64:8,9; Romans 9:19–29.) What is the proper relationship between potter and clay? Why?

JEREMIAH 2

The meaning of success

JEREMIAH'S SUCCESS. This second part of the prophecy is very largely biographical. We see what happens to the faithful messenger of God. He is successful in that he does what God has told him to do, neither more nor less; because what he has prophesied comes to pass; because God continues to use him as his special messenger and because he pleases God.

But looked at from the human angle he is not so successful. Jeremiah is contradicted by other prophets, abandoned by the authorities to the mob, threatened and imprisoned.

THE AUTHOR. Jeremiah's name probably means 'The Lord exalts'. It could have indicated his parents' hopes for Israel, but it is much more likely that it was their hope for him.

Jeremiah was called while still a young man, and spoke for God for some forty years. He remained usable right through his lifetime. And he remained usable beyond his lifetime. He is very frequently quoted in the New Testament.

Jeremiah grew up during the evil reign of Manasseh and therefore was in a position to welcome Josiah's reforms. But he eventually realised that these reforms were external only. They didn't touch the lives of the people, their hearts or their motives. And so Jeremiah's task is confirmed to be one of announcing inevitable judgement – with salvation beyond the horizon, but judgement first.

THE KINGS. Jehoiakim, third of the five kings under whom and to whom Jeremiah preached may be taken as typical of the others. In chapter 36 Jehoiakim is given the chance to study Jeremiah's words in depth. They are written for him and read to him. But notice the comment: 'The king . . . showed no fear . . .' (24).

Jehoiakim's response was to destroy the scroll on which Jeremiah's words were written. This attempt to deny the truth and escape the implications of Jeremiah's message failed.

In fact he hadn't even the satisfaction of destroying the book. He merely opened the way for a longer book on the same theme to be written. God's word does not go away when it is ignored or when it is attacked (Isaiah 40:8).

Outline

Message

Jeremiah shows us what it can mean to be God's messenger.

1. Jeremiah's call.
Jeremiah shares with Isaiah (Isaiah 6) the sense of being unfitted for the task, and experiences, too, God's touch. 1:1–10

2. The clay jar incident.
Jeremiah uses a visual aid. The smashed pot symbolised judgement. The response **ought** to have been repentance. It never came. Instead Jeremiah's own faith is attacked. He is imprisoned, and cries out (20:7–18) 'Why?' He is stripped of all hope, except for his hope in God. 19:1–20:18

3. The incident of the yokes.
Not only were the people unresponsive, Jeremiah was also opposed by other 'prophets'. Their accusations can be imagined: arrogance would be included. Today's preachers can receive the same treatment. 27:1–28:17

4. Jeremiah and the Recabites.
There is always some comfort: the Recabites with their simple loyalty to their forefathers were the encouraging exception. Never over-state the gloom (see Elijah, 1 Kings 19:1–18). 35:1–19

5. The incident of the scroll.
Jeremiah received no support from people, prophet, priest or king. News of the destruction of his book must have discouraged him but he kept going. 36:1–32

6. From dungeon to cistern.
What were his thoughts when instead of release he faced new suffering? And help came from an unexpected source, the Ethiopian. 37:1–38:13

7. No happy ending.
Like Jeremiah, some of God's messengers see only the light at the end of the tunnel . . . 41:1–44:30

Application

1. When to be a pessimist.
The book of Jeremiah offers a vital lesson to the preacher: there can be no preaching of the good news without the preaching also of the bad news.

Jeremiah knew all about the love of God, and the covenant of God, and God's power to save, and God's willingness to save. But **his** task was to announce not salvation so much as judgement.

The preacher of salvation may find himself popular, but the preaching of judgement . . .

that's an occasion for sticks and stones and prison. It is grand to be able to offer the people salvation. But condemnation and judgement: these are the other side of the same coin, as much part of the message of God as salvation. **Cheap** grace is heaven without hell, salvation without repentance, love without justice, discipleship without discipline.

2. The compassion of Jeremiah.
But then there are preachers without mercy.

They revel in preaching hell. Jeremiah was not such a man as that. He would have loved to think that Hananiah's prophecy of peace would be fulfilled: 'Amen! May the Lord do so!' (28:6). But he had to go on to insist that this was **not** to be God's way.

The preacher cannot revel in the thought of hell. God doesn't! It must be preached . . . but always with Jeremiah's spirit of compassion, never vindictively.

3. The humility of the preacher.
From first ('I am only a child', 1:6) to last Jeremiah knew his place. Always it was 'This is what the Lord says' (51:1, etc).

Key themes

1. A message set in history.
Although the book of Jeremiah is not arranged chronologically, it cannot properly be understood apart from its history. After all, Jeremiah was active for forty years, through the reigns of five kings and through probably the most violent period of Israel's history.

Trace the historical setting through 2 Kings 21–25 (the reign of Manasseh, when Jeremiah was a boy) and 2 Chronicles 33–36. Note the many indications of dating in the prophecies of Jeremiah (1:2,3; 3:6; 21:1; 24:1; 25:1; 26:1; 27:1; 28:1; 29:2; 32:1; 34:1,8; 35:1; 36:1, 37:1; 38:14; 39:1; 41:1; 45:1; 49:34). Try to relate the history to the prophecy.

2. Prophecy is also theology.
Notice that in the 'Second Book of Judgement' (chapters 46–51), in which judgement is pronounced against ten groups of people, the major place is given to Babylon (50:1–46; 51:1–64).

Babylon has a special theological significance in the Bible, starting with the rebellion against God at Babel (which is another name for Babylon) in Genesis 11, and concluding with the announcement of the fall of Babylon in Revelation 18. Note also the two Babylon taunt songs in Isaiah, one in each of the main parts of the prophecy (chapters 13 and 47).

Compare these passages with one another. Contrast the history of Babylon with the history of Jerusalem. What significance would you give to these two cities as theological symbols?

3. The return of the exiles to Israel.
Both Isaiah and Jeremiah have a great deal to say about the exile of God's people and their return. But the prophecies were not all fulfilled by their return under Ezra and Nehemiah. Note the seven statements made about the return (32:37–41). How much of this prophecy was fulfilled by the exiles who returned from Babylon? How much has been fulfilled through the present return to Israel? How much has still to be fulfilled? (See also Isaiah 43:1–21; 49:1–26; 52:1–12; 60:1–22.)

LAMENTATIONS

A city in mourning

TITLE. The book has no title in the Hebrew Old Testament but was known by its first word: 'How'. The title 'Dirges' or 'Lamentations' was given to it by early Jewish rabbis.

AUTHOR. The work is actually anonymous. It was given the place next to the book of Jeremiah in the Septuagint, possibly because the two books are connected historically. The author's attitude to the current king (4:20), and to reliance on other nations (4:17) is different from Jeremiah's, but he and Jeremiah (the so-called 'weeping prophet') are similar in temperament, and both see God's judgement behind the tragedy about which they write (see 2:1–8). If the book is a unity, the author was almost certainly a contemporary of Jeremiah.

DATE. The precise dating depends on whether one or several writers are involved in its composition. A reasonable view is that chapters 1–4 were written by an eye-witness of the capture of Jerusalem and the beginning of the Exile (i.e. c. 587 BC), and that chapter 5 was added c. 550 BC, when the Exile had been a fact of experience for some time.

STRUCTURE. The book is a carefully constructed collection of poems, written mainly in the 'qinah' or 'dirge' metre – chapter 5 is the exception. Chapters 1–4 are 'acrostic' poems, each successive stanza beginning with a letter of the Hebrew alphabet in order. (There are minor exceptions to this order and chapter 3 is a more elaborate acrostic.) The pattern was probably intended partly to aid memorisation in a liturgical setting.

BACKGROUND AND PURPOSE. 2 Kings 25:8–12 should be read as the background narrative to Lamentations. The Exile was the most devastating event in Judah's history, and one of the greatest influences in her developing understanding of God. The disastrous fall of Jerusalem in 587 BC demanded an explanation, and this is what the writer provides. Most of the visible signs of God's election of Judah were destroyed (city, Temple, services etc.). The writer faces boldly some harsh truths about Judah's sin, and God's hidden purpose of purification through judgement. To the question (often voiced by those under trial): 'Where is our God?', the writer replies with a profound challenge: 'Try to understand what God is doing.'

Outline

LAMENTATIONS

Message

1. Glorious past, tragic present.
- [ ] Splendour . . . affliction. 3:18,19
- [ ] Riches . . . poverty. 4:5
- [ ] Joy . . . mourning. 5:15

2. Causes of the tragedy.
- [ ] Judah's rebellion against God. 1:20; 4:6
- [ ] Irresponsibility of her leaders. 2:14; 4:13
- [ ] God's inescapable anger. 2:21,22; 4:11
- [ ] Vindication of God's righteousness. 1:18

3. Nature of the tragedy.
- [ ] Famine and death. 1:11; 2:21
- [ ] Ruin of city and Temple. 1:4; 2:6,7
- [ ] Loss of king and princes. 4:7,8,20
- [ ] Breakdown of community life. 5:1–5
- [ ] Scorn from the enemy. 2:15,16
- [ ] Isolation from others. 1:12,16,21
- [ ] Alienation from God. 2:9; 3:8,44

4. Reactions to the tragedy.
- [ ] Desire for revenge. 3:64–66
- [ ] Bewildered complaint to God. 2:13,20
- [ ] Depression. 3:20
- [ ] Recognition of God as judge. 3:1–3,38
- [ ] Confession of sin. 1:8; 5:17
- [ ] Renewed prayer to God. 1:9,20; 5:21
- [ ] Patient bearing of discipline. 3:26–30,39

5. Basis of hope.
- [ ] God's control of man's destiny. 2:17; 3:37
- [ ] God's everlasting rule. 5:19
- [ ] God's reluctance to punish. 3:33
- [ ] God's love and compassion. 3:22–25

6. Message of hope.
- [ ] End of the Exile. 4:22
- [ ] Judgement of Judah's enemies. 4:21,22
- [ ] God's continuing love. 3:32

Application

- [ ] Some tragedy is due to man's willingness to sin, not God's unwillingness to save.
- [ ] Tragedy can lead to black despair, or deepened trust in a God great enough to allow us to handle suffering.
- [ ] When the wall of life shows signs of collapse, we can either paper over the cracks, or help God rebuild the wall.
- [ ] God sometimes removes the signs of his grace, so that our faith and longing may be rooted in him, not in the symbols of his presence.
- [ ] 'I have sinned' may be among the most difficult words in a believer's vocabulary; they are also among the most creative.
- [ ] God does not enjoy disciplining his people, but caring discipline is one aspect of a parent-child relationship.
- [ ] God's love will outlast all our rejection of him. He waits and works to turn us back to himself.

LAMENTATIONS

Key themes

1. Honesty and hope in trouble.
Notice how openly and honestly the writer describes his sorrow, loneliness, sense of bereavement, etc. (especially in chapter 3). The 'bridge passage' between despair and hope is 3:19–24. Try to paraphrase this passage in language which is really meaningful to you.

2. The writer's identification with his people.
This is apparent throughout the book (eg. 2:11; 3:48,51), and is a frequent characteristic of the writing prophets. See, eg. Amos 7:1,2; Isaiah 6:5; Jeremiah 8:21,22.

How did Jesus show his concern for his contemporaries and for us? See Matthew 23:37; Mark 10:45; Philippians 2:6–8; Hebrews 2:14–18.

3. The writer's appeals to God.
There are several of these: eg. 1:9,11,22; 2:20; 3:56,64,66; 5:1,21. He asks God to act in different ways. What does each of the appeals teach about his state of mind and his view of God?

4. God's part in leading men back to himself.
5:21 strongly implies this. Study also Psalm 85:4; Jeremiah 31:18; Acts 11:18; Romans 2:4.

Can you find verses which stress **man's** responsibility to repent and turn back to God? Compare verses in Lamentations with Psalm 119:59; Isaiah 55:6–9.

EZEKIEL

The watchman's report

THE BACKGROUND. In 597 BC the Babylonian king Nebuchadnezzar deported to Babylon King Jehoiachin, with ten thousand of the leading citizens of Israel. The puppet government he left behind in Jerusalem rebelled, and in 587 BC Nebuchadnezzar totally destroyed the city and took another and larger group into exile.

THE AUTHOR. It has been suggested that the book of Ezekiel was compiled by several authors or written at a much later date, but the continuous use of the first person, the precise dating, the personal details given, and the same style found throughout are strong indications that Ezekiel himself made sure that his prophecies were written down and, sometime towards the end of his life, carefully arranged them in book form.

Ezekiel grew up in Judah and was probably influenced in his youth by Josiah's reforms and the prophecies of Jeremiah. He was a priest who was deported to Babylon, probably with Jehoiachin in 597 BC, and his writings were strongly influenced by his priestly background. He settled in exile in Tel-Abib by the river Kebar; five years later when he was thirty he was given a vision of God and called to be a prophet. He probably had an important position (8:1; 14:1), though most people rejected his warnings (3:25), or didn't take him seriously (33:30–32).

THE BOOK. We have in Ezekiel a record of the prophet's life and prophecies dating from 597 to 570 BC. There are four distinct blocks of material. Chapters 1–24 consist mainly of prophecies given before 587 BC where Ezekiel confronts the people with their sin, and shows how the fall of Jerusalem was an inevitable and a richly deserved judgement on them. Chapters 25–32 are prophecies of judgement on surrounding nations. Chapters 33–39 come after the fall of Jerusalem, and Ezekiel encourages the exiles to repent of their past sins, and to become a new community committed to serving God. The final section looks forward beyond the return from exile to the end times, and describes Ezekiel's vision of the new Jerusalem. We will learn more from Ezekiel if we see it as a message to a specific and a very needy people in an actual situation.

Outline

1 EZEKIEL'S CALL
1:1–3:27

1:1–3 The date
1:4–24 The vision of living creatures
1:25–28 The glory of the Lord
2:1–3:15 Ezekiel receives his commission
3:16–27 He is to bring a warning to Israel

2 PROPHECIES OF JUDGEMENT ON JERUSALEM
4:1–12:28

4:1–5:17 Pictures of the siege of Jerusalem
6:1–14 Prophecy against Israel's mountains
7:1–27 The end has come
8:1–9:11 Idolatry in the Temple
10:1–22 God's glory leaves the Temple
11:1–15 Punishment for Israel's leaders
11:16–25 A renewed Israel will return
12:1–28 Pictures of the Exile

3 THE SINS OF ISRAEL AND JERUSALEM
13:1–24:27

13:1–23 False prophets are condemned
14:1–11 Idolaters are condemned
14:12–23 Judgement cannot be avoided
15:1–8 Jerusalem is like a useless vine
16:1–63 Jerusalem is like a prostitute
17:1–24 A parable of two eagles and a vine
18:1–32 Individual responsibility for sin
19:1–14 A lament for Israel's princes
20:1–29 Israel's rebellious past
20:30–44 God's judgement and restoration
20:45–21:32 Judgement by fire and sword
22:1–31 Jerusalem has sinned greatly

23:1–49 Israel and Judah are two adulterous sisters
24:1–14 Jerusalem is like a rusty cooking pot
24:15–27 Ezekiel's wife dies

4 PROPHECIES AGAINST THE NATIONS
25:1–32:32

25:1–7 Against Ammon
25:8–11 Against Moab
25:12–14 Against Edom
25:15–17 Against Philistia
26:1–28:19 Against Tyre
28:20–26 Against Sidon
29:1–32:32 Against Egypt

5 PROPHECIES WHICH LOOK TO THE FUTURE
33:1–39:29

33:1–20 Ezekiel the watchman
33:21–33 Jerusalem's fall is explained
34:1–31 The good shepherd replacing bad shepherds
35:1–15 Edom's treachery will be repaid
36:1–38 New hope for Israel's mountains
37:1–14 New life for dry bones
37:15–28 A renewed nation with a new king
38:1–39:20 A prophecy against Gog
39:21–29 God's purposes for Israel

6 PLANS FOR THE NEW JERUSALEM
40:1–48:35

40:1–42:20 The new Temple
43:1–12 God's glory returns to the Temple
43:13–46:24 Arrangements for worship
47:1–12 The life-giving river
47:13–48:35 The division of the land

Message

1. The nature of God.
The people in exile may have been tempted to doubt God's power. Ezekiel was very concerned to proclaim God's greatness even in this situation of apparent failure.
- [ ] God is glorious and awesome. 1:25–28; 3:23
- [ ] God is holy. 5:11; 36:23
- [ ] God is powerful in every place. 3:12–27; 5:5
- [ ] God is powerful over all nations. 25:1–32:32
- [ ] God is just. 18:25; 33:20
- [ ] God guides and directs his people. 2:2; 11:1,5
- [ ] God acts in order that men might know him. 6:7,14; 20:38
- [ ] God cares for his people like a good shepherd. 34:11–16
- [ ] God gives new life. 36:25–32

2. The seriousness of sin.
Ezekiel's message of doom and punishment seems hard and unfeeling when we think of the people suffering in exile, but it was necessary to bring home to them the point of the exile as a punishment. In order to shame them into true repentance, Ezekiel presents the people as rotten to the core.
- [ ] They had brought shame on God's name. 20:9; 36:20
- [ ] They had defiled God's Temple. 5:11; 23:38
- [ ] They were idolaters. 20:7,18; 22:4
- [ ] They took part in child-sacrifice. 20:26,31
- [ ] They ignored the law. 44:6–8
- [ ] They oppressed the poor. 22:7,12

3. The necessity of judgement.
Because God is just, Israel must be punished. It was only because of God's great patience that he bore with the corrupt nation for so long, but Ezekiel brings the message that God's patience with Israel has at last run out.
- [ ] Judgement cannot be shrugged off. 12:22,27
- [ ] Judgement cannot be avoided. 7:14–27; 22:14
- [ ] Judgement is coming not 'sometime soon' but 'now'. 9:10; 24:14

4. The promise of new life.
God still longed to save Israel. The judgement and exile meant that their sin was punished and there could now be a message of restoration. All were challenged to repent and by faith to join the new community of God's people which would:
- [ ] Be made up of individuals whose hearts have been transformed by God. 36:25–27
- [ ] Be given life by God's Spirit. 37:5
- [ ] Be undivided. 37:15–17
- [ ] Have an eternal covenant with God. 14:11; 37:23
- [ ] Be led by a Davidic Messiah-King. 37:24–28
- [ ] Bring new life to the world. 47:1–12

EZEKIEL

Application

Ezekiel has a lot to say about the way in which the rulers of Israel failed to act as God's representatives, and the people of Israel failed to live as God wanted. However, he also points the way forward showing how life should be lived.

1. Characteristics of a renewed person.
☐ He is directed by God.
☐ His heart is turned towards God.
☐ His aim is to glorify God.
☐ He joyfully accepts God's will.
☐ He is known by his purity and obedience to God.

☐ He lives in the security of knowing God's care for him.
☐ He shows concern for his neighbour.

2. Characteristics of a good leader.
☐ He is obedient to God in everything.
☐ He looks to God for his strength.
☐ He is dedicated to his task.
☐ He identifies with the people.
☐ He cares for the people.
☐ He makes decisions based on justice.
☐ He is not afraid to speak out.

Key themes

1. God's honour.
The Israelites had thought that the honour of Israel was the same thing as the honour of God, so God would never let Israel be destroyed. This was a mistake; Israel had herself brought dishonour to God's name. For the sake of his own glory God acted, first to punish and then to save. Look up 20:40–44; 28:25,26; 36:16–23; 38:17–23; 39:7,8,25–29.

Are there ways in which Christians today bring dishonour to God's name?

2. God's care.
God continued to care for Israel, even when he had to punish them. Look up 11:17; 16:60–63; 28:24–26; 34:11–31; 37:25–27.

Compare the picture of God as a shepherd of Israel, found in chapter 34, with the teaching about the Good Shepherd in John 10:7–18.

3. Responsibility.
Every man is responsible before God for what he does. Neither family nor circumstances can in the end be blamed for the way a man turns out. He himself must make a choice – to serve God and to keep on serving God, or not. Read 18:1–32; 33:7–20.

4. The watchman.
Ezekiel took very seriously his own call to be a watchman, or a 'look-out', warning his fellows that God's judgement was coming, and giving them the chance to turn and accept the way of escape that God was providing. Look up 3:12–21; 33:1–9.

From these and other passages make a list of some of the responsibilities God gives to his servants in the world.

DANIEL

The man of vision

WHO DANIEL WAS. Daniel was a prisoner of war, captured by Nebuchadnezzar of Babylon when Jerusalem fell. Along with many other Jews from the upper classes, Daniel was taken off to Babylon, educated, and put into government service. He served under Nebuchadnezzar, Belshazzar and Darius from 605 BC until about 536 BC.

His name means 'God is my judge', but in Babylon he was given a new name. Just as his own name contained the name of the God of Israel, **El**, so his new name contained the name of the Babylonian deity, **Bel**, 'Belteshazzar', possibly meaning 'May Bel protect the king'.

Note three things about Daniel: he was a man of **great wisdom, great integrity,** and a man of **prayer.**

THE ANSWER TO A PATHETIC QUESTION. Psalm 137, like this prophecy, was written in Babylon:

'By the rivers of Babylon
we sat and wept
when we remembered Zion.'

The Jewish exiles were completely demoralised by their captivity. It seemed that God had abandoned them. So they hung their harps up and refused to sing:

'How can we sing the songs of the Lord
while in a foreign land?'

That was their pathetic question. Daniel answers their question. He demonstrates that God is still God even in Babylon.

DANIEL AND ANTIOCHUS EPIPHANES. The second part of the book is filled with prophetic imagery which we can now see was fulfilled in minute detail in Antiochus Epiphanes who ruled most of Asia Minor, Syria and Palestine from 175 BC until 164 BC. Many writers on Daniel deny that there is any prophecy here at all, and suggest that the book was, in fact, written about 165 BC, not by Daniel but by some unknown author. Their main objection seems to be to the concept of prophecy as a real foretelling of future events, especially with such detail.

But these prophecies are taken seriously by Jesus (Matthew 24:15) and ought to be given at least two and probably three points of fulfilment: in the time of Antiochus, at the fall of Jerusalem in AD70 and at the final End Time. The four beasts of Daniel 7 should probably also be interpreted in three ways, as the great world empires, past, present and future.

Outline

1 **DANIEL IN BABYLON**
1:1–21

1:1–7 How Daniel came to Babylon
1:8–16 Daniel turns vegetarian
1:17–21 God's gifts

2 **NEBUCHADNEZZAR'S DREAM OF A STATUE**
2:1–49

2:1–13 The dream
2:14–23 Daniel as a man of prayer
2:24–45 The dream interpreted
2:46–49 Daniel as a man with power

3 **THE FIERY FURNACE**
3:1–30

3:1–7 The king's command
3:8–23 Accused, sentenced
3:24–27 Delivered
3:28–30 Rewarded

4 **NEBUCHADNEZZAR'S DREAM OF A TREE**
4:1–37

4:1–18 The dream described
4:19–27 The dream explained
4:28–37 The dream fulfilled

5 **BELSHAZZAR'S FEAST**
5:1–31

5:1–9 Writing on the wall
5:10–12 Call for Daniel
5:13–28 Daniel explains it all
5:29–31 Reward and ruin

6 **DANIEL WITH THE LIONS**
6:1–28

6:1–4 The man of total integrity

6:5–9 The plot
6:10–18 The lions' den
6:19–23 God leads out again
6:24–28 A royal proclamation

7 **THE VISION OF THE FOUR BEASTS**
7:1–28

8 **THE RAM AND THE GOAT**
8:1–27

9 **PAUSE FOR PRAYER**
9:1–19

10 **THE SEVENTY SEVENS**
9:20–27

11 **PRELUDE TO PROPHECY**
10:1–21

10:1–3 The circumstances
10:4–17 Daniel's collapse
10:18–21 A strengthening touch

12 **A VISION OF KINGS**
11:1–12:4

11:1–35 The two kings
11:36–45 A king-usurper
12:1–4 A king-deliverer

13 **A VISION AT THE RIVER**
12:5–13

DANIEL

Message

1. Man's fatal interest in religion. 3:1–30
- [ ] An object of worship provided. Note its construction – soft but impressive gold; and its size – unwieldy but again outwardly impressive. 3:1–3
- [ ] A decree proclaimed. A new liturgy! 'Tell us what to do and we'll do it!' Nebuchadnezzar was right in thinking that awe and fear combine to promote worship. 3:4–6
- [ ] Obedience offered. The people are like sheep and they will follow a 'shepherd'. A warning to leaders here. 3:7
- [ ] An accusation laid. Thank God for the 'non-conformists', people who know right from wrong, even when the wrong comes from the king. 3:8–12
- [ ] An alternative offered. Recant or die! It's not often that the alternatives are as stark as these but **we often deny Christ** when the option is not death but merely being laughed at, or thought odd. 3:13–15
- [ ] An answer given. And what a grand answer! **We will not**! Trumpets! 3:16–18
- [ ] Sentence executed. The faith of these three is tested to the limit; there is, apparently, to be no deliverance. 3:19–23
- [ ] Deliverance effected. A fourth figure, a divine figure, walks with the three in the fire (a remarkable illustration of Isaiah 43:2). 3:24–27

- [ ] A new decree. Nebuchadnezzar is very ready to add the God of Israel to his collection, even to recognise his unique power to save. But he remains 'The God of Shadrach, Meshach and Abednego'. 3:28–29
- [ ] A new promotion. From prison to power, from disgrace to honour. Joseph had a similar experience (Genesis 41). 3:30

2. God's total knowledge of the future. 9:20–27
- [ ] Prelude to revelation. Again we find Daniel at prayer; not asking for things but confessing; getting right with God. 9:20–23
- [ ] A concise summary. Seventy sevens, not merely 490 years, but a figure standing for the complete period of time in God's plans. 9:24
- [ ] Guidance for interpretation. The programme has three parts: 49 years, 434 years and a final 7 years. Verse 27 probably refers both to Antiochus (who desolated the altar by instituting heathen rites), and to the times of Titus when, on July 17, AD 70, the Temple sacrifices ended, and to the end time of the Book of Revelation. Daniel must be interpreted in the light of Revelation. 9:25–27

Application

1. The Christian as an exile.
As Paul put it, 'our citizenship is in heaven' (Philippians 3:20), and Peter advises us, 'live your lives as strangers here in reverent fear' (1 Peter 1:17).

That's what Daniel was: an exile, a stranger, a foreigner. The early part of this book is a marvellous guide to how God's people ought to behave themselves in a hostile world.

These early chapters teach us:
- [ ] Don't be impressed by the world's applause, or influenced by its gifts (5:17).

DANIEL

☐ Don't be intimidated by the world's threats; say what has to be said (3:16–18).

☐ Don't be infected by the world's religions; stay with God and leave the consequences to him (6:1–10).

2. God's people as God's partners.

Throughout Daniel there is the awareness that God is there, with his people, sharing his plans with them, sharing their experiences. That was the lesson Moses had to tell the exiles in Egypt. They had suffered and prayed, and yet God had not saved them. God told Moses:

'I have indeed seen the misery of my people in Egypt. I have heard them crying out because of their slave drivers, and I am concerned about their suffering. So I have come down to rescue them' (Exodus 3:7,8).

Daniel reminds us that although God may sometimes allow us to suffer, he is always at hand, always able to free us. And as his partners he sometimes allows us a glimpse of coming glory.

Key themes

The end times.

☐ The book of Daniel is prophetic, but in a special way, containing unusual pictures and symbolism. It is primarily concerned with the end times. In this it is similar to Revelation, but must also be compared with Mark 13, Matthew 24 and Luke 21.

☐ From our Lord's words (Mark 13:32–4) an important principle emerges: we are not intended to know exactly when the end will come. The information we are given in Daniel is not enough to allow us to work out the precise time of the end.

☐ But we are not left without any indication. There are some who laugh at prophecy and deny the idea of an apocalypse, a catastrophic end to the age. All goes on as it always has done (2 Peter 3:1–13). There are others who want to know more than we are allowed to, and try to work out the precise time of the end.

☐ Many solutions to the mystery of the 'sevens' have been proposed. The first period of seven sevens may refer to the period of exile, from 587/6 BC when Jerusalem fell, to 538/7 BC when Cyrus ordered the rebuilding of Jerusalem.

There is widespread agreement that the Anointed One (the meaning of the Hebrew word, **Messiah**) must refer to Christ. And it is commonly suggested that between the 69 weeks and the final week, that is, between the first and second comings of Christ, there is a long 'pause' during which the good news is to be preached.

☐ The events of 9:27 and the reference to the 'middle of the week' are often compared with Revelation 11:1–13, and certainly Daniel's words cannot be interpreted without reference to this and other passages in Revelation. Study and compare: Daniel 9:20–27; Matthew 24:1–44; 2 Peter 3; and Revelation 11. Note how the number seven has a symbolic importance in the Bible. Trace the many sets of seven referred to in Revelation. The prophecies are certainly more easily understood if the number seven is taken symbolically and not literally, to represent 'completeness'.

List what we **do** know about the end times. Do we need to know more? Knowing this much, what sort of people ought we to be (2 Peter 3:11–15)?

HOSEA

A faithless people; a faithful God

THE DATE. The kings listed in 1:1 give a maximum range for Hosea's prophecy of 780-692 BC, but it is likely that most of his work was done in the time between the last years of Jeroboam's reign and the fall of Samaria – i.e. from about 755-722 BC. Hosea is the second of the four writers known as the eighth-century prophets (Amos, Hosea, Isaiah and Micah).

THE WRITER. Hosea is the only prophet from the northern kingdom of Israel whose writings have survived. His father's name was Beeri but we are told nothing about his town or his early background. Some people think that Hosea was a baker because he shows a detailed knowledge of the trade (7:4–8), but he also has many references to farming (10:11–13; 13:3), so we cannot be sure about this. It is perhaps most likely that Hosea worked as a professional prophet.

THE SITUATION TO WHICH HE WROTE. Almost all the prophecies in Hosea are aimed at Israel (usually called Ephraim – the name of the largest tribe), although there are a few references to Judah. The religion of Israel had become totally corrupt; officially they served God but everywhere their worship was mixed up with idolatry and Baalism. The country had been fairly stable and prosperous under Jeroboam, but in the years after his death there was a rapid decline, both economically and politically. They wavered between the powers of Assyria and Egypt, but ignored God. They were finally overrun by Assyria in 721 BC.

HIS FAMILY. Hosea had rather a tragic family life. God told him to marry a woman who was unfaithful to him. Hosea loved his wife, Gomer, and they had three children whose names were really a message to Israel. But after a while Gomer ran away and became a prostitute. Hosea still loved her, and eventually, though she had become little more than a slave, he bought her back. She was then restored to her status as his wife, although she had to go through a time of cleansing before this could happen.

HIS MESSAGE. Hosea's own marriage relationship provides a very vivid picture of the relationship between God and Israel. God loved Israel and even when they deserted him and served other gods, he still loved them and longed to have them back as his people. Because of his own suffering, Hosea could explain clearly the way in which God was suffering because of his love for a faithless people. Thus Hosea strongly attacks the idolatry of Israel and calls them to repent and return to serving God who loves them and will gladly forgive them and restore them.

Outline

1 HOSEA'S FAMILY AND GOD'S FAMILY 1:1–3:5

1:1 Introduction: The setting
1:2–9 Hosea's wife and children
1:10,11 Israel as God's children
2:1–13 Israel, the faithless wife
2:14–23 God, the loving husband
3:1–5 Hosea buys back his wife

2 THE CORRUPTION OF ISRAEL 4:1–5:15

4:1–3 The case against Israel
4:4–9 The case against the priests
4:10–19 They are behaving like prostitutes
5:1–12 Warning of judgement to come
5:13–15 Assyria can't protect Israel

3 GOD'S LOVE IS REJECTED 6:1–8:6

6:1–3 Repentance?
6:4–6 Their love for God is not heartfelt
6:7–11 Israel and Judah are both faithless
7:1 God longs to restore them
7:2–7 The people want nothing of it
7:8–13 They depend on foreign nations

7:14–16 They even turn to Baal
8:1–6 Israel spurns God's love

4 JUDGEMENT IS INEVITABLE 8:7–10:15

8:7–10 Their allies will prove useless
8:11–14 Punishment must follow their sin
9:1–6 Stop! Festivals aren't what God wants
9:7–9 The message is unpopular – but true
9:10–17 Israel will be cast off by God
10:1–15 They have kept on being unfaithful

5 REPENTANCE IS STILL POSSIBLE 11:1–14:9

11:1–5 God loved Israel as a father
11:6,7 Yet they rejected him
11:8,9 God longs for the people now
11:10–12 He loves them in spite of their sin
12:1–6 The door for return is wide open
12:7–14 But faithlessness must be punished
13:1–16 Only God's love can save Israel
14:1–3 A final plea for repentance
14:4–9 God will restore all who seek him

HOSEA

Message

1. God's love is constant.
- [ ] In the past God has blessed and cared for Israel. 2:15; 11:1; 13:4,5
- [ ] In the present God longs to restore Israel. 7:1; 11:8,9
- [ ] In the future, because of God's gracious love, and only because of that, there is hope of salvation. 11:10,11; 14:4–9

2. God's love is demanding.
God is holy (2:19,20), and if they are to be his people, Israel too must live holy lives. A relationship with God can only exist on his terms, and these terms are that his people give exclusive service and live upright lives. 4:7–10; 5:4 11:5–7

3. Sin is serious.
Breaking faith with God is as serious as adultery in a marriage. 1:2; 2:1–5

Hosea brought Gomer back (3:1–5), but for her own sake the old relationship could not be fully restored without discipline. So it is with Israel. God's love for them meant their sin must be dealt with, not ignored. God longed to forgive them, but repentance must come first. 14:1–9

4. Repentance and service must be real.
- [ ] Repentance is not an easy or a shallow thing. It must be witnessed, not by a renewed show of religion, but by new lives. 6:1–4
- [ ] Sacrifices without commitment and obedience are quite unacceptable to God. 6:6

Application

1. What God cannot allow his people:
- [ ] To worship anyone else. He alone is to be honoured; shared worship is no worship at all.
- [ ] To serve anyone else. Full obedience can only be given to one Lord; to serve another is to be unfaithful to God.
- [ ] To depend on anyone else. God can be trusted; to lean on others is to doubt his care.

2. What God will be to his people:
- [ ] A husband
- [ ] A father
- [ ] A doctor
- [ ] A shepherd

In other words he will fulfil all their needs. We cannot limit God to one picture. His love is greater than anything we can imagine.

HOSEA

3. What God wants from his people:
- Repentance, involving a real change of behaviour.
- Knowledge of himself: they must make the effort to study and understand the things God has told them about himself and his will for them.
- Obedience, involving right behaviour towards others as well as towards God.
- Devotion: God loves them and wants a wholehearted love from them in return.
- Faithfulness; loyalty was out of fashion in Hosea's time as it is today, but service of God cannot be half-hearted. It involves a total and an unswerving commitment.

Key themes

1. Relationship.
Hosea makes it clear that the basis of religion is a real relationship with God. This relationship makes demands on God's people, but it is also costly to God, who suffers when his love is rejected and his people are unfaithful. 7:1–7; 8:1–5; 11:3–7

From these and other passages you may find, note the ways in which God wanted to relate to Israel, and the way in which they responded.

2. Israel's unfaithfulness.
Israel's turning away from God affected their religious, political and moral lives. Lcok for verses where Hosea speaks out against their sin in each of these areas.

3. The love of God.
God loved Israel in spite of their sin. Make a list of all the references in Hosea to God's love, and note the different ways in which God's love is expressed, involving both blessing and judgement.

4. The need for knowledge.
Hosea was sure that the heart of Israel's problem lay in their failure to understand God. If they really knew him, then their behaviour would be transformed. Look up 2:13,20; 4:1,6,14; 5:4; 8:14; 13:6.

JOEL

Judgement and mercy

WHO WAS JOEL? The name Joel means 'Yahweh is God'. It was the name of Samuel's eldest son (1 Samuel 8:2), but we know nothing about the prophet Joel beyond the short description he gives us of himself in 1:1.

It is generally thought that he was one of the earliest of all the Old Testament prophets, and he might well have known both Elijah and Elisha in his youth.

He prophesied in the southern kingdom, Judah, perhaps during the reign of Joash (2 Kings 11 and 12).

WHAT WAS HIS BACKGROUND? The key phrase is 'the day of the Lord'. The country had recently been devastated by a plague of locusts, and for Joel this had a spiritual significance. He believed that the locusts had been a divine judgement, God's response to the people's sin. But greater judgement was at hand: Judah was surrounded by hostile nations like hordes of locusts. Their only hope lay in repentance. This book focuses on judgement past (the locusts), judgement at hand (the nations), the availability of God's mercy and God's demand for repentance (1:13-20; 2:12-17).

WHAT WAS HIS MESSAGE? Nevertheless, Joel was a prophet of hope. In fact he has been called 'the prophet of religious revival' (2:18-32).

We can see this particularly in the events of the day of Pentecost when some of Joel's prophecies were fulfilled. Of course some still await fulfilment (Joel 2:28,29; Acts 2:16-21).

But we may also see in the book of Joel the forecast of an eventual re-gathering of the Jewish people in their own land, and of the judgement of the nations (Joel 3:2-7; Matthew 25:32).

A PROPHETIC GEM. As literature, Joel is a gem. Nowhere else is there to be found such a graphic description of the devastation caused by the swirling clouds of locusts. And it was Joel's genius to see in these locusts an unforgettable illustration of the enemy hordes gathering round Judah to inflict judgement from the Lord.

Outline

JOEL

Message

Joel's message focuses on 'the day of the Lord', the time when the Lord would finally intervene in the world, when the Lord would reign as king, and his people would be vindicated. Of course this same theme is present in other prophets (Isaiah 2:6–22; Amos 5:18–20; Zephaniah 1:2–18).

1. Preparation for the 'day of the Lord'.
☐ The plague of locusts was intended as a warning (see Amos 7:1–3). 1:1–12; 2:1–11

☐ God's demand was that the people should repent (see Zephaniah 2:1–3). 1:13–20; 2:12–17

2. The Lord's answer.
☐ Blessing for the nation. 2:18–27
☐ The outpouring of the Spirit. 2:28–32
☐ The judgement of the surrounding nations. 3:1–8
☐ The valley of decision: God's people vindicated. 3:9–21

Application

1. When things go wrong.
'God whispers to us in our joys, but shouts to us in our sorrows.' When things go wrong for us or for our nation it may well be God calling to us. He uses disaster and sorrow to turn people to himself, but we often miss his voice because we are content with a neat scientific explanation of 'natural' events. Joel's task was to show the people what God was saying to them through the plague of locusts.

2. Putting things right.
Joel's task was to tell the people what they were doing wrong, but the task of the people was to put things right! When God gives a clear warning the only response should be repentance.

3. Repentance and forgiveness.
These two are inextricably linked in the Bible.

If we repent we **will** be forgiven. And if we **won't** repent then we **can't** be forgiven.

4. Joel's message to the church.
Joel preached to a nation, God's chosen people. Natural disaster was shown to be due to spiritual decay. This has an important lesson for God's chosen people today, the church.

Do we suffer spiritual famine? Do we experience spiritual defeat? Do the unconverted people around laugh at the church? Are we depressed, discouraged? If so, sin, unbelief, disobedience may be the reason. If so, repentance is the response. And if God's people hear, respond, repent and obey, God will forgive and restore us to the place of blessing.

JOEL

Key themes

1. The day of the Lord.
The phrase appears five times here. (1:15; 2:1,11,31; 3:14. See also 3:18, 'that day'.) There are many other Old Testament references: Isaiah 2:12–22; Ezekiel 13:1–7; Zephaniah 1:14–2:3; Zechariah 14:1–21. What are five characteristics of the Day of the Lord?

2. The outpouring of God's Spirit.
Joel expects a great outpouring of God's Spirit. Notice that this is to be 'on all people' (2:28) and it will take place 'before the coming of the great and dreadful day of the Lord' (2:31).

On the day of Pentecost Peter said that Joel's prophecy was being fulfilled (Acts 2:1–21). What part of Joel's prophecy has **been** fulfilled, what is now demanded of everyone, everywhere (Acts 2:38) and what part of Joel's prophecy has still to be fulfilled? (See also Mark 13:3–37.)

3. God's judgement.
When God decided to discipline his people he sometimes used famine or plagues (like Joel's locusts), but he sometimes used other nations. The book of Judges is filled with examples of this. But sometimes those nations got the wrong idea. They became proud, boastful and then they, in turn, had to be punished. See this in 3:1–14.

Do we get the idea that because God has used us in some way he will always use us? What other things can make us proud? How might God punish us?

4. The King and his kingdom.
Right through the Bible there is a stream of chapters and verses that reveal a hope, an expectation, that one day God will reign on earth. 3:17,18 is part of this stream. (See also Isaiah 9:6,7; 35; 40, and the thousand years prophecy of Revelation 20.) It is usually understood that Jesus will actually be the ruler.

Why, then, did Jesus not clearly accept the title King of the Jews? Why did he not allow people to reveal his power (eg. Mark 1:44; 3:12; 5:43; 7:24,36)? Does Acts 1:6 help in understanding the secrecy?

Read Romans 8:18–22. What is meant by the 'frustration' of the whole of creation? How can this frustration be ended?

AMOS

Prophet to the affluent society

THE PROPHET. Amos was not a professional prophet. He was a shepherd (1:1) and probably a sheep-breeder who went to the markets to sell his sheep. It may have been on such a visit that he began preaching.

His home was in Tekoa, twelve miles south of Jerusalem. Since he preached in the northern kingdom of Israel he was especially unwelcome – a southerner preaching in the north (7:12)! Although he was not a professional prophet (7:14), he had heard the voice of God and so felt that he had no option but to preach (1:1,2).

THE DATE. Amos dates his preaching as 'two years before the earthquake'. The earthquake made a great impression at the time (see 8:8; 9:5; Zechariah 14:5), but can no longer be dated exactly. It was probably around 760 BC. Two kings are mentioned: Uzziah reigned 783-742 BC and Jeroboam II 786-746 BC.

THE SITUATION. Amos was preaching to a society which had never had it so good.

1. It was a time of peace. The superpower, Assyria, was led by weak rulers, and so Israel was left alone.

2. It was a time of prosperity. Trade had increased and Israel was for a short time quite wealthy.

3. It was a time of problems. The wealth was not fairly distributed to all in the society. The rich got richer, whilst the poor not only got poorer but were deliberately kept under by the rich. At the same time they began to leave God out of their lives. They kept up the outward show of religion, but it really meant nothing to them.

THE STYLE. Amos must have been a courageous man. His preaching is straight to the point. He never minces his words even when arguing with a priest (7:17). His prophecy is full of judgement and doom. He presents God as a roaring lion, and one can just imagine him roaring his sermons at unwilling and embarrassed listeners whose peace he had rudely disturbed.

For all that there are moments of tenderness in his prophecy and the book ends with a message of hope.

Outline

1 THE PROPHET: HIS TIME
AND MESSAGE
1:1,2

2 THE NATIONS CALLED
TO ACCOUNT
1:3–2:5

1:3–5 Syria: neglected human rights
1:6–8 Philistia: sold people for money
1:9,10 Phoenicia: broke her promises
1:11,12 Edom: hated her brother
1:13–15 Ammon: cruel to the defenceless
2:1–3 Moab: spiteful to the dead
2:4,5 Judah: unfaithful to her God

3 ISRAEL IN
THE DOCK
2:6–16

2:6–9 Their serious crimes
2:10–12 Their short memories
2:13–16 Their stiff sentence

4 THE VERDICT OF
THE JUDGE
3:1–4:3

3:1,2 The responsibilities of love
3:3–8 The inevitability of judgement
3:9–4:3 The description of judgement

5 WHEN WILL THEY
EVER LEARN?
4:4–13

4:4,5 Carry on ignoring God
4:6 God has spoken through famine . . .
4:7,8 . . . and drought . . .
4:9 . . . and crop failure . . .
4:10 . . . and war . . .
4:11 . . . and disaster
4:12,13 Get ready to meet God

6 THE FUNERAL OF
RELIGION
5:1–27

5:1–3 The funeral hymn
5:4–6 An invitation to seek God
5:7–13 The causes of death
5:14,15 An invitation to seek good
5:16–27 Post mortem on religious
hypocrisy

7 THE FATE OF
THE RICH
6:1–14

6:1–7 The emptiness of luxury
6:8–10 The horror of judgement
6:11–14 The folly of injustice

8 THE VISIONS OF
THE PROPHET
7:1–8:6

7:1–3 A vision of locusts
7:4–6 A vision of fire
7:7–9 A vision of a plumb-line
7:10–17 Interlude: the persecution of Amos
8:1–6 A vision of ripe fruit

9 THE SILENCE OF
GOD
8:7–9:10

8:7,8 God's memory
8:9–14 God's silence
9:1–10 God's destruction

10 HOPE FOR
THE FUTURE
9:11–15

AMOS

Message

1. God judges sinful nations.
☐ God has a right to judge all the nations of the world, not just his chosen nation, because he is the Creator (1:3–2:3).
☐ He judges them because of the way they treat their fellow human beings.
☐ The sentences passed on each nation were worked out in the course of history.

2. God wants social justice.
☐ The sins he condemns:
   – Money was supreme. 3:10,15; 6:4–6
   – The poor were exploited. 2:7; 4:1; 5:11
   – Justice was perverted. 2:7; 5:7,10; 8:4–6
   – Morals were lax. 2:7; 4:1
☐ The behaviour he expects:
   – Love goodness. 5:14,15
   – Guard justice. 5:15,24
   – Live righteously. 5:24

3. God hates religious hypocrisy.
Israel were:
☐ Unfaithful to their agreement. 2:4,5; 3:1,2
☐ Disrespectful in the Temple. 2:8
☐ Ungrateful for the past. 2:9–12
☐ Pretending in their worship. 4:4,5; 5:21–27; 8:5
☐ Self-satisfied in their attitudes. 6:1
☐ Spiteful to the prophet. 7:10–17

4. God loves undeserving Israel.
Even though Amos basically preaches a message of judgement he does speak about God as a God of love.
☐ God freely chooses to love. 3:2
☐ God patiently tries to teach. 4:6–11
☐ God graciously offers to help. 5:6
☐ God generously promises to restore. 9:11–15

Application

1. How to live in the world.
Remember:
☐ Human rights matter
☐ Even-handed justice is important
☐ Poor people are valuable to God
☐ Luxury living is dangerous living
☐ Judgement is on its way

2. How to live before God.
Remember:
☐ Put God before gain
☐ Make sure your worship is real
☐ Listen for the voice of God
☐ Be prepared to meet God
☐ Don't trust religion – trust God

AMOS

Key themes

1. Breaking the law of God.

Amos condemns the nations for their sin
(1:3,6,9,11,13; 2:1,4,6), that is, for their
rebellion against God's law. Breaking God's
law lies at the root of sin. The transgressions
were both personal and national. List the sins
for which the people are condemned here.
What are the corresponding sins today?

2. Facing the punishment of God.

When people sin:

- ☐ Punishment is inevitable because sin
  brings it in its train (1:3,6,9,11,13;
  2:1,4,6).
- ☐ Punishment is inescapable because God
  chooses to let it run its course (3:13–15).
- ☐ Punishment is greater for those who have
  had the privilege of being in a special
  relationship with God (3:2).
- ☐ Punishment is only carried out by God
  with great reluctance (7:1–6).

How might we realistically speak of God's
punishment in today's world?

3. Hearing the voice of God.

One of the worst fates possible for man is to
endure a period in which God is silent
(8:11,12). But in Amos' day God had spoken
through:

- ☐ Events (4:4–11)
- ☐ The prophet (7:14,15). Amos was no
  professional but a man taken from an
  ordinary job, with a burning desire to
  speak God's word.

Does God still speak in these ways
today? Think of examples. What does Amos
himself teach us about being a servant of God?

4. Doing the will of God.

Amos called on Israel to repent. Repentance
is more than just saying 'sorry'. It is a
complete change of mind which results in
people turning their back on their old way of
living and starting to live as God intends.
What God wanted from Israel was action
(5:14,15,24). What should be the fruits of
repentance in your life?

OBADIAH & NAHUM

The Avenger has come

AUTHOR.
- OBADIAH. His name means 'servant of the Lord', but his precise identity is uncertain. Several men in the Old Testament bear this name.
- NAHUM. His name means 'comforter'. Nothing is known about him, except that he was a native of Elkosh, probably the town twenty miles south west of Jerusalem.

  Both 'names' may, in fact, refer to the function of each prophet rather than his personal identity.

DATE.
- OBADIAH. Much depends on the date of the capture of Jerusalem referred to in verses 10-14. This is either the capture by the Babylonians in 587 BC (in which case Obadiah is to be dated in the mid-sixth century), or that by the Arabians and Philistines in the ninth century. The majority of scholars hold to a sixth century date.
- NAHUM. The date of writing is between 663 BC, when Thebes was captured by Assyrians (see 3:8–10), and the conquest of Nineveh, capital of Assyria, by a combined force of Medes and Babylonians in 612 BC, vividly described in 2:6–8.

BACKGROUND. Common to both books is an atmosphere of hatred of the enemies of God's people. Obadiah attacks Edom, and Nahum, Assyria. Both nations, at the height of their power, were arrogant and oppressive. The Edomites were 'first cousins' of the Israelites – Esau, from whom Edom was descended, was Jacob's brother – and the hostility between the brothers was reflected in the frequent wars between Israel and Edom. Assyria at her peak was a source of terror to the whole of western Asia, and guilty of gross atrocities in war, especially against Egypt.

FEATURES. Both prophecies are in the form of poetry, and contain the most realistic description of the siege and attack of a city in the whole of the Old Testament.

Both prophets breathe a desire for revenge, relishing each detail of the downfall of Israel's enemies.

Both books are unusual in the absence of condemnation of Israel and of calls to repentance so common in the eighth century writings of Amos and Micah. Neither book is directly referred to in the New Testament.

Outline

OBADIAH

 DESTRUCTION OF EDOM
1–9

1 Decree of judgement
2,3 Edom, proud but despised
4 No escape!
5,6 Nothing left!
7 Treachery among friends
8,9 Failure of Edom's 'props'

 REASONS FOR EDOM'S DESTRUCTION
10–14

10 Unbrotherliness
11 Indifference
12 Scorn
13 Robbery
14 Violence

 THE TERRIBLE DAY OF GOD
15,16

 RESTORATION OF ISRAEL
17–21

17 Escape of the survivors
18 Final defeat of Edom
19,20 Restoration of the land
21 God's universal kingship

NAHUM

 A PORTRAIT OF GOD
1:1–8

1:1–3 God's anger and mercy
1:4–6 God's power over nature
1:7 God's protection of the faithful
1:8 God's pursuit of his enemies

 DESTRUCTION OF NINEVEH
1:9–15

1:9–11 Powerlessness against God
1:12,13 Deliverance of Judah
1:14 Obliteration of Nineveh
1:15 Rejoicing in Judah

 ATTACK ON NINEVEH
2:1–3:4

2:1–5 Preparations for battle
2:6,7 Assault and conquest
2:8–10 Flight and plunder
2:11–13 Desolation in the city
3:1–4 Slaughter in the city

 GOD VERSUS NINEVEH
3:5–19

3:5–7 God the avenger
3:8–11 The example of Thebes
3:12–15 Futility of resistance
3:16–18 Uselessness of leaders
3:19 Joy of Nineveh's enemies

OBADIAH & NAHUM

Message

Obadiah

1. God is Edom's enemy.
- [ ] He will bring Edom down. 2–4,8
- [ ] He will use other nations. 1,7

2. Edom cannot escape from God.
- [ ] Her natural defences cannot save. 3,4
- [ ] Her sources of boasting will vanish. 6,8,9

3. Edom's punishment is deserved.
- [ ] Israel was her brother. 12
- [ ] She gloated over Israel's misfortune. 12,13
- [ ] She failed to help Israel. 11
- [ ] She actively helped Israel's enemies. 14
- [ ] She will be treated similarly. 15

4. Israel will rise again.
- [ ] She has known ruin and disaster. 12,13
- [ ] Mount Zion, her home, will be holy. 17
- [ ] She will expand her territory. 17–20

5. God will be supreme.
- [ ] All nations will face his judgement. 15,16
- [ ] He will rule as universal king. 21

Nahum

1. The two sides of God's character.
- [ ] The sure protector of his people. 1:7
- [ ] The destroyer of his enemies. 1:2,6

2. The crime and judgement of Assyria.
- [ ] She has lied, plundered, led astray. 3:1,4
- [ ] All have suffered at her hand. 3:19
- [ ] She has plotted against God. 1:11
- [ ] She must now deal with God. 3:5
- [ ] Her gods cannot save her. 1:14
- [ ] Her lion's strength has waned. 2:11–13
- [ ] She will be ashamed and despised. 2:10; 3:5–7
- [ ] Her defeat will be absolute. 1:14,15

3. The tragedy and triumph of Israel.
- [ ] She has been troubled and afflicted. 1:7,12; 2:2
- [ ] She will keep a joyful festival. 1:15

Application

1. We live in a moral universe.
It is a universe controlled by God who will ultimately right all wrongs.

2. God is holy as well as loving.
He is not the condoning, short-sighted God we sometimes imagine him to be.

3. God is in control of history.
This is sometimes accomplished through international politics. 'In the end, God . . .' will be the final comment of all history.

4. Pride always leads to a fall.
This is especially true if pride leaves no room for God.

5. We are all answerable to God.
We are all answerable for the way we treat each other, and we cannot escape confrontation with God.

6. God's people are not immune from trouble.
But God is a mighty source of security to those who belong to him, and he can be trusted with their ultimate happiness.

7. The 'how long?' of the sufferer.
One day the cry will change to a triumphant 'At last!'

Key themes

1. The light and shade of God's character.
Paul speaks of 'the kindness and sternness of God' (Romans 11:22). Obadiah and Nahum major on the sternness, but there are indications of his kindness, especially in Nahum. Find examples of this, and go on to study the following: Isaiah 55:7; Micah 7:18; Psalms 125:2; 139:1–8; Isaiah 54:5–10. What different aspects of God's kindness do these verses teach?

2. The Lord is a jealous God.
What do you think is meant by 'jealous' in Nahum 1:2? The following verses may help you to answer this question: Exodus 34:14; Zechariah 8:2,3; 1 Corinthians 10:21,22; Titus 2:14; 1 Peter 2:9,10.

3. Man's accountability to God.
Obadiah and Nahum make it clear that Edom and Assyria must face **God's** judgement because of their crimes. Psalm 33:13–15;

Galatians 6:7; Hebrews 4:13 will help to emphasise the truth that our final point of reference is God.

4. God's care for all people.
Obadiah and Nahum give only part of the biblical teaching on God's attitude towards those who do not belong to him in a special way. For balancing evidence, study Jonah 4:11; Isaiah 19:25; 45:22; John 3:17; 1 Timothy 2:3–6.

5. The kingdom will be the Lord's.
Obadiah 21: The Bible often refers to God's rule over men in terms of 'kingship' or a 'kingdom', and makes it clear that this rule is centred in Christ. What truths about God's kingdom can you discover in the following verses: Matthew 12:28; John 18:36; Romans 14:17; Revelation 12:10?

JONAH

How can God bless the wicked?

THE PROPHET WHO IS DIFFERENT. Although the book of Jonah is
included in the Old Testament collection of prophets, it is not
like the others. For a start, it is an account of incidents in the
prophet's life. His actual message is very short indeed (3:4).
Again, it seems to have been written up by someone else who
speaks about Jonah in the third person, unlike the other books
in this section of the Bible. Apart from this book all we know
about Jonah is that he preached in the northern kingdom during
the reign of Jeroboam II (2 Kings 14:25), which would date him
around 780 BC. But this does not mean that the book was put
together as early as this. It may have been much later, when
Israel needed the lesson which Jonah had to learn the hard way.

WHAT ABOUT THE WHALE? Modern people find the story of Jonah
very difficult to take because it is hard for them to believe that
he could have survived for that time 'in a whale' (1:17). Actually
the Bible calls it 'a big fish' or sea monster (Matthew 12:40), so
we do not know quite what it was. Because, it is argued, this
kind of thing does not happen, it would be better to think of the
book as a sort of parable rather than as actual fact. It is the
message that matters, not the fish.

Although this is certainly true, it would be unlike other
parables, in that Jonah is described as a real, historical person.
What is more, Jesus seems to take him and his adventures
seriously when comparing his resurrection with this event
(Matthew 12:39–41). If God is Lord of his own creation, which is
part of the message of the book, there is no reason at all why he
could not arrange events in this way.

NINEVEH. Of all the peoples of ancient times, there were none who
delighted in sheer cruelty as much as the Assyrians. Later on
they were going to wipe out the northern kingdom and crush
Judah. In Jonah's day, their power was on the increase, and they
presented a terrible threat to God's people. If anyone did not
deserve God's goodness it was those who lived in Assyria's
capital city. We can understand, therefore, something of
Jonah's natural revulsion when he was told to go and preach
there, especially as he had a feeling that God would forgive
them (4:2).

Outline

1 **THE RUNAWAY PROPHET**
1:1–17

1:1,2 God's commission
1:3 Jonah's disobedience
1:4–16 All at sea
1:17 No ordinary fish

2 **THE GRATEFUL PROPHET**
2:1–10

2:1–6 Jonah drowning
2:7–10 God rescuing

3 **THE OBEDIENT PROPHET**
3:1–10

3:1,2 A second chance
3:3,4 Jonah preaching
3:5–9 Nineveh repenting
3:10 God forgiving

4 **THE HARD-HEARTED PROPHET**
4:1–11

4:1–4 Jonah is angry
4:5–8 The lesson of the vine
4:9–11 God is merciful

JONAH

Message

1. We learn about God.
☐ The whole book assumes that God is just, that he will punish wrong-doers, and that all nations are answerable to him – not just Israel. 1:2; 3:2,9,10
☐ God is sovereign in the world he has made. He can control his creatures, the weather, even plants. Later in Israel's history he would even use a cruel, pagan people like the Assyrians. 1:4,9,17; 2:10; 4:6–8
☐ God is also merciful and compassionate, caring for all mankind – even for animals – as well as being Israel's God in particular. 2:8,9; 3:9,10; 4:2,10,11

2. We learn about Jonah.
☐ Jonah is a representative of God's people who knows God's grace, who can boast of his relationship with God – and who can pray to him in time of trouble. We even find him praising God and recommitting his life to him. 1:9; 2:1–9
☐ Jonah is also inconsistent and disobedient. He tries to run away from the God who made all things! He is angry when God is merciful. He is more concerned about a plant than he is about people. 1:3,10; 4:1–3,9

3. We learn about pagans.
They come out in a better light than the prophet does, whether it is the heathen sailors or the repentant Ninevites. They surprise us with their sense of what is right, and their ready response to God's message. Yet Jonah wrote them off because they were not Israelites. 1:13,14,16; 3:5–9

Application

1. We are also inconsistent.
Like Jonah, we are often prepared to profess our faith in God without being prepared to see what that will mean. We also can be wilfully disobedient. We can be just as illogical as someone trying to run away from the Almighty. Worse, we can be just as hard and unfeeling towards others, even when we say that we know God's grace and mercy.

2. We are just as selfish.
Probably one of the reasons why Jonah wanted judgement to fall was that otherwise his reputation as a prophet would suffer. Like him, we can get just as upset over little things which do not matter, while we are unconcerned with people.

3. God cares for all.
God is concerned about everybody, not only because he intends to judge them, but because he genuinely loves what he has made. This does not mean that everyone will be saved, but it does mean that everyone should have the opportunity of getting right with him. If we are one with him, this will mean witness and mission, not to say simple care for non-Christians.

4. God gives second chances.
God gave Jonah another opportunity to fulfil his commission. Whereas we must not play with God and assume his mercy, we know that he often deals with us in the same way.

JONAH

Key themes

1. Grace.
The reason why Jonah knew that God was 'gracious and compassionate . . . slow to anger and abounding in love' was that God had been gracious to **him**. Study the psalm in chapter 2. This makes his harsh dealing with others harder to take. Compare Jesus' teaching in Matthew 18:21–35.

2. Unfulfilled prophecy.
God's promise of judgement through Jonah never happened (3:10). This reminds us that not all prophecy needs to be fulfilled. Although God cannot be manipulated – 'Who knows?' (3:9) – he does respond to human repentance, and is able to fulfil his purpose by different means.

3. Jonah and Jesus.
Jesus used Jonah's experience as an illustration of his own (see Matthew 12:39–41; 16:4). Just as Jonah was marked out as God's servant by his miraculous deliverance, Jesus' claims and message would be endorsed by his resurrection from the dead (eg. Romans 1:3,4).

MICAH

A message of judgement and hope

THE DATE. Chapter 1, verse 1 puts outside limits on the time that Micah worked as a prophet. Jotham's reign began in 742 BC and Hezekiah's ended in 687 BC. Jeremiah speaks of Micah prophesying in Hezekiah's reign (Jeremiah 26:18), and it is likely that most of his work was done in the years between 725 BC and 701 BC.

THE SITUATION. Micah lived at a time of crisis. The two super-powers, Egypt and Assyria, were battling for supremacy, and Micah's country was still fairly prosperous–a hangover from the long and stable reign of Uzziah (d. 739 BC). But all was not well. Hezekiah was a good king from a religious point of view (2 Kings 18-20), but politically he was weak. He did, perhaps under Micah's influence, lead a religious reformation, but his reforms didn't change the people. The country was corrupt – the rich got richer by cheating the poor, judges favoured those who paid the most, and even prophets and priests put money before God. The people ignored God's laws and idols were everywhere, but they still thought that God would protect them. In 722 BC the northern kingdom of Israel was destroyed. This should have warned Judah, but instead they followed the same corrupt road.

THE MAN. Micah came from Moresheth-Gath, a country town on the border with Philistia. It was in a fertile valley, on a trade route. As a countryman, Micah was suspicious of the city and saw much of Judah's corruption as stemming from city life (1:5; 6:9). Strongly aware of his prophetic calling and of God's power in his own life (3:8; 7:7), he was willing to stand on his own against popular opinion.

THE BOOK. The book of Micah is not a single speech delivered at one time. It is a collection of various messages. This means that it often hops quite quickly from one topic to another.

The book alternates between prophecies of the judgement coming to Judah because of her sins, with graphic descriptions of both the sins and the punishment, and prophecies of a bright future after this judgement.

Outline

 1 INTRODUCING MICAH
1:1

 2 JUDGEMENT ON THE CAPITAL CITIES
1:2–16

1:2–8 Samaria will be flattened
1:9 Jerusalem is heading the same way
1:10–16 The Assyrians march on Jerusalem

 3 WHY IS GOD SO ANGRY?
2:1–11

2:1,2 They plot and cheat their fellows
2:3–5 So God will take what is theirs
2:6,7 Micah is not exaggerating
2:8,9 They oppress the poor
2:10 So God will evict them
2:11 They don't want the truth

 4 A QUICK LOOK AHEAD
2:12,13

2:12,13 Hope for the future

 5 THE LEADERS ARE MOST TO BLAME
3:1–12

3:1–4 Butchers or shepherds?
3:5–8 The prophets all take bribes
3:9–12 Their religion is all pretence

6 A BLACK PRESENT – A GOLDEN FUTURE
4:1–5

4:1 Jerusalem: centre of a world at peace
4:2–4 Every nation will come to worship and learn
4:5 Let's start by doing God's will now

7 GREAT TIMES TO COME
4:6–5:15

4:6–8 Weakness will become strength
4:9,10 Distress will become deliverance
4:11–13 The conquered will be the conquerors
5:1–6 The ruled will become the ruler
5:7–9 The small group who come through will become prosperous
5:10–15 Corruption will be rooted out

8 GOD TAKES ISRAEL TO COURT
6:1–16

6:1,2 The courtroom is the world
6:3–5 The speech for the prosecution – God has done nothing to offend
6:6,7 The defence – we are very religious. What more does God want?
6:8 God wants the same as always – justice, kindness and humility
6:9–16 Israel is denounced

 9 MICAH'S SAD POEM
7:1–7

7:1–4 He is upset by his people's sin: no one does what is right
7:5,6 You can't trust anyone any more – no even your own family
7:7 But you can still trust God

10 LOOKING TO THE FUTURE
7:8–20

7:8–10 Watch out nations!
7:11–13 Everyone will come to Jerusalem
7:14–17 Please God, be our Shepherd
7:18–20 Let's end by praising God

MICAH

Message

1. God is holy.
The people are kidding themselves if they think they can get away with their selfishness, cruelty and corruption. God is pure and good and cannot allow wrong-doing. All sin must and will be punished. 1:2–5; 5:10–15

2. God is just.
Unlike the rulers of Israel, God does not take bribes. The rich and powerful will get no special treatment. In fact, God will make their punishment fit their crime. 2:3–7; 3:4,9–12

3. God is demanding.
He expects not just lip-service from his people, but that their attitudes and behaviour, their whole lives, should match up to what they say. 6:8

4. God is in control.
It may look as if the world is out of control and in a real mess with godless nations taking over, but things are not always what they seem. This is God's world and he is in charge even of history. 4:8–13; 7:8–10

5. God cares.
God has always loved his people and always will. They must be punished, but after that there is hope for the future. There will be a glorious new life for all those who really follow the Lord. 2:12,13; 6:3–5; 7:14,15

6. God is concerned for the whole world.
The plans which God has include not just Israel but all the nations. The crimes of the nations will be punished, but there will also be a place for them in the wonderful future time. 4:1–4; 7:16,17

7. God will send a Saviour.
After a long time somebody will be born who will deliver the people and be a real shepherd to them. He will be a humble person, from little Bethlehem, but someone 'whose origin is from of old'. 5:2–6

Application

Micah teaches us that:

1. Surface religion is useless.
Religion and life-style must be linked. All the sacrifices in the world and all the religious meetings are useless unless there is also justice and kindness and humility (6:8). There is no way we can say 'The Lord is with us' and claim his protection if our lives show that we don't really care what God wants (3:11).

2. Business life matters as well.
God cares how we treat other people, and he isn't interested in excuses like, 'everybody does it' or 'you couldn't exist in business without . . .' (2:1–5). Treading on other people may help you climb the ladder, but the rewards will not be quite what you expect. Material wealth is not always the greatest blessing (6:9–15).

MICAH

3. The easy answer isn't always right.
We must never look just for the answers we want to hear. The kind of message that leaves a warm feeling isn't always from the source we think (2:11)!

Any message that claims to be from God must fit with what the Bible tells us of God's love and God's justice (3:5–8).

4. The character of God's messenger.
He knows God is faithful – even when all around is in chaos (7:7). He speaks the truth – even when people don't want to hear it (2:6). He is conscious of a power not his own – and his messages reflect God's justice (3:8).

Key themes

1. Judgement.
The crimes of the people of Judah involved every aspect of their lives (2:1–11; 3:1–12; 6:9–16).

From these references make a list of all their sins and the action that God says he will take against them. Note how the punishment fits the crime, and also how many of the things which God refused to tolerate then, are still problems today.

2. Justice.
God is a God of justice and he expects justice from his people.

Make a list of all the references to justice in Micah. Note that it is seen very much in a practical way, not just as an abstract concept.

3. Hope.
Micah had a clear hope for the future, based on what he knew of God and his Word. See 2:12; 4:4,6.

Read 4:1–5:15. How did Micah envisage the future for
☐ Jerusalem (4:1–3,8,13)?
☐ The remnant (2:12; 4:6,7,10; 5:7,8)?
☐ All nations (4:2–4)?

4. Forgiveness.
Micah ends with a description of God's gracious forgiveness. These verses are read by Jews on the Day of Atonement, when they seek cleansing from the sins of the past year.

Read 7:18–20. What do these verses tell us about God? Is there anything earlier in the book which points towards this final message?

HABAKKUK

How can God use the wicked?

THE UNKNOWN PROPHET. Apart from one brief reference, we know absolutely nothing about Habakkuk or when he preached. Some have suggested that because chapter 3 is written like many of the psalms for public worship – complete with musical directions (3:1,3,9,13,19) – he might have been a Levite who worked in the Jerusalem Temple and who was also a prophet. The only hint we have refers to the Chaldeans or Babylonians (1:6), and there is some debate as to whether Habakkuk foresees their rise to power, or is describing what is happening in his days. Either way, it seems to place him towards the end of the seventh century BC. It was then that the Assyrian empire gave way to the Babylonians (612 BC). After they defeated the Egyptians at the battle of Carchemish (605 BC), they went on to conquer Palestine. By 597 BC they had Jerusalem in their control, while ten years later they destroyed it. The Babylonians were therefore to close an era in Jewish history.

WHAT HAD HE TO SAY? Some have thought that the book as we have it has been made up from different writings, but there does seem to be one theme running through it. It is the problem of suffering once again, seen both in society and on a much more fearsome scale in international politics. Whereas the prophet was convinced that God was sovereign, and that therefore nothing could happen without his permission, he also knew that God was holy and righteous. How could God use wicked agents without getting his hands dirty?

The first part of the book is a dialogue with the prophet complaining to God and insisting on an answer, although no real solution to the problem is given. In the face of man's continual inhumanity to man, we can only trust that God will put the record straight in his own will and time.

Outline

1 WHY,
LORD?
1:1–4

1:1–3 So much suffering
1:4 So much injustice

2 THERE IS MUCH
MORE TO COME!
1:5–11

1:5 An unexpected turn of events
1:6–11 The Chaldeans are coming!

3 HOW CAN YOU
DO IT, LORD?
1:12–2:1

1:12 You are in control
1:13 But you are holy
1:14–17 How can you allow it?
2:1 I want an answer

4 GOD KNOWS WHAT
HE'S DOING
2:2–5

2:2,3 His word is true
2:4,5 His judgement will follow

5 GOD HATES
INJUSTICE
2:6–20

2:6–8 Those who love to murder and steal
2:9–11 Those who feel secure in their crime
2:12–14 Those who are heartless
2:15–17 Those who shame others
2:18–20 Those who worship false gods

6 OUR GOD IS
ON THE WAY
3:1–19

3:1–15 God comes in judgement
3:16–19 Trembling, trust and triumph

HABAKKUK

Message

1. The world is full of suffering.
Everywhere the prophet looks in society there is suffering, and what is worse, it is often unjust. Because the wicked seem to get away with it, and his prayers for justice are unanswered, Habakkuk is faced with the awful dilemma: 'If God is just, why does he allow it to go on?' 1:2–4

Far from making things easier to take, God gives him a vision of much worse. The Babylonians, who would care little for human life or rights, would overrun the land. 1:5–11

Added to this horror was the fact that these invaders had no time for God. They were supremely self-confident. 1:7,11,15,16

2. God is in control.
Habakkuk believed that his God was Lord of the whole earth, and that because of this, he must have allowed these things to happen. He sees God as using these evil forces to his own ends. 1:5,6; 2:20; 3:19

He was also aware that God is just, and that he would judge this injustice and wickedness. The repeated 'Woe' seals their fate. 1:12; 2:6–20; 3:3–15

This still left him with the problem of how God could get involved at all, seeing that he is holy and righteous. 1:13

3. The message of trust.
Although Habakkuk complains to the Lord and waits for an answer, God does not really give him one. 2:1

Instead, the truth which he reveals – and commands to be written plainly so that all may easily read it – is that the righteous man would be preserved through it all in his faithfulness to God. 2:2–4

Habakkuk was given a glimpse of a wonderful future when all would acknowledge God and his law. In the confidence of who God is and what he will do, he finds it possible not only to endure through the perplexing times, but actually to rejoice. 2:14; 3:17–19

Application

1. This world is a fallen place.
We must be realistic about human wickedness, whether in society or in international affairs. Men and women do not care for God or his law and, given the opportunity, will trample on others in order to gain wealth, security, power or pleasure.

2. It is not wrong to ask.
Habakkuk's questionings were not sinful doubt but believing perplexity. We must also think through our faith, facing up to the hard questions which life throws at us, even though we may not have ready-made answers.

3. We can trust in God too.
Even when we cannot understand what God is doing, we can be confident that he is working things out in his own way and time. We can also learn to rejoice, not in our circumstances, but in him, in who he is and in what he will do.

4. History demands a judgement.
So much of man's wickedness never gets what it deserves in this life or in this world. If God is just there must be a judgement one day. The problem of suffering points us beyond this life to the next.

HABAKKUK

Key themes

1. God.

Habakkuk's whole problem arose because he had a clear idea of who God is. See the way that he describes him as holy (1:12,13; 3:3), just (1:12), sovereign (2:20; 3:19), unchanging (1:12; 3:6), merciful (3:2), saving (3:13,18), judging (2:13,16; 3:3–15), and revealing truth (2:2).

2. Faith.

God's answer to the prophet's question was that 'the righteous man will live by his faith (or faithfulness)' (2:4), that is, his loyalty to God in spite of the godlessness of others. The readers of the letter to the Hebrews were told to hang on in a similar way (10:35–39), while Paul used this verse to illustrate his understanding of 'justification by faith' (Romans 1:17; Galatians 3:11). For him faith meant obedient commitment. Hence, whereas in Habakkuk the rightous man is loyal to God, in Paul's writings the thought is reversed. The man who is committed to Christ is righteous.

ZEPHANIAH

God: strong to smite, strong to save

AUTHOR. Zephaniah's name means 'the Lord hides'. He is the only prophet whose descent is traced back four generations, possibly to indicate his royal connections. Hezekiah (1:1) is perhaps to be identified with the king of that name who ruled Judah from 715–686 BC. This would make Zephaniah a distant cousin of the reigning king, Josiah.

His reference to specific areas of Jerusalem – Fish Gate, New Quarter, market district (1:10,11) – suggest that he lived in that city.

DATE. Zephaniah was probably the first of the seventh-century prophets, beginning his ministry slightly earlier than Jeremiah and Nahum. Several of the false religious practices denounced by him were abolished during Josiah's reformation, which began about 629 BC; therefore we are fairly safe in dating the start of his ministry about 630 BC. He was probably one of the prophets who identified themselves with Josiah's reforming movement (see 2 Kings 23:2).

SITUATION. Josiah was the most godly of the kings of Judah. When he became king, Judah was suffering the effects of the reign of Manasseh (686–642 BC), the worst king to rule the southern kingdom. The country's religion was syncretistic (i.e. a mixture of the worship of the Lord and of other gods), and the people showed a general disregard for God. Josiah did his best to put the situation right, but the people had advanced too far down the path to spiritual ruin, and his reform resulted in correct religious observance rather than a change of heart.

Zephaniah saw that Judah could not ultimately escape the judgement of God, which he saw primarily in the context of 'the Day of the Lord', and which was to affect the whole world.

Outline

1 **THE DECREE OF GOD'S JUDGEMENT**
1:1–18

1:1–3 Threat of universal judgement
1:4–6 The false worshippers
1:7–11 Judah's corrupt leaders
1:12,13 The complacent and wealthy
1:14–18 The terrible day of the Lord

2 **SUMMONS TO JUDAH**
2:1–3

2:1,2 To repent while there is time
2:3 To seek the Lord

3 **THE SCOPE OF GOD'S JUDGEMENT**
2:4–15

2:4–7 West: the Philistines
2:8–11 East: the Moabites and Ammonites
2:12 South: the Ethiopians
2:13–15 North: the Assyrians

4 **NO EXEMPTION FOR JUDAH**
3:1–8

3:1–4 The rebellion of her leaders
3:5 The holiness of her God
3:6,7 The failure of God's discipline
3:8 The certainty of judgement

5 **THE PROMISES OF A MIGHTY GOD**
3:9–20

3:9,10 The nations will turn to God
3:11–13 God's purified people will be safe
3:14–20 A restored remnant will rejoice

ZEPHANIAH

Message

1. Judah's treatment of God.
- [ ] As though he doesn't exist. 1:6
- [ ] As though he doesn't care. 1:12
- [ ] As though he isn't supreme. 1:4,5,9
- [ ] As though he isn't trustworthy. 3:2

2. God versus Judah.
- [ ] Destroying the idol worshippers. 1:4–6
- [ ] Punishing the leaders. 1:8
- [ ] Searching out the sinners. 1:12

3. The day of God's anger.
- [ ] Approaching fast. 1:7,14
- [ ] Inescapable. 1:18
- [ ] Catastrophic. 1:15–17

4. God's universal judgement.
- [ ] Reaching to every nation. 1:18; 2:4–15
- [ ] Affecting the world of nature. 1:2,3

5. God's universal sovereignty.
- [ ] He accepts the world's worship. 2:11; 3:10
- [ ] He receives the world's service. 3:9

6. God's remnant.
- [ ] Honoured by all men. 3:19,20
- [ ] Cleansed from sin. 3:11–13
- [ ] Secure in God's protection. 2:3; 3:13–15
- [ ] Rejoicing in God's salvation. 3:14
- [ ] Causing God to rejoice. 3:17

Application

- [ ] 'Believers' are practical atheists when they live as if God were a nonentity in his own world.
- [ ] God's purpose in the world can be hindered by the complacency of his followers just as effectively as by the enthusiasm of his enemies.
- [ ] Men need to be confronted by God's warnings as well as comforted by his promises. How else will they be persuaded to take him seriously?
- [ ] There is no hiding place from God's scrutiny. This can be a comforting as well as a challenging thought.

- [ ] Seeking the Lord while he may be found is an option open to all. There may come a time when 'now' is too late.
- [ ] God will bring in his day of reckoning. He has also provided a way of escape from his judgement, and a source of security in his love.
- [ ] Man's ability to bring delight and joy to a sovereign God may be an incredible mystery; it is also a biblical truth.

ZEPHANIAH

Key themes

1. The Day of the Lord.
Make your own summary of what this 'day' will be like (1:14–15). It is a theme present in several of the biblical writings. Study the aspects of it indicated by Amos 5:18–20; Joel 2:2; Isaiah 13:9–13. What light do the following verses throw on the darkness of the 'day': Isaiah 2:12–18; Joel 2:28,29,32?

The New Testament equivalent is 'the day of Jesus Christ'. What comfort and challenge can the Christian gain from such verses as 1 Thessalonians 1:10; 1 John 4:17; 2 Timothy 1:12; Philippians 1:6,10; 1 Peter 2:12?

2. God's complaints.
From the following verses, find out what made God angry with his people in Zephaniah's time: 1:6,9; 3:2,4,7. How many of these complaints do you think he could make today?

3. God's commands.
Find out what they are from: 1:7,14; 2:1–3; 3:8,14. What do you learn about God's character and rights, and man's privileges and responsibilities from these verses?

4. God's rule over all.
Zephaniah 2:11; 3:9,10 speak of God receiving the homage of **all** men. What other aspects of the concept of God's universal rule can you find in Isaiah 11:9; 45:22; Micah 4:1–4?

5. A new lifestyle.
Zephaniah 3:11–13 speak of God bringing about a radical change of character in his people. God's people today can be changed as a result of his activity and their co-operation. See 2 Corinthians 5:17; Ephesians 4:22–24; Colossians 3:9,10 for the evidence.

HAGGAI

Lessons for practical atheists

THE PROPHET. Haggai only makes a brief appearance in the Bible. Apart from the book which records his messages he is only mentioned by Ezra (5:1; 6:14) who, in passing, pays tribute to the good effect his preaching had.

His name suggests that he was born on the day of a religious festival. It is a fair guess that he was a priest, but we cannot be sure. Certainly he was in close touch with God.

It is difficult to know how old a man he was when he began to preach. His message about the old Temple (2:3) which was destroyed in 587 BC has led some to believe he was an old man who remembered it. But others because of the same verse have argued that he was probably a young man who went to Jerusalem for the first time when he joined the other returning exiles in 538 BC.

He preached at about the same time as Zechariah.

THE SITUATION. Haggai dates his sermons. They were delivered between August and November in 520 BC.

At that time Jerusalem was a small struggling community with a population of about 20,000. They had suffered poor harvests and partial crop failures, so virtually all their time and energy was taken up with trying to scratch together a living. The situation in Jerusalem was not helped by unrest on the international scene.

The people were therefore probably very low in spirit when Haggai began to preach to them.

THE STYLE. Haggai is not a typical blood and thunder type of prophet. Although he speaks of very big issues he does so by using quiet argument rather than heated accusations. He is sometimes thought of more as a teacher than a prophet. He leads his audience step by step to where he wants them and then manages to provoke them into a definite response.

Outline

HAGGAI

Message

Haggai teaches the people about God:

1. He is the Lord of Hosts.
This is Haggai's favourite name for God. It is a name which describes the greatness of God. He is a God more powerful than any earthly nation and richer than the earth itself. 1:2,7,9,14; 2:6–9,11,23

2. He is a God who makes demands.
No matter what their situation, God expects to assume a priority in the lives of his people. He also demands purity. 1:2,3; 2:10–14

3. He is in control of economic conditions.
Haggai tells the people that their poor harvests were not caused by the accidents of nature or by blind fate but by the living God who was trying to communicate through them to his people. God uses economic conditions to teach spiritual lessons. 1:5–11

4. He keeps his promises.
Haggai encourages the people that God is with them because he is a reliable God who keeps his promises. 2:5

5. He is a living God.
Many associated God with the old Temple which had been destroyed. They seemed to forget that he was a living God who was active today and had great things in store for them tomorrow. He was in no way tied to the spiritual museums of yesterday. 2:3–9

6. He wants to bless his people.
What prevented him from doing so in the past was their impurity. But now they have laid the foundation of the Temple again, they are in a position for God to bless them. 2:10–19

7. He takes care of individuals.
Haggai's final message is basically a message to an individual, Zerubbabel. He is told that even though nations are going to be turned upside down, he will be safe and raised to a position of authority and usefulness. In all God's concern for the affairs of nations he never forgets the individual. 2:20–23

Application

The prophecy is a message to practical atheists, that is, those people who say there is a God but then live as if he did not exist.

If God exists:
☐ There can be no half-measures in following him.
☐ You must put his interests before your own. Matthew 6:33

☐ You cannot make excuses for delaying to do God's work.
☐ You must review your life to see how God may be speaking to you.
☐ You must not be bound by the past.
☐ You must prove your repentance by action, not words.
☐ You need not be discouraged – even in difficult times God remains in control.

HAGGAI

Key themes

This short prophecy contains many memorable sayings. Use the following verses, or others of your own choosing, as the basis of prayerful thought . . .

1. About money:
'Is it a time for you yourselves to be living in your panelled houses, while this house remains a ruin?' 1:4

2. About life's achievements:
'Give careful thought to your ways.' 1:5,7

3. About your attitude to God:
'The people feared the Lord.' 1:12

4. About Christian service:
'Be strong . . . and work.' 2:4

5. About God's resources:
' "The silver is mine and the gold is mine," declares the Lord Almighty.' 2:8

6. About the future of God's work:
'The glory of this present house will be greater than the glory of the former house.' 2:9

7. About human stubbornness:
'Yet you did not turn to me.' 2:17

8. About God's promises:
'From this day on I will bless you.' 2:19

9. About God's love and purpose:
'I will take you . . . and I will make you . . . for I have chosen you.' 2:23

ZECHARIAH

Prophet and priest

THE AUTHOR. Zechariah was the grandson of Iddo (1:1) who is probably the priest named in Nehemiah 12:4 as having accompanied Zerubbabel and Jeshua from Babylon to Jerusalem. If Iddo was a priest, then Zechariah was both priest and prophet. This would explain Zechariah's concern to get the Temple rebuilt (Ezra 6:14).

THE SITUATION. The Jews were carried off to exile in Babylon in 587/6 BC but the Babylonian empire was suddenly smashed by Cyrus, God's 'Messiah' (Isaiah 45:1). He at once announced that the exiles were free to return to Jerusalem, and from 538 BC onwards there was a steady stream of Jews returning home.

But the work of rebuilding the Temple went slowly. In the second year of Darius, Zechariah, still a young man, began to encourage them to push on with the work.

THE CHARACTERISTICS OF THE PROPHECY. The prophecy very readily divides into two parts (chapters 1–8 and 9–14). The first part consists of seven striking visions, plus a court scene in which the High Priest Joshua is being accused by Satan.

The second part is concerned primarily with the two themes of judgement and salvation; judgement for the unbeliever but salvation for the people of God. The prophecy closes with a view of the Day of the Lord and a distinctive call to holiness.

The difference in style which some claim to have observed between these two parts of the prophecy could well be due to the first being written when Zechariah was only in his twenties and the second part being written many years later.

An unusual characteristic of the second part of Zechariah is that the **result** of a certain event is described before the event itself. In chapter 9, for example, verses 1–8 describe the judgement of Israel's enemies, but the coming of the king to judge them appears in verses 9–13. In chapter 14 the restoration of Jerusalem is described **before** the plagues with which the nations who fight against Jerusalem are afflicted, the plagues which force them to end their attack.

Mention must also be made of the remarkable 'oracle of the shepherds' (chapters 10,11), which has many points of contact and contrast with the New Testament theme of the Good Shepherd. Here, however, the sheep weary of the Good Shepherd and pay him off with thirty pieces of silver (11:12,13; see John 10; Matthew 26:14–16; 27:3–10).

Outline

1 THE BOOK OF
THE SEVEN VISIONS
1:1–8:23

1:1–6 Introduction: a call for repentance
1:7–17 First vision: a man on a red horse
1:18–21 Second vision: the four horns
2:1–13 Third vision: a man with a
measuring line
3:1–10 Interlude: Joshua the Priest
accused and acquitted
4:1–14 Fourth vision: a lampstand and two
olive trees
5:1–4 Fifth vision: a flying scroll
5:5–11 Sixth vision: a woman in a basket
6:1–15 Seventh vision: four chariots
7:1–14 Postscript: The call for repentance
renewed two years later
8:1–23 Jerusalem's glorious future

2 THE BOOK OF ORACLES: I
AN ORACLE OF JUDGEMENT
9:1–17

9:1–8 The judgement of the nations
9:9–13 A Saviour for Zion
9:14–17 The coming of the Lord

3 THE BOOK OF ORACLES: II
THE SHEPHERDS
10:1–11:17

10:1–5 A shepherd for Judah
10:6–12 The sheep gathered in
11:1–9 The sheep that chose destruction
11:10–17 Pricing the shepherd

4 THE BOOK OF ORACLES: III
AN ORACLE OF SALVATION
12:1–13:9

12:1–9 Jerusalem saved
12:10–14 The way of salvation: repentance
13:1–6 The consequence of salvation:
Jerusalem cleansed
13:7–9 The means of salvation: the
suffering shepherd

5 THE BOOK OF ORACLES: IV
AN ORACLE OF
THE DAY OF THE LORD
14:1–21

14:1–7 The Day of the Lord: darkness
14:8–11 The Day of the Lord: the Lord of the
living waters
14:12–19 The Day of the Lord: judgement
14:20,21 The Day of the Lord: holiness

ZECHARIAH

Message

The message is two fold. The first part deals with the restoration of Jerusalem, particularly the rebuilding of the Temple.

1. Part One.
☐ **The first vision:** a man on a red horse. The world is at peace, but in view of the oppression of the Jewish people it ought **not** to be. God responds: judgement is on the way. 1:7–17
☐ **The second vision:** the four horns. The horns symbolise kingdoms, possibly the four great empires of Daniel, more probably the kingdoms of the four corners of the earth. They are about to be destroyed by God's four craftsmen. 1:18–21
☐ **The third vision:** a man with a measuring line, attempting to measure Jerusalem. 'Impossible! Jerusalem will soon overflow those walls!' Blessing too great to be contained! 2:1–13
☐ **Interlude:** Joshua the priest. This vision explains how the Jews, so clearly guilty, can be so blessed. God forgives; God in grace gives Israel new garments. 3:1–10
☐ **The fourth vision:** the lampstand and the two trees. These are the end times; this passage is distinctly taken up in Revelation 1:12 (the lampstand) and

11:1,4 (both the measuring line and the olive trees). The vision points to the Holy Spirit who alone provides power for the church. 4:1–14
☐ **The fifth vision:** a flying scroll. This is a reminder of the role of obedience in holiness. The scroll is open so that all may see the consequence of disobedience. 5:1–4
☐ **The sixth vision:** a woman in a basket. Symbolically the sin of Judah is carried away to Satan's anti-city, Babylon. 5:5–11
☐ **The seventh vision:** the four chariots. The mountains between which the chariots emerge symbolise the majesty of God and the law of God, as at Sinai.
   The chariots, symbolising unrest, move into the world, driving God's people to seek for rest in the city of peace, Jerusalem, where they join in the task of rebuilding the Temple. 6:1–15

2. Part Two.
☐ Begins with judgement. 9:1–17
☐ Presents a Shepherd-Saviour. 10:1–11:17
☐ Prescribes repentance. 12:1–13:9
☐ Describes the Day of the Lord. 14:1–21

Application

1. Prophecy and the role of Jerusalem.
In this comparatively brief book Jerusalem is named forty times. The book is primarily concerned with apocalyptic visions of the end times. It is difficult to read these chapters and others throughout the Bible without realising that the Jews in general, and Jerusalem in

particular have central roles still to play in God's plans.

2. Satan.
Chapter 3 is a dramatic portrayal of Satan at work. His name (**Satan** in Hebrew, **Diabolos** in Greek) means 'accuser'. Here we see him

ZECHARIAH

accusing Joshua, the High Priest, who is seen symbolically dressed in filthy clothes. Why shouldn't the judge (the Angel of the Lord) condemn him (Romans 8:31–39)? In fact, it is Satan who is condemned while Joshua is symbolically given rich clean clothes (see 1 John 2:1,2).

3. Interpreting the visions.
The seven visions are difficult to interpret. Some have sought significance in every detail. But note the very limited interpretation offered by the angels. In the first vision we are told who the horsemen are; and the myrtle trees probably stand for Israel. But what about the colours of the horses? Why is the scroll thirty feet long and fifteen feet wide (5:2), or the basket cover made of lead (5:7)? As with the New Testament parables we should look for the main meaning without pressing the details.

Key themes

1. Three important people.
This prophecy focuses attention on three people: Zechariah himself, Joshua the High Priest, and Zerubbabel who became Governor of Judah (Haggai 1:1).

Zechariah is the shepherd of ch. 11, and so becomes a type, or picture, of Christ. Like Christ, he suffers the mockery of the very sheep he was trying to shepherd and like Jesus he is sold off at the price of a slave (Matthew 26:15; Exodus 21:32).

Joshua the High Priest also becomes a type of Christ and is given the messianic title 'The Branch' (6:12). (See also Isaiah 11:1; Jeremiah 23:5; and 33:15.)

Zerubbabel ('Seed of Babylon') was a descendent of King Jehoiakin, and was with the first party to return from the Exile in 537 BC. He was the dependable sort: he both began the task of rebuilding the Temple **and** finished it. His special designation is 'The signet ring' (Haggai 2:20–23), an indication that as Governor he ruled on behalf of God.

Study the many references to these three important people: Ezra 2:1,2; 3:1–9; 4:1–3; 5:1,2; Haggai 1:1; 2:1–5, 20–23; Zechariah 3:1–10; 4:6–10; 6:9–15; 11:4–17; Matthew 1:12. See how each depended on the others.

2. Comparing biblical themes.
The Christian is not entirely free to interpret a passage of Scripture as seems best to him. Very often our freedom is limited because the passage we are examining is commented on or expanded or interpreted elsewhere in the Bible.

Zechariah 4 is a good example of this. The golden lampstand has its obvious parallel in Revelation 1:12, and the two olive trees in Revelation 11. Note how Revelation adds detail to the earlier prophecy and how Revelation 11:4, like Zechariah, brings together the lampstand and the olive trees. Each passage helps in interpreting the other, but neither contradicts the other.

Isaiah 7:14 is similarly interpreted by Matthew 1:22,23. Search the Bible for other examples (the Exodus; Jonah; the High Priest; Isaiah 53).

MALACHI

Will you rob God?

WHO WAS MALACHI? Malachi means 'my messenger'. Perhaps this was the prophet's actual name, but more likely it was simply a way of describing himself. At all events nothing is known of the prophet.

WHEN DID HE WRITE? Malachi's prophecy belongs to the period after the Exile when many of the Jews had returned to their own land. He refers to a 'governor' and this clearly indicates the post-exilic period (1:8). Zerubbabel was thus described (Haggai 1:1). There is no reference to the rebuilding of the Temple, so presumably this had taken place some years previously. The conditions described in the book would apply particularly to the days of Ezra and Nehemiah. It was a time of spiritual decline when the Jewish religion had become merely formal. Malachi was the last of the prophets. Four hundred years were to elapse before the birth of Christ, and therefore Malachi is, in a sense, the bridge between the Old and New Testaments.

WHY DID HE WRITE? Malachi was appalled at the religious coldness and social laxity of the nation. He comes on the scene as a reformer, calling the people to repentance. His mission was very similar to that of John the Baptist. The book is largely in the form of a dialogue between God and the people in which God combats the various sceptical statements made by Israel. Malachi emphasises the covenant relationship which existed between God and the nation and calls on the people to fulfil their obligations under that covenant. He accuses them of having robbed God. Malachi's prophecy represents the end of an era. The next 400 years have been called 'the period of silence'. During that time no biblical prophet spoke or wrote.

For many the most striking feature of Malachi's prophecy is the challenge to 'put God to the test'. If we are to do this and receive the blessings he promises, there must be total commitment on the part of his people (Mal. 3:10).

Outline

1 GOD'S LOVE FOR
ISRAEL
1:1–5

1:1 Title
1:2 Love questioned
1:3–5 Love proved

2 THE PRIESTS
REBUKED
1:6–2:9

1:6–14 Polluted sacrifices
2:1–9 Inevitable retribution

3 THE PEOPLE
REBUKED
2:10–16

2:10 Treachery in society
2:11–16 Infidelity in family life

4 THINGS TO
COME
2:17–3:5

2:17 The Lord weary of double standards
3:1 The advent of the forerunner
3:2–5 The advent of the Lord himself

5 THE NATION'S
CONTROVERSY WITH GOD
3:6–15

3:6–9 Robbing God
3:10–12 The key to blessing
3:13–15 Speaking against God

6 THE FAITHFUL
REMNANT
3:16–18

7 THE DAY OF
THE LORD
4:1–6

4:1 Its effect on the wicked
4:2–4 Its blessings for the righteous
4:5,6 The prophet who prepares the way

MALACHI

Message

1. A message of love.
The prophet begins by reminding the people of God's great love for them, as demonstrated in the fact that of the two sons of Isaac and Rebekah, Jacob was the favoured one. 1:1–5

2. A message of admonition.
Malachi begins by speaking of God's indictment of the priests who had offered in sacrifice to God what was of no value to man. They had not shown him the reverence and honour which was his due. They therefore were objects of God's wrath and were liable to his judgement.

The prophet then turns to the people and rebukes them for their unfaithfulness, both in worship and in the keeping of their marriage vows. 1:6–2:16

3. A message of judgement and hope.
God's appointed messenger will prepare the way for the coming Day of the Lord. The call is to repent and put matters right. When the Day of the Lord does come he will vindicate the righteous. There will be a turning of the tables and no longer will the righteous be oppressed. 3:1–4:5

Application

The background to Malachi's prophecy is strikingly similar to our own, therefore he has a very clear message for today.

1. Remember God's love.
We have evidence of God's love which was not available then, so there are even more compelling reasons for us to remember his love than they had.

2. Return to him.
Religion had become purely formal and God was not impressed. The priests were offering to God blemished sacrifices. The people were worshipping him with their lips but denying

him in their lives. This sad state of affairs affected social and family life also. There was a general air of scepticism and cynicism. At such times there can be only one possible remedy. People must repent and return to God with contrite hearts.

3. Put God to the test.
God is longing to pour out spiritual blessings on his people. He challenges us to fulfil our obligations to him and put him to the test. Here is a challenge to the people of God in every generation.

MALACHI

Key themes

1. Divine love.
God reminds his people that he had a special love for them, and this was why he dealt with them as he did (1:2–5).

2. Divine displeasure.
God was far from pleased with his people for a number of reasons. They lacked reverence for him and for his house (1:6–14). They lacked sound teaching (2:7–9). They were unfaithful (2:10–16), cynical (2:17; 3:14,15), indifferent to human need (3:5), and they withheld God's rightful dues (3:8,9).

3. Divine promises.
The message of judgement is relieved with promises that God would intervene and bless. See 1:5,11; 3:1–4, 10–12.

4. Divine remembrance.
God knows all about those who are his (3:16–18), and he will vindicate them (4:2,3).

THE NEW TESTAMENT

MATTHEW

The fullest of the Gospels

WHY THE GOSPEL WAS WRITTEN. Matthew has a number of clear reasons for writing his Gospel:

1. To show the connection between Jesus and the Old Testament.

2. To record the extensive teaching Christ gave to his disciples.

3. To set out how Christ expected his disciples to behave.

4. To answer questions raised by members of the church, eg. about the early life of Jesus or his coming again.

5. To speak about the way the church should be run.

THE AUTHOR. The Gospel does not claim to have been written by Matthew but early tradition firmly states that he was its author. We know little of him, since he is only mentioned in 9:9 and 10:3, except that he was a tax collector who was personally called by Jesus. His name means 'gift of God'. Elsewhere he is called Levi (Mark 2:14).

THE READERS. The issues which concern Matthew most suggest that the majority of his readers would have been Jews. Most would already be Christians but he may be writing to persuade others that Jesus was the Messiah the Jews had expected for so long.

Yet he does not ignore the Gentiles altogether and he may be writing with a view to answering some of their questions about the Jewish origin of their faith.

WHEN WAS IT WRITTEN? We cannot say when it was written. It must have been written after Mark wrote his Gospel since Matthew is familiar with Mark. But it cannot be too late because the problems of the Jewish Christians with which he deals gradually became less important. Many dates between AD 50 and 90 have been suggested.

SPECIAL FEATURES. 1. Matthew is a very orderly Gospel. It sandwiches sections of Jesus' teaching between sections describing his activities.

2. In his desire to show that Jesus was the Jewish Messiah he frequently quotes from the Old Testament. There are 65 references in all to the Old Testament.

3. Matthew speaks about the kingdom of heaven (33 times), which is appropriate for the Jewish background he is writing from, whereas other Gospels speak about the kingdom of God.

4. Alone among the Gospels Matthew speaks of the church. He writes as a pastor, dealing with questions and problems.

Outline

Olivent Discourse

MATTHEW

Message

1. Jesus is the Messiah.
- [ ] He comes from Jewish ancestry. 1:1–17
- [ ] He fulfils Old Testament prophecy. eg. 1:23; 2:6,18,23; 4:15,16; etc.
- [x] He comes to save people from sin. 1:21
- [x] He goes first to Israel. 15:24
- [ ] He illustrates his attitude to the Old Testament. 5:17–48
- [ ] He challenges religious leaders who mislead God's people. 16:5–12; 23:1–36
- [x] He will one day act as judge. 25:31–46

2. Jesus speaks of a kingdom.
- [x] He explains what the kingdom of God is: not a place, but God actively ruling his world. 9:35
- [ ] He himself is also king. 2:2, 16:28
- [ ] He announces its revolutionary entry qualifications. eg. 5:3,10,20; 7:21; 19:14, 23,24

- [x] His kingdom is already present. 12:28
- [x] His kingdom is yet fully to come. 16:28
- [ ] Its growth is certain even if it is hidden. 13:1–23
- [ ] It deserves to be man's greatest priority. 6:33; 13:44–46

3. Jesus underlines the law.
- [x] He strengthens the law. 5:17–48
- [x] He summarises the law. 22:37–40
- [x] He interprets the law. 23:23

4. Jesus commissions his church.
- [ ] As a moral community. 5:20
- [ ] As a disciplined community. 18:15–18
- [ ] As a forgiving community. 18:21–22
- [ ] As a praying community. 18:19–20
- [ ] As a witnessing community. 28:19–20

Application

The message of Matthew can be applied to two main groups:

1. To unbelievers.
- [x] Jewish unbelievers: It shows that Jesus is the Messiah for whom they have been waiting. His coming was carefully prepared throughout history and salvation is now available through him.
- [ ] Gentile unbelievers: Deliverance from sin and its effects is available to Gentiles as well. Jesus is a universal Saviour. He welcomes those who express their faith in him.

2. To Christians.
- [x] The gospel will provide you with basic teaching about the life and words of Jesus.
- [x] The gospel will begin to show you the value of the Old Testament.
- [ ] The gospel will point out the need to live by a new law and to reach high moral standards.
- [ ] The gospel will show you how to live with your fellow Christians.
- [x] The gospel will encourage you to be involved in world mission.
- [x] The gospel will inspire you with the hope of the return of Jesus.

MATTHEW

Key themes

Matthew emphasises certain themes. Look through the following notes and use a concordance to follow up other references to study them in depth.

1. God is our heavenly Father.
This is Matthew's favourite way of talking about God: 5:16,45,48; 6:1,9; 7:11,21; 10:32,33; 12:50; 16:17; 18:10,14,19.

2. The various descriptions of Jesus.
Jesus is called the Son of David (1:1), the Saviour (1:21), the King of the Jews (2:2), a Nazarene (2:23). What other titles for Jesus can you find?

3. The quotations from the Old Testament.
Matthew often says 'this was to fulfil what the Lord had spoken by the prophet' (2:15) or something similar. Search out the other references and see what they teach about Jesus.

4. The teaching of Jesus.
Five times Matthew says 'when Jesus had finished saying these things' (7:28; 11:1; 13:53; 19:1; 26:1). Each follows a collection of the sayings of Jesus. Summarise what each 'sermon' says.

5. The parables of Jesus.
Jesus taught his disciples by parables. But remember not everyone got the point of them (13:10–17). Some parables are to be found at: 7:24–27; 13:3–52; 18:23–35; 20:1–16; 22:1–14; 25:1–30. Summarise what these and other parables teach.

6. The miracles of Jesus.
Matthew records many miracles of healing and several other types of miracle through which Jesus demonstrates that he is Lord over all creation. There are twenty miracles in all: 8:1–17, 23–34; 9:1–8, 18–33; 12:10–13, 22; 14:15–33; 15:21–39; 17:14–21; 20:29–34; 21:18–22. List the miracles and in a sentence say what each one shows about Jesus.

7. The kingdom of heaven.
This phrase summarises the essential teaching of Jesus. Use a concordance to find out where he speaks of it and build up a picture of what Jesus intended to say about it.

MARK

The Christian teacher's handbook

WHO WAS JOHN MARK?

1. He was the cousin of Barnabas (Col.4:10).

2. He lived in Jerusalem with his mother, Mary (Acts 12:12). The church met in his home.

3. He went with Paul and his cousin on the first missionary journey (Acts 13:5).

4. Mark left the others after their time in Cyprus (which was the homeland of Barnabas, Acts 4:36), perhaps because he did not approve of Paul taking over the leadership.

5. He went back to Jerusalem (Acts 13:13).

6. In Jerusalem he would have had plenty of opportunity to talk with Peter.

7. It might even have been Peter who first brought Mark to faith in Jesus: Peter calls him 'my son Mark' in 1 Peter 5:13.

8. It is generally accepted that Mark wrote down the good news as he heard it from Peter.

9. It is sometimes suggested that Mark was the young man mentioned in Mark 14:51,52, but there is no way of proving this.

DATE. It is probably the earliest gospel, written between AD 65 and AD 70, before the Jerusalem Temple was destroyed. Matthew and Luke both seem to have used Mark's Gospel.

MARK'S MYSTERY. Mark shows us Jesus-with-a-secret. In Mark's Gospel we find Jesus discouraging publicity . . .

1. Demons are commanded to keep silent (1:25, 34; 3:12).

2. Those who have been healed by Jesus are told not to talk about it (1:44; 5:43; 7:36).

3. Jesus' own followers are told not to tell others that he is the Messiah (8:30).

4. And Jesus tells his followers privately about 'the **secret** of the kingdom of God' (4:10–12).

So how do we interpret this idea of secrecy? The problem for Jesus was that the Jewish people had the wrong idea about the Messiah. As Jesus confronts their wrong idea we have:

1. **Not approval of it** because the popular idea of the Messiah was political and human, instead of spiritual and divine.

2. **Not denial of it** because Jesus **was** the Messiah: his many miracles (at least 17 are recorded by Mark) witnessed to that.

3. **But re-formulation of it** because Jesus had to show them a serving, saving and suffering Messiah who was fully man but fully God.

SPECIAL FEATURES. It is the shortest Gospel, compressed and concise. Mark makes the essentials available for immediate reference. The word 'immediately' occurs more than forty times and seems to hurry us on from one amazing story to the next.

Outline

MARK

Message

1. Jesus: the Son of God.
Mark starts with the words: 'The beginning of the gospel about Jesus Christ, the Son of God.' 1:1

2. Jesus: the Son of Man.
Mark also shows us the humanness of Jesus:
- [ ] He is grieved. 3:5
- [ ] He has compassion on the crowds. 6:34
- [ ] He is troubled. 14:33
- [ ] Mark uses the title 'Son of Man' fourteen times; this is his preferred title for Jesus.

3. The actual words of Jesus.
Mark records for us Peter's memory of some of the actual Aramaic words used by Jesus:
- [ ] **'Talitha koum!',** Wake up, little girl!' 5:41
- [ ] **'Ephphatha!',** 'Open!' 7:34
- [ ] **'Eloi, Eloi, lama sabachthani?',** 'My God, my God, why have you forsaken me?' 15:34

4. The kindness of Jesus.
Mark records Peter's memory of Jesus' special kindness to him and Peter's awareness that he did not deserve it. Peter makes Mark leave out Jesus' words about Peter being a rock because Peter remembered when he was not a rock. (See Matthew 16:18,19.)

Application *portraits him as a servant*

Mark shows us:

1. The importance of right doctrine.
- [ ] It couldn't come from demons even though they **had** to submit to his power.
- [ ] It couldn't come from those who had been healed even though they were grateful.
- [ ] It couldn't come from the apostles, until they had been properly taught.

Christian doctrine is not common sense **but** divine wisdom.

2. That miracles are natural with God.
- [ ] Mark never apologises for a miracle, never attempts to explain it away.
- [ ] Jesus' miracles point to his nature. Take away his miracles and you cast doubt on his deity.

- [ ] Miracles are, were and always will be amazing. Mark repeatedly follows up the story of a miracle with the observation that the people were 'amazed', 'filled with awe'.
- [ ] Notice particularly the collection of miracles in chapter 5 which show Jesus' power over – demons (1–20)
  – disease (24–34)
  – death (35–43)

3. That opposition often comes from religious people.
- [ ] The Scribes 2:6
- [ ] The Pharisees 2:24
- [ ] The Herodians 3:6
- [ ] The Chief Priests 11:18
- [ ] The Sadducees 12:18

197

MARK

Key themes

1. Jesus' miracles.
Make a list of the miracles recorded in Mark. Compare this with the number of parables given in Mark.

Why does Mark place so much emphasis on Jesus' miracles?

Why did Jesus perform miracles? Try to find at least three distinct reasons.

2. The people's response.
Locate those places where Mark comments on the amazement of the people when they saw Jesus' miracles (eg. 1:27; 2:12; 4:41; 5:15; 6:50 and so on). List the various reactions of the people and explain why they reacted in so many different ways.

3. Special titles for Jesus.
Go through Mark's Gospel and note the special titles Mark records for Jesus. How many times does he use The Son, My Son, Son of God, Son of Man?

Who uses the title Son of Man?

Why? (Study Daniel 7:13–28 carefully.)

4. Jesus' authority.
Study carefully all those passages which refer to Jesus' authority: 1:22; 1:27; 2:10; 3:15; 6:7; 11:27–33 and 13:34. Note especially this last reference:

'It is like a man going away: he leaves his house in charge of his servants'. This last phrase is literally 'gives his servants authority'.

LUKE

The most human of the Gospels

WHO WROTE LUKE? The Gospel was written by a doctor, called Luke, who was a friend and colleague of the apostle Paul (Colossians 4:14; Philemon 24 and 2 Timothy 4:11). Luke was not himself an eyewitness of the life of Jesus (1:1–4). Tradition tells us that he was a Gentile who remained unmarried and lived until he was eighty-four.

WHY WAS THE GOSPEL WRITTEN? Luke had several purposes:

1. He wanted to write a well-organised life of Jesus which was based on good eye-witness evidence (1:1–4).

2. He wanted to record the beginnings and development of Christianity, which he did in two parts. Acts is the second volume. Luke shows how God has been at work in history and especially in the way in which the followers of Jesus rapidly spread from Galilee to Rome.

3. He wanted to demonstrate that Jesus was a Saviour for all types of people and not just for a select group.

4. He wanted to show the Roman authorities that Christianity was not a threat to good political order.

WHO WERE LUKE'S READERS?

1. Luke addresses his Gospel to Theophilus (1:3), probably an upper-class Gentile convert to Christianity. His name means 'loved of God' but we know nothing else about him.

2. In addition Luke would have had a wider circle of readers in mind which would have included other Gentiles and perhaps Roman officials in particular.

WHEN WAS IT WRITTEN? Luke must have written his Gospel before he wrote his second volume and since the last event mentioned in Acts took place around AD 62 it is a fair guess that Luke itself was written between AD 60–65.

SPECIAL FEATURES. 1. Luke's story-telling is second to none. His ability with words is also shown by his very good Greek style.

2. Luke is also more interested in the human life of Jesus and tells us more about his early life and childhood than others.

3. In other ways, too, Luke is more complete than the other Gospels and records more parables, more news about people and more about Jesus' resurrection than others.

4. Luke shows more interest in individuals than the other Gospel-writers, particularly children, women, and social outcasts.

5. He has other special interests, for example, prayer, the Holy Spirit and the theme of joy.

Outline

LUKE

Message

1. Good news about salvation.
The message of Luke is that God has come to rescue man from his sin and situation.
- [ ] God is a Saviour. 1:47
- [ ] Christ was born to save. 2:11,30; 3:6
- [ ] He came to save the lost. 19:9,10
- [ ] Salvation comes by faith. 7:50; 8:12
- [ ] Salvation means losing life now. 9:24
- [ ] Salvation is possible because Christ did not save himself. 23:35–43
- [ ] Salvation is available now. 4:21; 19:9

2. Good news about a kingdom.
The central section (9:51–19:44) has much to say about the kingdom of God which was central to Jesus' preaching. 4:43; 8:1
- [ ] God's kingdom is everlasting. 1:33
- [ ] It belongs to the poor. 6:20
- [ ] His disciples should preach it. 9:2,11
- [ ] Its interests should come first. 9:60–62; 12:31
- [ ] Men should pray for it. 11:2
- [ ] It is the gift of God. 12:32; 22:29
- [ ] God's kingdom is like . . . 13:18–30
- [ ] Rich men do not enter easily. 18:18–30
- [ ] It is near now. 10:9,11; 11:20; 17:20,21
- [ ] But it is also to come. 24:31

3. Good news seen in Jesus.
The good news was not a myth or fairy story but was well supported by events which took place in the life of Jesus.
- [ ] History is important. 1:1–4
- [ ] God planned it ages ago. 3:23–38
- [ ] God was at work in the life of Jesus. Many eye-witnesses saw it:
  – at his birth. 2:30
  – at his baptism. 3:22
  – in his miracles. 4:36; 7:16
  – in his death. 23:39–49
  – in his resurrection. 24:1–49
- [ ] Jesus still works through his disciples. 24:48
- [ ] Jesus is working all over the world. Jerusalem was just a beginning. 24:47

Application

The message of Luke can be applied to two main groups:

1. To those who do not believe in Jesus.
To put your faith in Jesus:
- [ ] is to build on the witness of history
- [ ] is to know the forgiveness of God
- [ ] is to be able to start life again
- [ ] is to be involved in the kingdom of God
- [ ] does not demand prior goodness or respectability
- [ ] does demand humility and a willingness to give up everything for Jesus
- [ ] pays great rewards in the future

2. To those who do believe in Jesus.
Your faith in Jesus means you should:
- [ ] be joyful and thankful in life
- [ ] imitate Jesus' love for all men
- [ ] get involved in spreading the good news of the kingdom
- [ ] put self to death every day
- [ ] pray as Jesus taught
- [ ] make God's kingdom your clear priority
- [ ] trust that God is in control of the world

LUKE

Key themes

Among Luke's other special concerns are:

1. Prayer.
He often speaks about the prayer life of Jesus: 3:21; 5:16; 6:12; 9:18–22,29; 10:17–21; 11:1; 22:39–46; 23:34,46. He also records parables Jesus told about prayer: 11:5–13; 18:1–8. What can you learn about when to pray, how to pray and what to pray from these verses?

2. The Holy Spirit.
The work of the Holy Spirit in the life of Jesus is emphasised by Luke. List the times in the life of Jesus when he is mentioned: eg. 1:35; 4:1,14,18; 10:21,22; 24:49. What do these verses teach about the Holy Spirit?

3. Praise and joy.
Luke's Gospel opens with a number of songs of praise: 1:46–55, 68–79; 2:14 ; and 2:29–32. What other references to joy can you find in the Gospel?

4. Forgiveness.
The good news is basically about the forgiveness of sins. Why was the teaching of Jesus about forgiveness so revolutionary? Be careful to note all that Jesus says about it: 5:17–25; 6:37; 7:36–50; 11:4; 17:3–4; 23:34; 24:47.

5. Money.
Luke speaks more about money than any of the other Gospels and has a special place for the poor. Again his message is quite revolutionary. Trace his teaching in the following verses: 1:53; 4:18; 6:20; 12:13–34; 15:8–10; 16:1–15, 19–31; 18:1–14; 19:1–27; 20:19–26.

6. Women and children.
Make a note of the number of women to whom Luke refers in his Gospel. The society of Jesus' day would not normally consider them worth so much attention. But Luke emphasises God's love for all people – even women, outcasts and children. Look at the following verses about children and summarise their teaching: 8:40–56; 9:37–43, 46–48; 18:15–17.

JOHN

God's last word to man

THE GOSPEL THAT IS DIFFERENT. John has his own approach to the life and work of Jesus. Compared with the other Gospels, the long flowing accounts of what Jesus said have made some feel that John is not accurate. Until recently many scholars believed that John was late (around AD 100), the most un-Jewish Gospel, that he used the others, that he was not an eyewitness and that these were not really Jesus' words. So we were left with an interesting collection of thoughts about Jesus by an early Christian.

Archaeology has changed that picture. Many now say that John was independent of the others, that he knew Southern Palestine well in the time of Jesus, that he was an eyewitness and that he wrote very early on, at least as early as the others.

JOHN'S GOSPEL? We have a clue in the book itself about who wrote it, or at least who provided the material. It was 'the disciple whom Jesus loved' (21:20–24, see 13:23–25). Many have argued as did the early church that this was John, the brother of James. Although prominent in the other Gospels, he is not named in this one. What is more, it is likely that he would have had the place at Jesus' side at the Supper. He would certainly have been able to supply some very intimate details about the way in which Jesus spoke and worked.

WHY DID HE WRITE IT? He tells us himself – 'that you may believe that Jesus is the Christ' (20:30,31). So we are not just dealing with a biography here. It is more like a carefully prepared Gospel tract. He tells us that he has specially selected the evidence. He includes only seven of Jesus' miracles, and he usually follows them up with discourses which give us the inner meaning of what Jesus was doing. John brings forward his witnesses one by one, and the reader must make some decision about Jesus Christ by the end. This is why, although he probably wrote it first of all for non-Jews (he explains many of the Jewish terms and customs), it has led so many to faith in Christ ever since.

AN EARLY ADDITION. In John's Gospel we have one of the most telling stories about Jesus' compassion for a sinner, that of the woman taken in adultery (7:53–8:11). Strange to say, it does not form part of the oldest manuscripts, and it does not always appear at this point. Most are agreed, however, that it was an actual incident in Jesus' life which was remembered, written up and added to the Gospel at a very early date.

Outline

 INTRODUCTION
1:1–51

1:1–5 Christ and creation
1:6–18 God became man
1:19–34 The Lamb of God
1:35–51 The Christ

 SOUTH AND NORTH
2:1–4:54

2:1–12 First glimpse of glory
2:13–25 The Lord of the Temple
3:1–21 Nicodemus by night
3:22–36 The One from above
4:1–42 The Messiah and the outcast
4:43–54 The second sign

 A LAME MAN ON THE SABBATH
5:1–47

 THE FIVE THOUSAND FED
6:1–71

 AT THE FEAST OF TABERNACLES
7:1–9:41

7:1–52 Living water
7:53–8:11 The woman accused
8:12–59 The Light of the World
9:1–41 The giver of sight

 THE GOOD SHEPHERD
10:1–42

 THE LIFE-RESTORER
11:1–57

talks about the boy

Love themes

 THE LAST PASSOVER
12:1–50

12:1–11 Mary's love
12:12–19 The King comes to Jerusalem
12:20–36 The corn of wheat
12:37–50 Summing it up

 IN THE UPPER ROOM
13:1–30

13:1–20 Jesus, the servant
13:21–30 Judas, the betrayer

 GETTING READY TO GO
13:31–16:33

13:31–14:14 Time to leave
14:15–31 The Spirit promised
15:1–17 The True Vine
15:18–16:11 Trouble in the world
16:12–33 Promise and perplexity

11 **JESUS PRAYS FOR HIS OWN**
17:1–26

17:1–19 His disciples
17:20–26 The church to come

 ARREST, TRIAL, CRUCIFIXION
18:1–19:42

18:1–11 Confusion in the garden
18:12–27 Private viewing
18:28–19:16 The governor and the King
19:17–42 Dead and buried

13 **RESURRECTION**
20:1–21:25

20:1–18 Mary in the garden
20:19–23 Sunday evening
20:24–31 'My Lord and my God!'
21:1–14 Fish for breakfast
21:15–25 Feed my sheep

JOHN

Message

1. The evidence.

Witness in the courtroom sense is a key theme in John. There are a number of witnesses brought forward to prove the case that Jesus is the Christ and the Son of God.

- ☐ The Old Testament: 1:45; 5:39,46–47; 8:56, see 3:14; 6:32–35
- ☐ John the Baptist: 1:6–8,15,19–36; 3:25–30; 5:33–36, see 10:40–42
- ☐ People in general: 4:29,39; 9:13–33,38; 11:27; 12:9,17
- ☐ The apostles: 1:41–46,49; 15:27; 17:20; 20:24–25,28, see 1:14; 19:35; 20:30–31; 21:24
- ☐ The Father: 5:31–32,37; 8:18,50,54; 12:27–28
- ☐ The Holy Spirit: 14:26; 15:26; 16:12–15
- ☐ Jesus' works: 2:11,23; 5:36; 9:3,31–33; 10:25,37–38; 11:4,42,45; 14:11; 20:30–31
- ☐ Jesus himself, his words and claims: 3:11,32; 8:13–14,38; 6:35,48,51; 8:12; 9:5; 10:7,11,14; 11:25; 14:6; 15:1, see 8:58 (Exodus 3:14). See key themes.

2. The verdict.

- ☐ Those who rejected him: 1:10–11; 3:11; 4:48; 5:43; 6:36,64,66; 12:37,47–48; 15:19,24. And the reasons why: 3:19–21; 5:44; 6:37,44,65; 8:43–47; 9:39–41; 12:37–43; 18:37
- ☐ Those who responded to him:
  – By seeing and hearing him 1:14; 6:40,45; 10:3,16,27; 12:45,47; 14:9; 18:37
  – By believing in him 1:7,12; 2:11,22; 3:16,18; 5:24; 6:29,47; 8:24; 9:35–38; 11:25–27,40; 13:19; 14:1,11; 16:27,30; 17:8; 20:8,29,31
  – By coming to know him 6:69; 7:17; 8:19; 10:14; 14:7,9; 17:3,25 which means living in the light 1:4–5,9; 3:19–21; 8:12; 9:39; 11:9; 12:35–36,46 and learning the truth 1:14,17; 4:23–24; 8:32; 14:6; 17:17; 18:37
  – By loving Christ and one another 13:34–35; 14:15,21–24; 15:9–10,12; 21:15–17 which will mean abiding in him 15:1–10

Application   *New law " love another"* 13-14

1. Christ is God's last word to mankind.

He shows us:
- ☐ God's truth
- ☐ God's glory
- ☐ God's love

by his life and by his death. He is the only way back to God.

2. We must respond to him one way or the other.

The evidence is clear:
- ☐ If we reject him it is not because we cannot believe – we will not!
- ☐ If we accept him it will mean wholehearted commitment and obedience.

3. Eternal life begins here and now.

By the Holy Spirit Jesus offers us:
- ☐ satisfaction
- ☐ freedom from Satan and sin
- ☐ new potential
- ☐ answered prayer
- ☐ real joy

What he begins now he will complete when he comes back.

4. You must share your faith with others.

Even though the world will hate you as it hated Jesus, you too must become a witness with the help of the Holy Spirit.

JOHN

Key themes

1. Jesus and the Father.
The Gospel is full of the ways in which Jesus is God's Son. He was involved in creation, he came into this world and when he ascended he went back to his rightful glory. Build up the picture for yourself: 1:1–18; 3:13,31,35; 5:17–23,26–27,30; 6:38,46,57; 7:16–17,29; 8:28–29,38,42; 10:15,29–30,38; 11:41–42; 12:44–45,49–50; 13:3,31–32; 14:7–11,20,28,31; 15:23–24; 16:15,28,32; 17:1–2,4–5,10–11,21–23; 20:17.

2. Christ's death for sinners.
More than any of the other Gospels, John tells us why Jesus had to die and of the love which made him do it. See 1:29,36; 2:19–22; 3:14–17; 6:51,53–56; 8:28; 10:11,15,18; 11:50–52; 12:24,27,32–34; 15:13.

3. The Holy Spirit.
There is more about the Spirit in this Gospel than in the others. He is described as the One who would replace Jesus when he went back to the Father. 1:32–33; 3:5–6,8,34; 4:23–24; 6:63; 7:37–39, see 4:13–14; 14:16–17,25–26; 15:26; 16:7–15; 20:22.

4. Eternal Life.
This is what Matthew, Mark and Luke describe as the kingdom of God. It is connected with new or second birth. See 1:4,12–13; 3:3–7,16,36; 4:14,36; 5:21,24–29; 6:27,40,47,54,57–58,68; 10:28; 11:25; 12:25,50; 17:2–3.

5. God's timetable.
John gives us a picture of Jesus in control of the situation from first to last. He knew he was working out a master plan so that nothing, not even his death, took him by surprise. Note the following: 2:4; 7:6–8; 12:23; 13:1; 18:4.

ACTS

The story of a witnessing church

WHO WROTE THE BOOK? Dr. Luke wrote this book. It could have been entitled the Acts of the Holy Spirit, for it tells of what happened after the Holy Spirit came upon the apostles at Pentecost. Luke, the only non-Jewish writer in the New Testament, wrote Acts as a sequel to his earlier volume, the Gospel bearing his name.

"To" Be my witness's

WHAT IS IT ABOUT? The first 12 chapters deal mostly with the activities of the apostle Peter, whilst the remaining chapters are taken up largely with the work of the apostle Paul.

Jesus had told his disciples that when the Holy Spirit had come upon them, they would be his witnesses. The book of Acts shows how this came to pass.

From the book of Acts we learn a good deal about the early church, its joys and sorrows, its triumphs and tragedies, but above all its expansion so that in a few short years it was established right throughout the civilised world.

We know Dr. Luke to have been a very careful historian and we can be assured that here we have a factual account of the early days of Christianity.

WHAT ARE ITS SPECIAL FEATURES? The word 'witness' is used over 30 times in Acts, reminding us that a true church is a witnessing church and that every Christian is called to be a witness. It is astonishing that in one generation those early Christians carried the message of the Gospel right through the civilised world. It has been said that Acts is the best guide book to missions that has ever been written.

The book closes very abruptly – it appears unfinished. A fitting end since the church's witness must go on till Christ returns. The Gospels display what Christ began to do when he was on earth, and Acts shows what he continued to do by his Holy Spirit, through the disciples. The book opens with the preaching of the gospel in Jerusalem, the religious capital of the Jewish people; it closes with the gospel being proclaimed in Rome, the capital of the civilised world of that day.

WHEN WAS IT WRITTEN? Almost certainly Luke wrote Acts in the early or mid-sixties of the first century – at the close of Paul's two-year imprisonment in Rome. It covers the period from the founding of the church in Jerusalem to Paul's imprisonment in Rome – some thirty years.

Outline

1 BY WAY OF INTRODUCTION
1:1–26

The forty days and after:

1:1–11 The promise of the Spirit
1:12–14 The waiting disciples
1:15–26 A replacement for Judas

2 WITNESSING IN JERUSALEM
2–7

2:1–47 Power is given and preaching is powerful
3:1–26 The first recorded miracle in the early church
4:1–31 Opposition flares up
4:32–5:16 Blessing and blemishes
5:17–42 Obeying God rather than men
6:1–7:60 The first Christian martyr

3 WITNESSING IN SAMARIA
8

4 WITNESSING FURTHER AFIELD
9:1–13:3

9 A remarkable conversion
10:1–11:30 Peter's eyes are opened
12:1–25 Peter arrested
13:1–3 Paul and Barnabas commissioned

Peter

Paul

Home missions

Foreign missions

5 WITNESSING TO THE ENDS OF THE EARTH
13:4–28:31

13:4–15:35 The first missionary journey
☑ Cyprus (13:4–12)
☑ Perga (13:13)
☑ Pisidian Antioch (13:14–52)
☑ Iconium (14:1–6)
☑ Lystra (14:6–20)
☑ Derbe (14:20–21)
☑ The Council at Jerusalem (15:1–35)
15:36–18:22 The second missionary journey
☐ Paul and Barnabas separate (15:36–41)
☑ Paul visits Lystra (16:1–3)
☐ Various cities of Asia Minor (16:4–11)
☐ Philippi (16:12–40)
☐ Thessalonica (17:1–9)
☐ Berea (17:10–14)
☐ Athens (17:15–34)
☐ Corinth (18:1–17)
☐ Returning to Antioch.
18:23–21:17 The third missionary journey
☐ Paul visits Ephesus (18:23–19:41)
☐ sets out for Jerusalem (20:1–16)
☐ addresses the Ephesian elders (20:17–38)
☐ and eventually reaches Jerusalem (21:1–7).
21:18–28:31 Paul faces the authorities
☐ Charged and arrested (21:18–40)
☐ On the defensive (22–26)
☐ En route for Rome (27–28:15)
☐ Paul still preaching (28:16–31)

Paul made three missionary journeys.

Message

1. The church waits for and receives the power of the Holy Spirit.
- The great commission repeated. 1:8
- The risen Lord ascends. 1:9
- ☐ The disciples pray. 1:14
- ☐ The promised Spirit is given. 2:4
- ☐ Powerful preaching follows. 2:37

2. The church demonstrates Christian fellowship.
- ☐ In communal living. 2:44; 4:32
- ☐ In corporate worship. 2:46

3. The church soon experiences both triumphs and tragedies.
- ☐ The healing of the cripple. 3:2
- ☐ The deception of Ananias and Sapphira. 5:1

4. The church gets its first 'officers' – the 'Seven' (6:3).

5. The church has its first martyr – Stephen (7:60).

6. The church receives its most notable convert – Saul of Tarsus (9:1–19).

7. The church proves the power of prayer.
- ☑ The prayer meeting which opened a prison. 12:5

8. The church holds its first conference where Gentile liberty is safeguarded (15:19).

Application

1. Acts shows us what a New Testament church should provide:
- ☑ Teaching
- ☑ Fellowship
- ☑ Breaking of bread
- ☑ Worship (prayers)

2. Acts shows us what Christian fellowship should be like:
- ☐ Sharing and caring

3. Acts shows us how missionary work should be carried out:
- ☑ By anyone God calls – not a special élite
- ☐ Under the guidance of the Spirit
- ☐ Visiting strategic centres

4. Acts reminds us that even keen Christians sometimes differ and part company.
- ☐ Paul and Barnabas took different attitudes to John Mark when he deserted them but the rift was later healed.

5. Acts introduces us to the first leaders to be appointed in the Christian church and tells us what their qualifications were.

ACTS

Key themes

1. Witnessing.

The Greek word translated 'witness' gives us our English word 'martyr'. The book of Acts shows just how costly witnessing may be – it cost Stephen his life and was the cause of both Peter and Paul's imprisonments.

Look up the references where the word 'witness' is used. Compare Stephen's martyrdom with Christ's death on the cross (Luke 23:34; Acts 7:60).

2. Conversions.

The book of Acts records a number of notable conversions. These four demonstrate how God brings men and women to himself by different means:

- ☑ The Ethiopian eunuch who was led to Christ through reading the Scriptures (8:30).
- ☑ Saul of Tarsus, whose life was suddenly and dramatically changed (9:1–19).
- ☑ Lydia, the religious woman who was ready to respond to the gospel (16:14).
- ☑ The Philippian jailer who was driven by fear to seek salvation (16:29,30).

Look up the references to these four conversions and compare God's methods, then and now, in bringing people to himself.

3. Team evangelism.

We see in Acts a pattern for missionary work. Not only did Paul make for strategic centres and seek to spread the good news into the surrounding area, but he had with him associate workers.

Note the different campaigns of Paul on his missionary journeys as recorded in Acts.

ROMANS

The heart of the gospel

WHY ROME? In the book of Acts we see Paul setting up churches in what we now know as Turkey and Greece. But he had a long-standing plan in his mind about going further west to Rome itself, and then beyond. However, there were things to be seen to first. He had to go back to Jerusalem to take a gift which the Gentile Christians had collected for the poor believers there. After that he would be free to turn his attention to the capital, and after that he had his eyes on Spain (15:22–29).

The reason for this was that Paul always liked to break fresh ground and preach the gospel where it had never been heard before. This partly explains this letter – a church already existed in Rome, so Paul did not see a visit as top priority (15:18–21). We do not know when it was founded, but if you look through the list of pilgrims on the Day of Pentecost, you will see that it included people from Rome (Acts 2:10). From the names at the end of this letter, it seems as though Paul already knew a good number of church members there (16:3–15), but this was to be expected as all roads led to Rome. People were moving round the empire all the time, especially traders, and many of them ended up in the capital city.

WHY THIS LETTER? It looks as though Paul was preparing the way for his visit by spelling out his gospel for them. It could even be that some had criticised his teaching and that he wanted to put this right. At the same time this gave him the chance to put down a summary of the good news about Christ in greater detail than we have it anywhere else in the New Testament. Romans is one of the most orderly of Paul's writings, and because of this it has been a source book for Christians ever since he dictated it to his friend Tertius around AD 57 in Corinth.

PAUL IN ROME. Paul's plans did not quite work out as he intended. We know from Acts that when he got to Jerusalem he was arrested, and after some while in jail, asked, as every Roman citizen could, for his case to be heard by the emperor. So he was packed off to Rome as a prisoner. It appears that he may have been released and undertaken a further spell of work before later being killed in Rome.

ROMANS AND THE CHURCH. When Christians rediscovered letters like Romans at the time of the Reformation, it revolutionised the church. They realised that they could not earn their salvation by what they did. God had done it all for them in such a way that he could pronounce guilty sinners innocent (or 'justify' them). The secret, of course, is the cross.

Outline

ROMANS

Message

1. We all need to get right with God
(chapters 1–3)
- [ ] For Gentiles, there is enough about him
  - in nature. 1:19–20
  - in the way we are made. 2:14–15
- [ ] For Jews, there is more than enough
  - in his word. 2:12,17–24; 3:1–2
- [ ] Everybody falls short. 3:9–20,23
- [ ] No one
  - may judge another. 2:1–3
  - can be proud. 3:27
  - has any excuse. 1:20; 2:1; 3:19
  - can save himself. 3:20,23

2. God did it all (chapters 3–5)
- [ ] Christ's death pays the bill
  - he died in our place. 3:24–25
  - while we were sinners. 5:6–8
  - we can be acquitted. 3:24
- [ ] Abraham took God at his word
  - so must we in faith. 3:25; 4:16–25; 5:1
- [ ] Adam did something which affects us now
  - so did Christ on the cross. 5:12–19

3. The way to live differently (chapters 6–8)
- [ ] The problem is sinful human nature
  - which cannot be good. 7:18
  - which is hostile to God. 8:7
  - which cannot please God. 8:8

- [ ] The power comes from the Holy Spirit
  - who lives in us. 8:9–11
  - who provokes conflict. 7:13–23
  - who provides victory. 7:24–25
- [ ] We must co-operate with him
  - refusing sin. 6:13,16,19; 8:13
  - obeying Christ. 6:13,16–19, see 12:1
- [ ] We may
  - have victory. 6:14
  - receive life. 8:11
  - become God's children. 8:14–17
  - know his help. 8:26–27
  - be made like Christ. 8:28–30, see 12:2
  - be sure we are his. 8:31–39

4. God knows what he is doing (chapters 9–11)
- [ ] God gets his way with people
  - even disobedient Jews. 9:1–33
  - he has a master plan. 11:1–32
- [ ] We still need to respond
  - in obedient faith. 10:5–21

5. We are saved together(chapters 12–15)
- [ ] We are members of the body
  - belonging to one another. 12:3–8
  - loving one another. 12:9–21; 13:8–10
  - accepting one another. 14:1–15:7
  - sharing a new lifestyle. 13:1–7, 11–14

Application

1. The offer is free
(of getting right with God)
- [ ] Because of what we are, it has to be
- [ ] Because of what Christ did, it can be
- [ ] This means
  - we cannot earn it
  - we must take it by faith

2. The power is there
(to live a Christian life)
- [ ] Because we cannot do it ourselves
- [ ] Because the Spirit lives in us
- [ ] This means
  - denying our sinful natures
  - obeying Jesus Christ

3. The fellowship is ours
(with other Christians)
☐ Because we belong together
☐ Because we now know how to love

This means
– we should nurture and value it
– we should not misuse it or take it for granted

Key themes

1. Grace.
The truth is hammered home that if we are going to be Christians at all, God had to do it. God's grace is free; we cannot earn it. At the same time we must not take it for granted.

Trace this theme through the letter: 1:7; 2:4; 3:24,27; 4:16; 5:15,17,21; 6:1,15; 11:5–6.

2. Faith.
We take God's free gift by faith in Christ. At the same time, this is not just believing about him. It means taking God at his word, obeying him and confessing Christ.

Note how Paul stresses faith in the letter, and also how he defines it. Is our idea of faith big enough? 1:5 (see 15:18); 1:16–17; 3:22,26–31; 4:1–25; 5:1; 10:8–11; 10:17.

3. Acquittal (or Justification).
This is a word from the law-courts. God acquits – or 'justifies' – the sinner, pronouncing him 'righteous' because of what Jesus has done in his place.

See how Paul ties this in with Christ's death and faith: 1:17; 3:21–26; 4:1–25; 5:8–11,15–21; 10:1–10.

4. Togetherness.
Notice that Paul tells us that we sin and we are saved together. He uses the picture of the body when he wants to show how closely we must work with one another.

Although the things which upset and divided Christians in Paul's day are different from our own, does he give us any rules we can apply today? See 14:1–15:7 especially.

5. God is King.
We get the clear impression that in spite of people not believing, God gets his way in the world, as well as ordering the lives of Christians. This becomes a great assurance for those who believe even if we cannot understand how he does it.

Read through chapters 9 and 10 again. How do they balance one another out?

1 CORINTHIANS

Letter to a divided church

HOW THE CHURCH AT CORINTH BEGAN. Paul first visited Corinth during his second missionary journey (Acts 18:1). A handful of Jews, including Crispus who was the 'ruler' of the synagogue, and many non-Jews became Christians.

Paul began a Bible school for them, strategically if provocatively located next door to the synagogue (Acts 18: 1–18). He stayed about eighteen months and was succeeded as Bible teacher by Apollos.

HOW NEWS ABOUT THE CHURCH REACHED PAUL. Paul was somewhere in Asia (1 Corinthians 16:19), probably at Ephesus (16:8), at a later stage of his second missionary journey, when Stephanas and two friends arrived with a letter from the Christians at Corinth (16:17 and 7:1).

A DIVIDED CHURCH.

1. They were divided about leadership (1:12).

2. They were divided about moral standards (5:1–8).

3. They were divided into accusers and accused (6:1–8).

4. They were divided into weak Christians and strong Christians (8:7–12).

5. They were divided into rich and poor (11:17–22).

6. Even their spiritual gifts divided them (12:12–26).

FOUR LETTERS TO CORINTH? It appears that Paul wrote four letters to Corinth: we have only the second and the last.

1. The first letter is referred to in 5:9: 'I wrote to you in my letter'. But we have no further knowledge of this letter.

2. The second letter is our First Corinthians.

3. A third letter seems to be referred to in 2 Corinthians 2:3,4, often labelled the 'sorrowful letter'. This might simply have been 1 Corinthians, but that letter doesn't really fit what Paul says of the sorrowful letter.

4. The fourth letter is our Second Corinthians.

YOUR QUESTIONS ANSWERED. First Corinthians is so valuable because it answers many of the questions which are being asked today:

☐ What is the right attitude to have towards our leaders?

☐ What is the place of education in the life of the Christian?

☐ What about church discipline?

☐ Should a Christian take another Christian to court?

☐ What should our attitude be towards other religions?

☐ What is meant by freedom?

☐ May women pray in church?
☐ What are spiritual gifts?
☐ Which is the most important of the spiritual gifts?
☐ What happens after death?

Careful study will reveal the answers to these and many other questions in this letter.

Outline

 INTRODUCTION
1:1–9
1:1–3 Greetings
1:4–9 Some surprising comments

 THE SCANDAL OF A DIVIDED CHURCH
1:10–4:21
1:10–31 Man glorified: Christ crucified
2:1–3:4 Spiritual wisdom
3:5–4:5 Think of leaders like this
4:6–21 Puffed-up pride, poverty and power

 THE SCANDAL OF IMMORALITY
5:1–6:20
5:1–13 A notorious sexual scandal
6:1–8 Scandalous lawsuits
6:9–20 Purity for the Spirit's temple

QUESTIONS ABOUT MARRIAGE
7:1–40
7:1–9 Concerning rights and duties
7:10–24 Concerning divorce
7:25–38 What about single people?
7:39–40 Summary

 SET FREE ... BUT HOW FREE?
8:1–11:1
8:1–13 Liberated from idolatry, but . . .
9:1–27 Free from society's ideas, but . . .
10:1–13 Free by God's grace, but . . .
10:14–11:1 Free to serve men and to please God

 DISORDER IN CHURCH SERVICES
11:2–14:40
11:2–16 Long hair, hats and veils
11:17–34 Communion: in a divided church?
12:1–31 Spiritual gifts
13:1–13 The highest gift
14:1–40 Tongues and prophecy

THE RESURRECTION
15:1–58
15:1–11 This is the good news
15:12–19 If Christ has not risen . . .
15:20–34 But **he** has and **we** shall
15:35–50 What resurrection means
15:51–58 The glory of the resurrection

 CONCLUSION
16:1–24
16:1–9 Paul's plans
16:10–20 Some important people
16:21–24 A personal greeting

1 CORINTHIANS

Message

The letter is structured like an ellipse with two 'poles' instead of one centre.

1. The scandal of a divided church (chapters 1-4)
The church was divided into four groups, each with a different 'label'
□ I belong to Paul   □ I belong to Peter
□ I belong to Apollos   □ I belong to Christ
The section about weakness in chapter 1 might refer to what some of his critics said about Paul (see 2 Corinthians 10:10) and the section about wisdom in the same chapter might be a reference to Apollos and his education (Acts 18:24). Paul uses five striking labels for himself and the rest of the church leaders to show what our attitude should be:
□ Servants **(diakonoi)**. 3:5
□ Fellow-workers. 3:9
□ Master builders. 3:10
□ Servants **(huperetas)**, under-oarsmen, assistants. 4:1
□ Stewards. 4:1

2. The confusion about freedom (chapters 8-10)
□ 'Strong' Christians thought they were free to eat in the idol temples of Corinth, even if other 'weak' Christians were upset by it.
□ 'Liberated' women thought they could abandon the veil even if some of the 'trad' men did think that they were being fast.
Paul explodes this nonsense. He takes a simple example: his right to expect to be paid for his work as a preacher.
He produces seven arguments which prove the principle of paying the preacher:
□ The example of the apostles. 9:5
□ The illustration of a soldier. 9:7
□ The illustration of a gardener. 9:7
□ The illustration of a shepherd. 9:7
□ The teaching of the Law. 9:8
□ The example of the Temple priests. 9:13
□ The teaching of Jesus himself. 9:14
And having proved his right to payment he refuses to be paid (9:15). His point is clear:
Because I **have** a right does not mean that I **must** exercise it.
And here's the principle:
'Though I am free and belong to no man, I make myself a slave to everyone, to win as many as possible'. (9:19)

Application

1. Human cleverness inevitably clashes with the wisdom of God.

2. Christians who idolise their leaders:
□ divide the church
□ delude their leaders
□ devalue God.

3. Church discipline, which is largely forgotten in the west:
□ restores the rebel
□ is a warning to the waverer

□ witnesses to the world
□ glorifies God.

4. The Christian is set free:
□ not so that he can please himself
□ but so that he can serve God
□ and so that he can win others.

5. The resurrection is of the essence of Christianity,
□ it is NOT an optional extra.

1 CORINTHIANS

Key themes

☐ Read carefully through 1:17 to 2:13, noting all references to **wisdom, power, folly** or **weakness**. Paul uses each of these words in two ways: as man sees it and as God sees it. Try to explain these eight ideas.

☐ In chapters 5 and 6 Paul begins seven questions with 'Do you not know?':
– a little leaven leavens the whole lump. 5:6
– the saints will judge the earth. 6:2
– we are to judge angels. 6:3
– the unrighteous will not inherit the kingdom of God. 6:9
– your bodies are members of Christ. 6:15
– he who joins himself to a prostitute becomes one body with her. 6:16
– your body is a temple of the Holy Spirit. 6:19

On what grounds does Paul expect the Corinthian Christians to **know** these seven principles? If we **know** these seven principles what effect should that knowledge have on our behaviour?

☐ Four fundamentals of the gospel. In 15:3–5 Paul boils the gospel down to four basics.

1. Christ died for our sins in accordance with the scriptures.
2. He was buried.
3. He was raised on the third day in accordance with the scriptures.
4. He appeared . . .

Search back through the Old Testament and show that Christ **died for our sins** in accordance with the scriptures and that Christ was **raised on the third day** in accordance with the scriptures.

☐ The resurrection chapter, 15. What are some of the consequences of a belief that there is no resurrection (verses 12–19)?

Notice the three striking pairs to which Paul refers in verses 45–49:

1. The first Adam and the last Adam.
2. The first man and the second Man.
3. The man of dust and the Man from heaven.

Why is Jesus the **last** Adam but the **second** Man? (Study carefully Romans 5:6–21 for further insights into the amazing contrast between Adam and Christ.)

2 CORINTHIANS

Sad history of a brief revolt

THE STORY BEHIND THE LETTER. To understand the letter it is
essential to know the story behind it. Humanly speaking Paul
began the church at Corinth (Acts 18:1–17). Paul claimed that
he was an apostle (1 Corinthians 9:1 and note the opening
words of this second letter). But false apostles (2 Corinthians
11:12–15) moved into Corinth. These 'super-apostles'
(2 Corinthians 11:5) taught a different gospel (2 Corinthians
11:12–15) and defied Paul's authority.

Confusion followed. Paul's advice in 1 Corinthians was
ignored. Paul then paid a very painful visit to Corinth
(2 Corinthians 2:1). Apparently the 'super-apostles' simply
laughed at him (2 Corinthians 10:10). Paul left Corinth and then
sent Titus to the church with a very severe letter (2 Corinthians
7:5–13). And the Corinthian church repented. Titus brought the
marvellous news back to Paul (2 Corinthians 7:6,7). This letter is
a running commentary on the sad history of the disagreement.

WHEN THE LETTER WAS WRITTEN. We know that Paul was at
Corinth when Gallio was proconsul in Achaia (Acts 18:12) in AD
51 or 52. So his first letter to Corinth must have been written
around AD 55 and this second letter about a year later.

CORINTHIANS AND TITUS. Titus is clearly valued by Paul (2:13; 8:23)
and is named nine times in this letter. He was the messenger
who took Paul's 'severe' letter to Corinth. He shared Paul's
concern about the situation at Corinth, and Paul's relief when
the Corinthians repented (7:13). He was sent back to Corinth
again, to take 2 Corinthians and to complete the arrangements
for the collection for the poor in Jerusalem (8:6).

WHY THE LETTER WAS WRITTEN. The main purpose of the letter
was to tell the Corinthians just how much their change of mind
meant to Paul.

The letter also warns them against dealing too harshly with
those who had battled against him (2:5–11).

Thirdly, Paul wants to reiterate some of the teaching he had
given in his first letter (6:14, compare 1 Cor. 6:15–20).

The fourth reason is to deal with the unrepentant 'super-
apostles' who were, in fact, false teachers with a different
gospel (11:1–6).

Fifthly Paul wants to remind them about the planned collection to help the poor Christians in Jerusalem. This, too, had been
talked about in his first letter (1 Corinthians 16:1–3) and now he
wants them to send the money by Titus (9:1–5).

Outline

2 CORINTHIANS

Message

There are two important subjects dealt with here:

1. Privilege and pain.
Christian leadership like Paul's will always mean hardship, misunderstanding, suffering, as well as encouragement and joy. Paul refers to this suffering in seven separate passages spread through the letter:

- ☐ Near-despair when the Corinthians rebuffed him. 1:8–11
- ☐ Mental anguish as Paul awaited their response to his letter. 2:12–17
- ☐ Physical exhaustion caused by spiritual conflict. 4:16–18
- ☐ The hardship of unrelenting battle in Christ's name. 6:3–10
- ☐ 'Fighting without and fear within'. 7:5–8
- ☐ The pain of being misunderstood and falsely accused. 11:1–10
- ☐ The myriad sufferings of the missionary. 11:21–29

2. Glory (chapters 3–5).
Paul opens the way for this topic by referring to 'letters of commendation' written by churches to commend their members to other churches. Then he speaks of God 'writing' his commendation not on a piece of paper but in the life (the 'heart') of his true servants. That leads him to the Old Testament account of God writing the Law on stone tablets. Now see how the theme develops:

- ☐ God himself gave that Law to Moses.
- ☐ Moses saw God's glory.
- ☐ Such brightness, such glory, transformed Moses so that his face shone with it.
- ☐ That scared the people when they saw it.
- ☐ So Moses had to hide it with a 'veil'.
- ☐ It must have been a marvellous sight; but it was short-lived, it faded away because Moses didn't see God's glory like that any more.
- ☐ The Christian meets with God daily: so the glow should stay!
- ☐ Still, life isn't all glory: there's suffering, too.
- ☐ But don't lose heart: even death is simply the gateway to glory.
- ☐ The body is like a tent: death is the final collapse of the tent.
- ☐ But that simply means a move: a move into a new home, not a tent, but a permanent house.
- ☐ That is what God has saved us for.

Application

We learn several things from this letter:

- ☐ The church is not **just** a gathering of friends: there are leaders.
- ☐ Democracy in the church must be accompanied by authority and responsibility.
- ☐ Leadership in the church is not just privilege, but invites pain.
- ☐ Mission isn't easy: the faint-hearted had better leave it alone.
- ☐ The Christian really ought not to fear death. There's glory this side of death but greater glory the other side.

2 CORINTHIANS

Key themes

1. Suffering.
Study the two main passages on suffering in chapters 6 and 11. How many of the incidents referred to in these chapters can you identify from Paul's biography in Acts?

2. The Christian and relief work.
Paul was very concerned about the need for the churches in Asia to assist the Christians in Judea who suffered most because of a widespread famine (Acts 11:27–30). Study Acts 4:32–5:11 and 2 Corinthians 8:1–9:15 along with 1 Corinthians 16:1–4, Romans 15:24–29 and Acts 24:17 to see what general principles ought to guide Christian giving. Note also Jesus' words on this subject: Matthew 6:1–4.

3. Death.
2 Corinthians 4:7–5:10 is concerned with the weakness of the human body and the inevitability of death. Study this passage and compare it with 1 Corinthians 15:35–58. Both passages refer to 'glory'. What is it (Exodus 24:15–17; Ezekiel 1:26–28)?

With glory ahead of us, why do we still fear death? Did Paul (2 Corinthians 5:8 and 2 Timothy 4:6–8)?

4. Apostolic authority.
Use a concordance to study every reference to 'apostles'. Make a list of all those called apostles.

Note especially:
– Jesus (Hebrews 3:1)
– the Twelve (Matthew 10:2)
– Andronicus (Romans 16:7)
– Paul (1 Corinthians 1:1)

The twelve are a special group, meant to indicate the link between the twelve tribes of OT Israel and the NT church (Galatians 6:16, 'the Israel of God').

What were the errors of the 'super-apostles' who were, in fact false apostles (2 Corinthians 11:1–21)?

GALATIANS

A letter about the true Gospel

WHY THE LETTER WAS WRITTEN. Paul wrote this vital letter because the Galatian Christians were moving away from the true understanding of Christian faith (1:6). They were unsettled by Jewish Christians who wanted to burden them with the practice of circumcision and with obeying other Jewish laws (3:1), saying that only in this way could they enjoy the full privileges of a relationship with God.

Paul felt strongly that if they relied on Jewish law for their relationship with God they were denying the very point of the gospel; which was that a man's relationship with God depends on faith not works.

During the letter Paul explains his own relationships with the Jerusalem church. He also explains the nature of Christian freedom which results when people have faith in Christ rather than trying to please God through obedience to law.

THE AUTHOR AND HIS READERS.

1. The author: Galatians was written by the Apostle Paul (1:1), and contains the very heart of his teaching about faith. Its strong argument reveals his personality and shows him to be both a preacher and a man who was not afraid to go it alone. The letter gives us many details about his life which are not mentioned elsewhere.

2. The readers: Paul had preached to his readers (1:8,9; 4:13) and they enjoyed a very close relationship (4:15). Some say he was writing to the Christians of Northern Galatia (N.E. Asia Minor) who were Gauls and whom Paul had visited on his second missionary journey. Others say he is writing to the Roman province of South Galatia (including Antioch, Iconium, Derbe and Lystra) which Paul had visited on his first missionary journey.

THE DATE. When the letter was written depends on who it was written to. Most believe it was written to Southern Galatia and this means the letter was written around AD 48. If it was written to the north it would be a little later but it would still be among the earliest letters of the New Testament.

SPECIAL FEATURES.

1. It is a fighting letter. Paul refuses to compromise, writes in strong language and supports his one main theme by using many different arguments.

2. It is a loving letter. It is written with all the concern and care of a great pastor.

3. It is a brief letter. It has been called 'a rough draft' of Romans where the same message is developed more fully and to a less disturbing situation.

4. It is a memorable letter and contains many sayings which stick in the mind, eg. 2:20; 5:1; 5:22,23; 6:14.

Outline

1 PAUL GREETS HIS READERS
1:1–5
1:1–2 The apostle and his readers
1:3–5 Paul's greeting

2 PAUL STATES HIS PURPOSE
1:6–10
1:6 His concern
1:7–9 His conviction
1:10 His motive

3 PAUL OUTLINES HIS TESTIMONY
1:11–2:21
1:11–12 The source of his teaching
1:13–17 The story of his call
1:18–2:10 His relations with Jerusalem
2:11–14 His argument with Peter
2:15–21 His understanding of the gospel

4 PAUL DEVELOPS HIS ARGUMENTS
3:1–4:31
3:1–5 The experience of the Galatians
3:6–9 The example of Abraham

3:10–14 The curse of the law
3:15–18 The advantages of the promise
3:19–29 The purpose of the law
4:1–11 The nature of sonship
4:12–20 A personal appeal
4:21–31 Two kinds of 'son'

5 PAUL DESCRIBES CHRISTIAN FREEDOM
5:1–6:10
5:1 Don't let go of freedom
5:2–6 Freedom from circumcision
5:7–12 Another personal appeal
5:13–15 How to use your freedom: love
5:16–21 What freedom is not
5:22–24 What freedom is
5:25–6:10 Freedom and our relationships

6 PAUL AUTOGRAPHS HIS LETTER
6:11–18
6:11–15 Paul underlines his point
6:16–18 Final greetings

GALATIANS

Message

1. The law is a dead end.
Paul's chief concern was to show that people cannot possibly be put right with God through relying on good works or keeping the law. The law:
- ☐ Doesn't make men right with God. 2:16
- ☐ Is opposed to Christ's way. 2:19; 5:4
- ☑ Cannot give the Holy Spirit. 3:2,5; 5:18
- ☐ Only results in a curse. 3:10–14
- ☐ Was a temporary interruption to God's long-term plan. 3:17
- ☑ Has a purpose. 3:21–29
- ☐ Makes absolute demands on people. 5:3
- ☐ Is easily summarised. 5:14

2. Faith is the only way to God.
Christ's supreme achievement was to make faith the only way to God.
- ☐ Faith makes men right with God. 2:16; 3:11

- ☐ The Christian must go on exercising faith. 2:20; 3:3
- ☑ The Spirit comes through faith. 3:2,5,14
- ☐ The long history of faith. 3:6–9
- ☐ The effect of faith's arrival. 3:22–26
- ☐ The way faith shows itself. 5:6
- ☐ Christians form 'the household of faith'. 6:10

3. Jesus means freedom.
- ☑ Jesus brings freedom from the oppression of the law. 3:1–4:7
- ☐ Freedom's great tradition. 4:21–31
- ☐ Freedom needs to be guarded. 5:1
- ☐ The right and the wrong way to express freedom. 5:13–6:10

Application

Circumcision may not be a hotly debated issue today but Paul's message is still relevant:

1. For the Christian legalist.
Many still think that a man's ability to get into God's good books depends on how many rules he keeps and how respectable he is. Paul shows that what counts is faith not works.

2. For the loose-living Christian.
The freedom Christ brings does not mean that a Christian can behave as he likes. His life must not be motivated by selfish or physical desires. He has new responsibilities to express the fruit of the Spirit in his character, behaviour and relationships.

This letter also teaches us about two other matters of importance:

1. About Christian doctrine.
The church has no right to believe whatever it likes nor to democratically decide its doctrine. Christian truth has been revealed by God and is not open to negotiation. Paul emphasises that believing something different from what God has revealed is dangerous both because it is untrue and because it leads to judgement. The truth was first of all set out by the apostles and so, in Galatians, Paul emphasises his apostolic authority.

2. About the unity of the Bible.
Many believe there is little connection between the Old and New Testaments and that they speak of two Gods making two kinds of demands on men. Paul shows that God is one and that a unity exists throughout the Bible.

Key themes

Around Paul's one main message a number of other ideas are to be found.

1. The flesh.
Paul uses the word in several different ways. What are they? 1:16; 2:20; 3:3; 4:23,29; 5:13,16,17,19,24; 6:8,12,13.

2. Bondage.
This is how Paul describes the condition of people before they become Christians. What is the problem now? 4:8; 2:4.

3. The cross.
For most the cross is offensive (5:11; 6:12) but for Paul it is a cause of boasting (6:14). What else does he say about the death of Jesus?

4. A son of God.
This is Paul's favourite description of a Christian. It is the opposite of being a slave. How does Paul describe the privileges of being a son of God? 3:7,26; 4:5,6,22.

5. The Holy Spirit.
Galatians is full of references to the Holy Spirit. Look through the verses below and group them under the main themes of Paul's teaching about him. The themes are: receiving the Spirit; bearing the fruit of the Spirit; walking by and living in the Spirit. 3:2,3,5,14; 4:6; 5:16,17,18,22,25; 6:1,8,18.

EPHESIANS

A circular letter?

FOR WHOM WAS IT WRITTEN? Many people think this letter was intended for a wider circulation than the actual church at Ephesus. It was probably a sort of circular letter written for common use among different Christian groups in the neighbourhood of Ephesus. What Paul has to say in this letter is applicable to God's people generally and is not addressed to one particular church.

There are no personal greetings. It is probable that it is in fact the letter to which the apostle refers in Colossians 4:16 as being 'from Laodicea'. Tychicus was entrusted with conveying it to its destination (6:21,22).

The letter was written like the epistles to Philippi and Colossae from a prison cell and it has for its main theme the nature, character and destiny of the Christian church – 'God's new society' as it has been called.

THE CHURCH AT EPHESUS. Paul had stayed in Ephesus for 3 years (Acts 19:8,10; 20:31). It was a city very much given to pagan worship. Diana's (Artemis) temple was there. Those who practised magic were very much in evidence. However, on reading this letter there is not the same need to be familiar with the background of the church to which it is apparently addressed since the content of the letter is general in character.

MESSAGE. The letter deals with no particular problems but its purpose is to exalt the name of Jesus Christ and to point to the importance of the Christian church as God's instrument in the world. As in Paul's other letters, doctrine is followed by practical application. Christian faith and Christian living must always be considered together. The letter closes with a timely reminder that the Christian is engaged in an unending conflict with Satan and the powers of evil but God has provided the necessary armour to enable Christians to withstand all the onslaught of the enemy.

Within by Unity

Outline

1 A MESSAGE FOR FAITHFUL SAINTS IN CHRIST JESUS AND AT EPHESUS
1:1,2

2 OUR INHERITANCE AS CHRISTIANS
1:3–2:22

1:3–6 Chosen for a purpose
1:7–14 Redeemed for a purpose
1:15–23 Enlightened for a purpose
2:1–10 Made alive for a purpose
2:11–22 Reconciled for a purpose

3 A MYSTERY MADE KNOWN
3:1–21

3:1–6 Gentile believers are included
3:7–12 Paul's ministry is strategic
3:13–21 Full understanding is vital

4 THE NATURE OF THE CHURCH
4:1–32

4:1–6 United in the Spirit
4:7–12 Endowed with spiritual gifts
4:13–16 Geared for growth
4:17–24 Renewed in character
4:25–32 Transformed in outlook

5 CHRISTIAN CHARACTER, CONDUCT AND CONFLICT
5:1–6:24

5:1–20 Following Christ
5:21–6:9 Living with others
6:10–24 Facing the enemy

EPHESIANS

Message

1. Inherited riches to be enjoyed.
☐ The three Persons of the Godhead are involved in our salvation
 – God the Father. 1:4–6
 – God the Son. 1:7–12
 – God the Holy Spirit. 1:13,14
☐ Note the requests in Paul's prayer for the Ephesians
 – for enlightenment as to the extent of our inheritance. 1:17–19
 – for power as to the extent of its greatness. 1:19–21

2. Grace and peace to be experienced.
☐ What we have been saved from. 2:1–3,11,12
☐ Who we have been saved by. 2:4–9, 13–18
☐ What we have been saved for. 2:10,19–22

3. Spiritual resources to be explored.
☐ Unsearchable riches. 3:8–13
☐ Divine strength. 3:14–21

4. Spiritual unity to be maintained.
☐ Right attitudes are essential. 4:1–3
☐ Common ground is essential. 4:4–6
☐ Unity in diversity is envisaged. 4:11
☐ Christian maturity is envisaged. 4:13

5. Harmonious relationships to be sought.
☐ Light in place of darkness. 5:3–6
☐ Wisdom in place of folly. 5:15–17
☐ Spirituality in place of sensuality. 5:18–20
☐ Submission in place of browbeating. 5:21–33

6. Spiritual weapons to be used.
☐ The enemy we face. 6:10–12
☐ The armour we have. 6:13–20

Application

Ephesians teaches us:

1. How generous God is
☐ in giving us a Saviour
☐ in sending to us his Holy Spirit
☐ in assuring us of a heavenly home

2. How privileged we are
☐ to be members of God's family
☐ to have access to God's throne

3. How considerate we need to be
☐ in our attitudes to others
☐ in our relationships with others

4. How practical Christianity is in regard to
☐ marriage
☐ parenthood
☐ employment

5. How real Satan is in
☐ his influence
☐ his activities

6. How prepared we need to be
☐ with God's armour
☐ by prayer

EPHESIANS

Key themes

1. Grace.

Grace is the key word of the Bible since it refers to that quality in God's nature which makes our salvation possible. Because of human sin, if there were no grace there could be no hope. Grace means free unmerited favour. Man's response to God's grace is faith but even this is given to us by God. See especially Ephesians 2:1–10.

Note that grace is always contrasted with law (Romans 6:14). Justification is made possible for two reasons – the grace of God (Romans 3:24) and the death of Christ (Romans 5:9).

2. Unity.

Paul has made the point that God's people under the new covenant includes both Jews and Gentiles and now he emphasises the need for true unity to be maintained. As Christians we cannot create unity since this is the work of the Holy Spirit, but we are told to maintain it. The unity we have is not the same as uniformity. There is a diversity of gifts among the people of God but a basic unity.

Look at the other classic passage where the importance of unity is stressed – John chapter 17.

3. Relationships.

We do not live our lives in a vacuum but within a series of relationships – in the home, at work, in church and in society generally. Our Christian faith is vitally concerned about those relationships. We may find at any given point in time that biblical standards and those standards generally accepted by contemporary society are in conflict. In such cases we are bound to obey God rather than men.

Compare the passages in Ephesians on this subject with the corresponding verses in Colossians.

Note how, in selecting Christian leaders, relationships were taken very much into consideration (1 Timothy 3:1–5; Titus 1:6–8).

4. Conflict.

Paul speaks of a Christian as a soldier (2 Timothy 2:3,4). For him there was a war on continually, and the Christian was very much involved. The Bible never questions the existence of Satan. He was real enough in our Lord's experience and equally real to the disciples. In Ephesians Paul reminds us of the subtlety of the enemy. We dare not face him unarmed and unprotected.

Look up references made by Christ to the devil – Matthew 4:1–11; 12:24; 13:39; 25:41; Luke 8:12; 10:18; John 8:44.

PHILIPPIANS

A 'thank you' letter

THE CITY OF PHILIPPI. Philippi was a Roman colony, occupied very largely by Italian settlers who remained intensely loyal to Rome. It was a cosmopolitan city, a busy trading centre but not noted for its moral standards.

THE LETTER. It is clear Paul wrote from a prison cell (1:12), and this may well have been in Rome in which case the date would be AD 61-63. Some have argued that the letter was written from Ephesus in which case the date would be 10 years earlier. Basically it was a 'thank you' letter sent by Epaphroditus to the church at Philippi and expressing gratitude for the gift they had sent. The letter comes from Paul and his companion Timothy.

THE CHURCH AT PHILIPPI. Paul had been the means of founding the church at Philippi. It was there he met with a group of women who were worshipping by the riverside and one of their number, Lydia, responded to the gospel (Acts 16:14). Later Paul and Silas were hauled before the local magistrates on a trumped-up charge, beaten up and thrown into prison. At midnight, as they prayed and praised God, there was a great earthquake which rocked the prison to its foundations. The jailer, realising the prisoners could have escaped, was about to commit suicide. Paul restrained him and he cried out for help – 'Men, what must I do to be saved?' (Acts 16:30). On learning the way of salvation, not only the jailer but all his family responded and were baptised.

SPECIAL FEATURES. The apostle seems to have had a special love for the church at Philippi. The Christians there were a source of great joy and encouragement to him (1:3–5). The note of joy and rejoicing runs right through the letter. In the third chapter Paul presents a balance sheet putting on one side the things he prized most highly before he became a Christian, and on the other all that was now his as a Christian. Clearly, he had gained as a result of his surrender to Christ far more than he had lost.

Outline

1 **JOY IN SUFFERING**
1:1–30

Here we find the apostle
1:1,2 sending greetings
1:3–7 giving thanks *Christlike*
1:8–11 praying
1:12–14 triumphing
1:15–26 trusting
1:27–30 challenging

2 **JOY IN SERVICE**
2:1–30

Paul gives us some practical advice about Christian service
2:1–4 live together in harmony
2:5–11 follow Christ's example
2:12,13 live out your salvation
2:14–18 stop grumbling
2:19–30 honour the Lord's servants
   Timothy (2:19–24)
   Epaphroditus (2:25–30)

3 **JOY IN CHRIST**
3:1–21

3:1–11 The assets that became liabilities
3:12–16 The race that has yet to be completed
3:17–21 The citizenship that is to be highly prized

4 **JOY IN CONTENTMENT**
4:1–20

4:1–4 The source of joy
4:5–9 The secret of joy
  – careful for nothing
  – prayerful for everything
  – thankful for anything
4:10–20 The supply of joy
  – a gift gratefully received
4:21–23 Farewell greetings

Message

1. Things to be thankful for:
- [ ] fellowship in the gospel. 1:5,7
- [ ] overruling of adverse circumstances. 1:12
- [ ] evangelistic preaching even if motives are mixed. 1:15–18

2. Matters to pray about:
- [ ] for greater love. 1:9
- [ ] for true discernment. 1:10
- [ ] for God-honouring lives. 1:11

3. Attitudes to adopt:
- [ ] a selfless mind. 2:4
- [ ] a serving mind. 2:7
- [ ] a sacrificial mind. 2:8

4. Values to reassess:
- [ ] a religious background. 3:5
- [ ] an obvious sincerity. 3:6
- [ ] a moral life. 3:6

5. Glory to anticipate: 3:20,21

6. Lessons to learn:
- [ ] to live in harmony. 4:2
- [ ] to rejoice at all times. 4:4
- [ ] to overcome anxiety. 4:6
- [ ] to think positively. 4:8
- [ ] to be content. 4:11
- [ ] to trust God. 4:19

Application

Philippians teaches us . . .

1. What Christians should be like.
- [ ] affectionate
- [ ] discerning
- [ ] upright
- [ ] co-operative
- [ ] joyful
- [ ] humble
- [ ] contented
- [ ] Christ-centred

2. What Christian leaders should be like.
- [ ] caring
- [ ] self-effacing
- [ ] uncomplaining
- [ ] practical
- [ ] thankful

3. About people we can learn from.
- [ ] Timothy – a worthy spiritual son
- [ ] Ephaphroditus – a sympathetic messenger
- [ ] Euodia and Syntyche – women at loggerheads

PHILIPPIANS

Key themes

1. Joy.

It makes it all the more impressive when we know that the one who said 'rejoice always' wrote from a prison cell! It is easy to appear joyful when outward circumstances are favourable. Christians, however, should know the secret of an inward, deep and abiding joy which is unaffected by external conditions. It is the joy which Jesus himself promised his followers (John 15:11).

Trace the theme of joy through the whole of the letter and suggest the particular reasons for the apostle's joy over the church in Philippi.

2. Christlikeness.

Philippians 2:5–11 may have been part of a hymn in the early church. It is in fact one of the outstanding Christological passages in the New Testament. It traces the steps the Son of God took in effecting salvation for us. Yet it is given as an example which we are to follow. We are to have the mental outlook of Christ, in other words, to be utterly self-effacing.

Paul often wrote of imitating Christ and even of imitating himself (Ephesians 5:1; 1 Corinthians 4:16; 11:1; Philippians 3:17). Should we be able to suggest people might imitate us?

3. Values.

Conversion meant for Paul a complete change of outlook – the things he had once prized so highly now counted for nothing at all. With him it was his religious upbringing which he had boasted about, with some it is their social status, their educational background, their financial position. Christ directs our gaze to higher things and reminds us our citizenship is in heaven. Our Lord himself had much to say on this subject.

Study our Lord's teaching about earthly possessions (Luke 12:15; Matthew 6:19–21,33). Is this why it is so hard for rich people to become Christians? (Mark 10:23,24).

4. Contentment.

Paul gives the impression he had learned to be content and maybe it was not an easy lesson for him to learn. He says elsewhere, '. . . godliness with contentment is great gain' (1 Timothy 6:6).

Look up 2 Corinthians 11:24–28 and assess Paul's statement in the light of such experiences. Consider how it was he learned the lesson of contentment.

1 THESSALONIANS

A letter to young Christians

THE CHURCH AND ITS SITUATION.
    1. The city of Thessalonica was the capital of Macedonia. It was a wealthy city with a fine natural harbour situated on the Roman highway to the east. As a result it was multi-racial, very mixed in culture and open to receive all kinds of religious beliefs.
    2. The founding of the church: Acts 17:1–10 tells us that Paul and Silas founded the church on Paul's second missionary journey. Their visit to Thessalonica lasted less than a month before some Jews rented a mob which led to Paul and Silas leaving town in a hurry and their supporters being bound over to keep the peace.
    3. The church to which Paul writes: In view of its unpromising start the young church showed remarkable strength. Its members were chiefly Gentiles converted from heathenism and now facing a very pagan and hostile environment.

THE DATE AND REASON FOR THE LETTER. Ever since Paul left Thessalonica he was anxious to know how they were progressing. Timothy had now brought him news (3:6) and he wanted to express his satisfaction and to encourage them to persist in their faith. He wrote the letter shortly after leaving them, while he was in Corinth, around the year 50. This makes it, with Galatians, among the earliest of Paul's letters.

SPECIAL FEATURES. The letter is a simple follow-up letter to new converts. It contains little complex doctrine but much to encourage them. In particular Paul speaks of the second coming of Jesus (1:10, 2:19, 3:13, 4:16–18 and 5:23) as an incentive for Christian living and service.
    Even when correcting them the letter is written in a gentle and loving manner.

THE OTHER REASONS FOR THE LETTER. In addition to writing a letter of general encouragement Paul had some other purposes in mind. He wished:
    1. To defend himself against false accusations (2:1–12).
    2. To stress the need for a distinctive Christian morality (4:1–12).
    3. To correct misunderstandings over the second coming of Christ (4:13–18).
    4. To discipline youthful immaturity in the church (5:12–22).

Outline

1 GREETING
1:1

2 THE THESSALONIAN CHURCH – A CAUSE OF JOY
1:2–10
1:2,3 Their character
1:4,5 Their election
1:6,7 Their responsiveness
1:8–10 Their reputation

3 PAUL'S PERSONAL CONDUCT – A MATTER FOR DEFENCE
2:1–16
2:1,2 The courage he displayed
2:3,4 The motives he had
2:5–7 The style he adopted
2:8–9 The support he provided
2:10–12 The example he set
2:13–16 The effect he had

4 PAUL'S GREAT CONCERN – AN EXPRESSION OF FEELING
2:17–3:13
2:17,18 Paul's desire
2:19,20 Paul's motive
3:1–5 Paul's messenger
3:6–10 Paul's relief
3:11–13 Paul's prayer

5 CHRISTIAN SOCIAL BEHAVIOUR – A SUBJECT FOR INSTRUCTION
4:1–12
4:1–8 Sexual morality
4:9,10 Brotherly love
4:11,12 Earning one's living

6 CHRIST'S SECOND COMING – A FIELD OF INQUIRY
4:13–5:11
4:13–18 What happens to the dead?
5:1–3 When will it take place?
5:4–11 How then should we live?

7 THESSALONIAN CHURCH LIFE – AN AREA FOR IMPROVEMENT
5:12–22
5:12,13 Regarding leaders
5:14,15 Regarding others
5:16–18 Regarding circumstances
5:19–22 Regarding worship

8 CONCLUDING PRAYER AND GREETING
5:23–28

1 THESSALONIANS

Message

1. God is at work.
The first thing these young Christians need to know about is not the mechanics of the Christian life but the God in whom they have come to believe. Paul speaks of:
- [ ] the call of God. 1:4; 2:12; 4:7
- [ ] the word of God. 1:6,8; 2:13; 4:15
- [ ] the approval of God. 2:4
- [ ] the testing of God. 2:4
- [ ] the wrath of God. 2:16
- [ ] the will of God. 4:3; 5:18
- [ ] the teaching of God. 4:9
- [ ] the peace of God. 5:23
- [ ] the faithfulness of God. 5:24

2. Christ is coming back.
Although Paul spends several paragraphs talking about the second coming of Jesus to correct some false ideas which were around he also makes a number of briefer references to it. Jesus' return is:
- [ ] an inspiration for young Christians. 1:10
- [ ] a stimulus to Christian workers. 2:19
- [ ] a motive for brotherly love. 3:13
- [ ] a comfort for bereaved Christians. 4:18
- [ ] an incentive for holy living. 5:23

3. The nature of Christian experience.
Paul speaks much about what it is like to be a Christian so that they should know what to expect in their experience. Being a Christian:
- [ ] Begins with a decisive conversion. 1:9–10
- [ ] Involves progress and growth. 2:13; 4:1
- [ ] Requires alert perseverance. 3:8; 5:5–8
- [ ] Aims for holy living. 3:13–4:8
- [ ] Depends on the Holy Spirit. 4:8; 5:19
- [ ] Means commitment to Christian fellowship. 4:9; 5:11–22

Application

1 Thessalonians shows us that there are:

1. Examples to follow.
- [ ] The example of the church
  It was noted for:
  - – faith   – joy in suffering
  - – love   – listening to God
  - – hope   – standing firm
  - – hard work   in affliction
- [ ] The example of Paul
  As a Christian worker he was:
  - – courageous
  - – gentle and affectionate
  - – full of integrity
  - – an example
  - – eager to please God rather than men

2. Instructions to obey.
- [ ] Concerning a distinctive Christian morality in contemporary pagan society
- [ ] Concerning relationships and behaviour in the Christian church

3. Aims to pursue.
- [ ] A life which is worthy
- [ ] A mind which is open to God's word
- [ ] A faith which is durable

4. Prayers to pray.
There are three references to prayer in the letter. Why not make them the basis of your own prayer life? You will find them at 1:2,3; 3:11–13 and 5:23,24.

1 THESSALONIANS

Key themes

1. The gospel.
The good news which Paul preached is not clearly spelled out in the letter but you can work it out from what Paul says. Try to do so.

It is obvious that it concerns him more than anything else in life. See the references to it in 1:5; 2:2,4,8,9 and 3:2.

2. Conversion.
1:9,10 is a superb statement of how men should respond to the gospel. The three aspects mentioned there can be linked with other features of conversion as follows:

☐ turn   ☐ faith   ☐ past
☐ serve   ☐ love   ☐ present
☐ wait   ☐ hope   ☐ future

3. Christian service.
Paul paints several pictures of his relationship with the Thessalonians. He was:

☐ A gentle nurse. 2:7
☐ A conscientious labourer. 2:9
☐ An encouraging father. 2:11
☐ A hopeful prize-winner. 2:19

4. The word of God.
Paul uses this phrase on several occasions. Look up the references 1:6,8; 2:13 and 4:15 and list why he considers it so important, what needs to happen to it and what should accompany it.

5. Pleasing God.
Put as briefly as possible, the letter is about pleasing God. The Thessalonians were already doing so but were being encouraged to do so even more. Go through the letter and make your own list of how they were pleasing God already and what they now need to do to please him more.

2 THESSALONIANS

Information about the end

ANOTHER LETTER TO THESSALONICA. Paul wrote this letter to the same people he had written to in 1 Thessalonians, and probably not long after that letter. If you read the introduction there, you will see the sort of church he had in mind. Once again, he adds the names of his travelling companions, Silvanus (or Silas in the book of Acts) and Timothy, to his own.

WHY WAS HE WRITING AGAIN?

1. Reading between the lines, the church was still going through it. We do not know who was actually doing the persecuting – it might have been the Jews – but they were having a rough time. Perhaps they were beginning to wonder if it was worth being Christians after all. Anyone might have been tempted to give up in those circumstances.

2. When Paul wrote the first letter, they had been somewhat mixed up about Jesus' return. It seems that some had become fascinated with the subject – something which has always been a temptation to Christians – and had become so obsessed with it that they thought of little else. Although Paul had sketched out the broad details while he was with them, he did not have much time to tell them all he would have liked to. It seems that they had also forgotten what he **did** teach them! Some expected Jesus to come back straight away – tomorrow if not today! Their excitement was unsettling the church. Added to this there were some who were actually misleading the Christians by putting it about that Christ had already come back – and what is more, making out that this was what Paul was teaching. Like many since, they were no doubt those who wanted to fill in the gaps in order to work out just when it was all going to happen.

3. Some were not pulling their weight. It may even have been because of their obsession with Christ's return and the end of the world. It might simply have been that some had seen an easy way to a living in the generosity of the Christian fellowship. We do not know. What we do know is that Paul deals with them very sharply indeed. Let's remember that what he says is for those who could work but would not – not those who wanted to work but did not have any.

4. He had to tell them to maintain Christian standards even if that meant breaking with some who were not toeing the line.

HOW LETTERS WERE WRITTEN. In those days people often used secretaries to help them to write their letters. They would dictate what they wanted to say and after it was written down, they would take the pen and add a word at the end. Probably because others had been using Paul's good name to spread error, he makes quite a point of this at the end of this letter.

Outline

1 'FROM US TO YOU...'
1:1–2
Paul and his friends greet the church

2 'THANK GOD YOU'RE STANDING!'
1:3–4
1:3 Your faith and love
1:4 Your reputation

3 'JUDGEMENT IS ON THE WAY!'
1:5–10
1:5 Why you are suffering
1:6–7 God is fair
1:8–10 The great divide when Jesus comes

4 'WE'RE PRAYING FOR YOU...'
1:11–12
1:11 That you might grow
1:12 That Christ might be glorified

5 'BEFORE JESUS COMES, CERTAIN THINGS MUST HAPPEN.'
2:1–12
2:1–2 Don't get over-excited
2:3–7 The opposition will increase
2:8 But the Lord will crush it
2:9–12 The wicked will be taken in

6 'BUT WE'RE RELIEVED ABOUT YOU...'
2:13–17
2:13 You were certainly converted
2:14 God will finish the job
2:15–17 Hang on!

7 'WE NEED YOUR PRAYERS TOO.'
3:1–5
3:1–2 In our preaching
3:3–5 Because God is good

8 'STOP LOAFING ABOUT!'
3:6–15
3:6 Some have stopped work
3:7–10 We were never lazy
3:11–15 Make sure everyone follows suit

9 'GOODBYE AND GOD BLESS!'
3:17–18

2 THESSALONIANS

Message

1. Judgement is absolutely certain.
☐ God will deal with the wicked. 1:5–6,8–9
☐ God will give rest to Christians. 1:7
☐ Putting up with persecution proves this. 1:5
☐ We ought to get ready for Jesus' return. 1:11
☐ We will share Christ's glory. 1:10; 2:14
☐ We must be patient. 2:1,2
☐ We must watch out for Satan's lies. 2:10

2. God has a timetable.
☐ Jesus **is** coming back. 1:7,9; 2:1,8
☐ The devil has his plan too. 2:3–4,9–10
☐ Evil is being held back. 2:6–7
☐ Satan's man will be destroyed. 2:8,10
☐ Watch out for error. 2:3

3. Get on with your work!
☐ We should not
  – be workshy. 3:6
  – live off others. 3:12

  – grow weary. 3:13
  – encourage the lazy. 3:6,14–15

4. Go on as you have begun!
☐ Worthy of God's call. 1:11
☐ In aim and output. 1:11
☐ Glorifying Christ. 1:12
☐ Standing firm. 2:15
☐ Holding the truth. 2:15
☐ Steadily working and witnessing. 2:17

5. God is on your side.
☐ He is making you worthy. 1:5,11
☐ He chose you to be saved. 2:13
☐ He makes you his own by his Spirit. 2:13
☐ He called you. 2:14
☐ He is utterly reliable. 3:3
☐ He will strengthen you. 3:3
☐ He will guard you. 3:3
☐ He will give you peace. 3:16
☐ He will be with you. 3:16

Application

2 Thessalonians teaches us that . . .

1. You don't get away with it.
Because God is just
☐ The wicked get punished
☐ The faithful get rewarded
☐ The devil gets his deserts

2. Christians have a future.
In spite of trouble
☐ we can be sure
☐ we can look forward
☐ we can hang on
☐ we can be comforted

3. God is in the driving seat.
He is in control
☐ of our circumstances

☐ of world events
☐ even of evil men

4. Work is not just a necessary evil.
It is God's will
☐ that we do a job
☐ that we earn our own keep
☐ that we are not lazy
☐ that we do not live off others

5. Dealing with the awkward.
We must
☐ warn them
☐ encourage them
☐ shame them
☐ love them
☐ discipline them

2 THESSALONIANS

Key themes

1. Jesus' return.
The fact that Jesus is coming back turns up several times. There was no question about it, even if Paul did not know the actual date and time. 1:7,9,10,12; 2:1–2,8,14.

The key words are 'reveal', that is, to draw back the curtain and show us what was there all the time; 'coming', used of a state visit by a king or official; 'glory' in the Bible is the presence of God himself. Think through what these things will mean when Christ comes back.

2. Judgement.
Because God is just and sees all, he will one day judge all the doings of men and women. 1:5–10; 2:8,11–12. In some ways God's judgement is already at work in the world.

Work out what God's judgement will mean for believers and for those who do not believe. How can we get ready for it?

3. Satan.
The devil is a fact in this letter, and he uses people in his purpose. 2:3–12.

What does this tell us about the outlook for the world? Are we able to recognise his activity?

4. Sticking it.
Being a Christian means going on as you began. This may mean putting up with persecution, proving God in new ways or sheer hard work.

What encouragements does the letter give us in our Christian lives? What reasons are given for keeping up the fight?

COLOSSIANS & PHILEMON

Maturity and slavery

TWO LETTERS AND FOUR PEOPLE. When Tychicus was sent by Paul to Colossae he took three things with him: the letter to the Colossians, Onesimus, a slave who had run away from his master, Philemon, who lived at Colossae, and a letter to Philemon from Paul.

THE CHURCH AT COLOSSAE. The city of Colossae was about 100 miles inland from Ephesus. The church there probably began as a result of Paul's preaching at Ephesus; Luke commented that during this period 'all who lived in the province of Asia heard the word of the Lord' (Acts 19:10). However, Paul hadn't been there himself (2:1). In fact the church might well have been begun through Epaphras (1:7), who apparently came from Colossae (4:12).

Epaphras was with Paul when he wrote the letters so probably Paul got his information about conditions in the church at Colossae from him.

DATE OF WRITING. These two letters were written from prison (Colossians 4:10 and Philemon 1) but the date depends on just **where** Paul was in prison. Ephesus is possible. It would be a reasonable distance for a fugitive like Onesimus to cover. Paul **seems** to refer once to an imprisonment at Ephesus (1 Corinthians 15:32). Rome is the other possibility, but would a runaway slave escape to Rome, right into the lion's mouth? Against Rome, also, is the fact that when he was in prison there he expected to be released and to go west to Spain, not east to Colossae (Philemon 22).

If these letters were written in Ephesus they must be dated AD 55-6, during Paul's third missionary journey (Acts 19); if from Rome, then the date is around AD 63.

WHY THE LETTERS WERE WRITTEN. Both these letters are really meant for the whole church (Colossians 1:2, Philemon 1:2). We might even call them 'first and second Colossians'!

1. Paul wrote Colossians because heresy was being taught, and he had to correct it. We don't quite know what the heresy was, but they had some very odd ideas about Christian maturity, which they thought of in terms of special diet, sacred days and even worshipping angels (2:16-23).

2. Onesimus had, apparently, been a rather useless slave who finally ran off (perhaps because he had stolen something, Philemon 18). Somehow he reached Paul in prison. He became

a Christian: maybe Paul led him to Christ (Philemon 10). For the first time in his life he lived up to the meaning of his name Onesimus, 'Useful'.

Useful though he had become, Paul sent him back to his master with a letter. He would have needed that letter: a runaway slave could expect to be branded with the letter 'F' for 'Fugitive' . . . he **could** be crucified. What Paul hopes for is the reconciliation of two **brothers**.

Outline

COLOSSIANS

 PAUL AND THE COLOSSIAN CHRISTIANS 1:1–14

1:1–2 Greetings
1:3–8 What we have heard about you
1:9–14 What we pray for you

 THE GRANDEUR OF JESUS 1:15–29

1:15–20 Who Jesus is
1:21–23 What Jesus has done
1:24–29 Christ in you, the hope of glory

3 JESUS: SUFFICIENT FOR EVERY NEED 2:1–23

2:1–7 United, equipped, standing firm
2:8–15 What Christ has done for us
2:16–23 Live as those who have died with Christ

4 A NEW OUTFIT 3:1–4:6

3:1–4 Live as those who have risen with Christ
3:5–9 Putting off the old clothes
3:10–17 Putting on the new clothes

3:18–4:1 Tailoring the suit
4:2–6 Talking to God and to men: praying and witnessing

 SO MANY FRIENDS 4:7–18

4:7–9 Two friends are coming to you
4:10–14 Six friends remain with me
4:15–17 Greetings and encouragement
4:18 Don't forget me . . . in prison

PHILEMON

1 INTRODUCTION 1–7

1–3 Greetings
4–7 Thank you, Philemon

2 THE RUNAWAY SLAVE 8–22

8–14 A new Onesimus: useful to me
15–20 Welcome him back . . . please
21–22 And prepare to welcome me

3 GREETINGS AND GRACE 23–25

COLOSSIANS & PHILEMON

Message

1. There was an error to be corrected.
The Christians at Colossae did not understand the idea of the deity of Christ, so they didn't understand that everything they needed could be found in Jesus.
Paul corrects them:
- ☐ Doctrinally . . . chapters 1 and 2
- ☐ Practically . . . chapters 3 and 4

2. There was a maturity to be sought.
- ☐ It starts with the viewpoint of eternity. 3:1–4
- ☐ It has both negative and positive aspects:
  - – negatively, put to death 3:5–7, put off. 3:8–9
  - – positively, put on. 3:10–14
- ☐ It has two reliable umpires:
  - – the peace of Christ. 3:15
  - – the word of Christ. 3:15–17

3. Maturity relates to the real world.
The Colossians made maturity 'religious'. Paul points them to relationships:
- ☐ Wives and husbands. 3:18–19
- ☐ Children and parents. 3:20–21
- ☐ Servants and masters. 3:22–4:1

4. Christianity deals with the root not the fruit.
It is sometimes said that the Bible actually encourages slavery. That's not so. But notice how Christ deals with the problem of slavery:
- ☐ not by promoting a political revolution which might have meant death and suffering for thousands, but by producing personal transformation so that Philemon, who owns slaves, and Onesimus, who was a slave, become –
  - – followers of Jesus
  - – brothers in Christ
  - – friends instead of enemies.
- ☐ Revolution changes the outside but not the inside; salvation changes everything!

5. Christianity majors in humility not in authority.
Paul was an apostle. So why didn't he just order Philemon to forgive Onesimus?
- ☐ Paul had to act as a **brother** (Philemon 9) because he expected Philemon to act as a brother
- ☐ Arrogance was exactly the sin which labelled one man master and another man slave. Violence brings more violence, arrogance encourages arrogance.

Humility is the most elusive of all the virtues: the moment you know you've got it . . . you've lost it!

Application

Maturity

1. This is the real theme of Colossians.
Notice the key verse, 1:28 'We proclaim him, admonishing and teaching **everyone** with all wisdom, so that we may present **everyone** perfect (mature) in Christ.'

- ☐ The **scope** of it is universal: every Christian should move on to maturity.
- ☐ The **source** of it is Christ: Paul told Christians about Christ, expecting them to follow Christ's example.

☐ The **evidence** of it is social: the mature Christian relates well to husband or wife, to children and to his employer or employees.

2. Mature behaviour is what Paul expects of Philemon.
The mature Christian does not behave like everyone else. As Christ forgave Philemon so he must forgive Onesimus: but that might well shock his friends!

Key themes

1. The word 'all'.
Paul's repeated use of this little word is a reminder of his emphasis on mature, whole-hearted Christianity. The Greek word is translated in many ways: **always, all** the saints, **whole** world, **fully** pleasing, **every** good work, **everything.** The word occurs 38 times. List these occurrences and study their importance for our understanding of who Christ is, what Christ has done and how we should behave.

2. Our part in reaching maturity.
Paul uses three 'imperatives' or orders to explain what we must do to become mature:
☐ 'Put to death' 3:5
☐ 'Put off' 3:8–9
☐ 'Put on' 3:12

The words 'put off' and 'put on' could be used in Greek for taking off your dirty clothes at night and putting on clean clothes in the morning. Study 3:1–14 carefully. Why do I sin? Why do I continue sinning? How can I stop?

3. Christ's part in our salvation.
To make it possible for us to do our part in becoming **mature**, Christ first does his part in saving us. Identify **six** steps in our salvation, located in 2:13–15.

4. Great oaks from little acorns.
Philemon is a very short, personal letter, only 335 words in the Greek original. Why is it in the Bible? Well, obviously because God wants it there! But there's an interesting human reason too. Onesimus may have finished his life not as a slave, nor even merely as a free man, but as bishop of Ephesus. At the beginning of the second century a well-known Christian called Ignatius wrote a letter to the church at Ephesus and mentioned Bishop Onesimus, and even referred to the pun on his name, 'Useful'! From runaway slave to bishop!

Search the Bible and study the lives of others whom God brought from obscurity to fame . . . Gideon? David? Peter? Others?

1 TIMOTHY

A manual for Christian leaders

THE PASTORAL LETTER. The three letters, 1 and 2 Timothy and Titus, are known as pastoral epistles because they are largely taken up with advice given by a mature pastor to younger men who in turn would be training others for the pastoral office.

TIMOTHY. Timothy's father was a Greek but his mother Jewish. He was converted at about the age of fifteen when the apostle Paul visited his home town of Lystra (Acts 16:1-3; 1 Timothy 1:2). Seven years later he became Paul's missionary companion and there developed a strong bond of friendship between Paul who was now about seventy years of age and his younger colleague.

After his first imprisonment Paul visited, amongst other places, Ephesus and, not being able to stay there for very long, he left Timothy in charge of the work. Timothy found being left on his own a sore trial because he had leaned heavily on Paul for counsel. By nature he was rather shy and sensitive. Paul wrote to him from Corinth to encourage him and give him some advice.

The key verse is 3:15. Paul was keen to see his young spiritual son measure up to his responsibilities as a Christian leader. He was anxious that in every respect Timothy would set an example to the Christians who looked to him for leadership (1 Timothy 4:12).

SPECIAL FEATURES. There are several words and phrases which are only found in the pastoral epistles, such as 'God my Saviour' (1 Timothy 1:1; 2:3; 4:10; Titus 1:3; 2:10,13; 3:4), and references to 'sayings' worthy of special note (1 Timothy 1:15; 3:1; 4:9,10; 2 Timothy 2:11-13; Titus 3:3). Christian workers have consistently found the pastoral epistles to be a source of encouragement and practical advice.

Outline

1 **THE NEED FOR SOUND TEACHING** 1:1–20

1:1,2 Greetings!
1:3–11 A timely warning
1:12–17 A personal testimony
1:18–20 A solemn charge

2 **THE NEED FOR PRAYER** 2:1–15

2:1–8 Christians who pray
2:9–15 The ministry of women

3 **THE NEED FOR GOOD LEADERSHIP** 3:1–16

The necessary qualifications of a Christian leader.

4 **THE NEED FOR SPIRITUAL DISCERNMENT** 4:1–16

4:1–6 In warning others
4:7–16 In exercising self-discipline

5 **THE NEED FOR PRACTICAL INSTRUCTIONS** 5:1–25

How to treat different groups.

6 **THE NEED FOR RIGHT ATTITUDES** 6:1–21

6:1,2 On the part of slaves
6:3–21 Various instructions

Message and application

1. The church has to be warned against false teaching.

- [ ] False teaching has been a threat from the beginning (1:3–7) and is often closely allied with wrong behaviour. 1:8–11
- [ ] A life transformed by the grace of God is the most effective answer. 1:12–17
- [ ] False teachers need to be disciplined. 1:20

2. The importance of prayer.

- [ ] Prayer must be all-embracing. 2:1
- [ ] Prayer for those in authority is a priority. 2:2
- [ ] Prayer must be backed by consistent lives. 2:8–10

3. Directions for church officers.

- [ ] Overseers must be beyond reproach in the community and in respect to family life. 3:1–7
- [ ] Deacons must have comparable moral and spiritual qualifications. 3:8–13

4. A good minister will . . .

- [ ] Possess discernment. 4:1–5
- [ ] Steer clear of false teaching. 4:6,7
- [ ] See the value of godliness. 4:8–10
- [ ] Be an example to the flock. 4:11–15
- [ ] Get his priorities right. 4:16
- [ ] Be careful in his treatment of others. 5:1–22
- [ ] Seek to maintain good health. 5:23

5. A final briefing.

- [ ] Be practical in teaching. 6:1,2
- [ ] Keep free from avarice. 6:6–10
- [ ] Fight the good fight of faith. 6:12
- [ ] Remain true to the calling. 6:20

1 TIMOTHY

Key themes

1. False teaching.
The New Testament abounds in warnings against false teaching. Today's world is being challenged by all sorts of 'isms and 'ologies. In this easy-going age of tolerance, the apostle's warnings need to be taken seriously. Sincerity is not enough: we must 'tests the spirits' (1 John 4:1).

Consider various New Testament references to false teachers – eg. Acts 20:28–30; Matthew 24:4,5,23,24; 2 John 7–11). A failure to understand the person and work of Christ is at the root of almost every heresy – look at 1 Timothy 3:16 in this connection.

2. Prayer.
So often our prayers are limited to the immediate family circle, but here we are encouraged to pray much more widely. Rulers should have a special place in our prayers. It is well to remember that Nero was the emperor of Rome at this time! In prayer we have direct access to God but if our prayers are to be effective they must be backed by consistent lives. The hands we lift in prayer must be '**holy** hands'.

Consider practical ways and means of ensuring that prayers do not become insular. When did we last pray for our rulers?

3. Leadership.
If the church is to glorify God it must have the right kind of leadership. Note that spiritual and moral qualifications are stressed by the apostle. Note also the danger of appointing a recent convert to a responsible position (1 Timothy 3:6).

Compare the qualifications called for in both elders and deacons. Note the emphasis placed on a well-ordered home life and also on the reputation the leader has in the secular world.

Is the weakness of the church a reflection partly on its leadership? Are we careful enough in ensuring that leaders measure up to New Testament requirements? Is our method of appointment conducive to finding the right kind of appointees?

2 TIMOTHY

Famous last words!

HOW IT WAS WRITTEN. After writing the first letter to Timothy, Paul left Corinth and in company with Titus set sail for Crete where he left Titus to look after the church. The apostle had intended to spend the winter at Nicopolis but whilst still there it seems he made a short visit to Troas where he was arrested and taken to Rome. Whilst waiting in a Roman dungeon believing the time of his departure was near, Paul wrote this second letter to his beloved spiritual son. The arrest had been quite sudden, he had not had time to pick up books and parchments which he greatly treasured (4:13), nor even his outer cloak. Earlier when he was imprisoned in Rome he had enjoyed a certain measure of freedom in that his friends were free to visit him (Acts 28:23,30), but now the situation was very different.

THE APOSTLE ALONE. He was alone (4:10–12) and expected to be executed. He had already appeared once before the emperor, Nero, but his case had been postponed (4:16,17). He expected to appear again in the winter and so he wrote urging Timothy to come and bring Mark with him and also some of the things he had left behind. This is Paul's last letter and is very personal in character yet even in facing death he is keenly interested in the welfare of others. There are altogether 23 references to individuals in the letter.

Outline

1 A FATHER COUNSELS HIS SON
1:1–18

1:1–7 A sincere faith
1:8–14 A special responsibility
1:15–18 A sad statement

2 ADVICE TO CHRISTIAN WORKERS
2:1–26

Some word pictures to ponder
☐ The soldier (2:3,4)
☐ The athlete (2:5)
☐ The farmer (2:6)
☐ The artisan (2:15)
☐ The vessel (2:20–21)
Some instructions to follow
☐ Be strong (2:1)
☐ Communicate (2:2)
☐ Remember Jesus Christ (2:8–13)
☐ Avoid disputes (2:14–19)
☐ Be gentle (2:23–26)

3 A PICTURE OF THE LAST DAYS
3:1–17

3:1–9 Vices with which we are all too familiar
3:10–17 The call to endure

4 LAST WORDS
4:1–22

4:1–5 A solemn farewell charge
4:6–8 Paul's farewell message
4:9–22 Concluding comments and greetings

2 TIMOTHY

Message and application

1. Remember Jesus Christ (2:8).

Paul, facing the likelihood of martyrdom, counsels Timothy to 'remember Jesus Christ', since he himself was being sustained in this way. He never forgot that he was first and foremost 'an apostle of Christ Jesus' (1:1). He was not ashamed of testifying to his faith in Christ (1:8). He was convinced that Christ would keep him to the end (1:12). Christ was, for Paul, an example to follow, especially in suffering. The glorious appearing of Christ was the great goal to which he looked forward.

2. Avoid senseless controversies (2:23).

False teaching was rife when Paul wrote this letter. There were those who loved controversy and no doubt wasted hours discussing issues which had no particular relevance. Such people had an unsettling effect on the church (2:18). As Paul points out there are two firm foundations, two facts that are beyond all controversy – 'the Lord –

and he alone – knows those who are his', and if we are his, then we must 'depart from wickedness' (2:19). It is important not to get bogged down with protracted discussions over such matters as the interpretation of prophecy, predestination and free will.

3. Keep the faith (4:7).

Paul regarded the gospel message as a sacred deposit with which he had been entrusted and which he must be careful to pass on to others intact. The truth was something to be guarded (1:14), particularly in the light of so much false teaching. The Christian minister has a God-given responsibility to pass it on to others who in turn will share it with yet others (2:2). The efficient Christian teacher has learned how to rightly handle the word of truth (2:15). There can be no greater consolation at the end of the day than that of knowing you have 'kept the faith' (4:7).

2 TIMOTHY

Key themes

1. Suffering (1:8,12; 2:9; 3:11).
The writer of the letter is at the time of writing suffering for his faith in a prison cell in Rome. Timothy, his spiritual son, must be prepared if need be to suffer the same fate (1:8). Such suffering will not always be physical but may be occasioned by bitter disappointment and loneliness. Former colleagues like Phygelus and Hermogenes had deserted Paul (1:15). Demas was another who had caused the apostle pain through his desertion (4:10).

Consider the place of suffering in the life of a Christian. Our Lord himself made it clear the path would not be easy. Peter makes it clear that to suffer as a Christian is nothing to be ashamed of (1 Peter 4:16). Is it not true that some of the finest Christians are those who have suffered for their faith?

2. Service (2:2–6,15, 20–21).
It is significant that four of the word pictures of Christian workers in chapter 2 portray occupations that involve strenuous activity. Furthermore, in the illustration of the vessels, the accent is on availability and usability. Christians are truly 'saved to serve'.

Consider the aptness of the word pictures used in chapter 2 and particularly focus on the reference to the soldier and its implications. What does it mean to 'get involved in civilian affairs'?

3. Apostasy.
Surely the features mentioned in 3:1–9 have characterised every generation; how then are these things particularly true of 'the last days'? Scripture consistently warns us of the conditions we may reasonably expect to encounter prior to the Lord's return (Matthew 24:1–51).

Consider the message and methods of false teachers today in comparison with 2 Timothy 3:5–9.

4. Scripture.
Timothy had the advantage of godly forebears (2 Timothy 1:5). Note the part played by the scriptures in his early life (3:14,15). Note the special nature of scripture – 'God-breathed' and its wide-ranging function (3:16,17).

Think of examples from your own experience of how scripture has been used for 'teaching, rebuking, correcting, and training in righteousness'. What do you understand by the expression 'God-breathed'?

TITUS

The call for practical Christian living

WHO WAS TITUS? This letter was probably written about the same time and from the same place as 1 Timothy. Like Timothy, Titus was also one of Paul's converts (1:4). He was no doubt converted fairly early on in Paul's ministry. He accompanied Paul and Barnabas to Jerusalem seventeen years after Paul's conversion (Galatians 2:1). Paul gave Titus the difficult task of trying to sort out the problems in the church at Corinth, and in his second letter to that church we hear something of how he fared there (2 Corinthians 7:6,7). Clearly Paul had great confidence in Titus' abilities because later he was left in Crete to play a leading part in the life of the church (1:5). The Cretans in general were noted for being a turbulent people, difficult to handle.

Unlike Timothy, Titus was a pure Gentile and was not circumcised (Galatians 2:3). He has been described as 'the most enigmatic figure in early Christian history'. It has also been said of him that he was 'a red rag to the Judaizers but the flag of freedom for the Gentiles'. In modern parlance we could describe him as a 'trouble shooter' – the man to handle a delicate situation. He was certainly a great source of encouragement to the apostle Paul.

PRACTICAL ADVICE. When Paul heard that Apollos was about to go to Crete, he seized the opportunity of sending a letter by him to Titus. The letter is full of practical advice and warnings against false teaching. One gains the impression that Titus was probably a stronger character than Timothy, for Paul seems less anxious about him and how others might treat him.

The letter contains two of the most comprehensive statements about the gospel in the New Testament – 2:11–14 and 3:4–7. It is sometimes argued that the apostle Paul was less concerned about Christ's return in his later life, but we see from this letter that this was not so (2:13).

Outline

Message and application

1. The importance of spiritual leadership (1:5–16).

Titus was given the task of appointing elders in Crete and he was given detailed instructions as to the kind of qualifications they should have. Furthermore Titus was left with no illusions about the problems likely to be encountered among the Cretans.

Truly spiritual leadership is of paramount importance to the life of the church and the criteria set out by Paul are still relevant.

2. Christian life in action (2:1–10).

It is possible to speak or write in such general terms that the message does not get applied by individuals. Paul singles out different age groups each with their peculiar problems and gives to the groups essentially practical advice which needs to be translated into conduct.

3. The gospel in a nutshell (2:11–14).

In one sentence, a long one, Paul sets forth the various aspects of the Christian message. God has taken the initiative. We need to note that only the grace of God can bring about salvation and that this is embodied in a person – Jesus Christ the Lord. Furthermore, this message is addressed to all men everywhere. To be saved, however, is not merely a mystical experience, it has essentially practical overtones. Negatively it means turning one's back on our former way of life; positively it means living a righteous life.

Christians have a glorious hope – the personal return of their Lord and Saviour. This hope is an incentive to holy living. It powerfully affects Christian character and conduct.

4. It takes all sorts . . . ! (3:8–15).

The Christian church has its problem people as well as its key workers. In Crete there were those who loved arguing and wrangling, and some whose teaching was definitely heretical. On the other hand there were such stalwarts as Artemas, Tychicus, Zenas and Apollos. These men were not necessarily household names in the early church, but they were men who could be relied on. It is very important to have such men and women in key positions in the local church and not merely powerful personalities who may well aspire to be prima donnas.

TITUS

Key themes

1. The importance of home life.
It is noteworthy that in the list of qualifications for eldership there are several words and phrases which relate to home life. An elder must be 'the husband of but one wife'. His children must be in full sympathy with his Christian profession. He must be 'hospitable'. The witness of the Christian home in the ancient world was all-important, and Christian leaders must show the way. This is just as true today.

Look up the qualifications for the wives of church leaders (1 Timothy 3:11). How far should the church today take seriously the need for Christian leaders to be recruited from a happy home background?

2. Consistency of conduct.
The fact that belief and behaviour, creed and conduct, are not always in full accord is a frequent scriptural theme. This was the basis of our Lord's controversy with the Pharisees (see Matthew 23:1–39). James makes a similar point when he insists that faith apart from works is futile (James 2:14–26). Paul in his letter frequently referred to the same issue. In Titus 1:16, Paul speaks of those who 'claim to know God, but by their actions they deny him'. Our Lord said 'By their fruit you will recognise them' (Matthew 7:20). Creed and conduct must harmonise or else we may rightly be dismissed as hypocrites.

In what ways do those who profess to know God deny him in their lives? Try to account for the fact that Christian belief and Christian conduct often seem wide apart. Try, by studying Matthew 23, to pinpoint some of the ways in which the Pharisees failed so abysmally.

3. The importance of sound doctrine.
It is clear from reading the New Testament that, in the early church, they knew what they meant by 'the faith'. They could sum up what to them were the basic tenets in their creed. Paul does this extremely well in Titus 2:11–14. Here is one of the clearest statements of the grace of God in the New Testament. A healthy church is built on the foundation of sound doctrine. Our Christian faith relates not only to what God has done at a certain point in history, but also to what he is now doing in the lives of his people and to what he will yet do in the future. The hope of the believer is the personal return of Christ and he lives his life in the light of his coming.

The purpose of God's grace in Christ was 'to redeem us from all wickedness and to purify for himself a people that are his very own, eager to do what is good' (Titus 2:14). How far do Christians today see themselves in that light? What are the implications for us of being 'a people belonging to God'? (See 1 Peter 2:9; 1 Corinthians 6:19.)

HEBREWS

Good news about better things

WHO WROTE HEBREWS? We simply don't know for although this is a letter with a warm greeting at the end it has no address at the beginning!

It is very commonly assumed that Paul wrote it, but Hebrews 2:3 says that the author heard the gospel from others who had themselves heard Jesus. Paul insisted that he hadn't heard the gospel from others (Galatians 1:12).

The author might have been the Levite Barnabas (Acts 4:36) who would have known all about the priests and their work. Luke is a third possibility; the style of Hebrews is like the style of Luke and Acts.

Fourthly, Apollos knew Timothy well (13:23). Again, Acts 18:24 tells us that Apollos was 'well versed in the scriptures'. Whoever wrote Hebrews was certainly **that!**

And there are many other suggestions. In the end we have to say that no one knows **who** wrote it!

WHO RECEIVED THE LETTER? Since there is no address on the letter we don't know this. The writer describes his letter as a 'word of exhortation' (13:22). But who is he **exhorting?**

They were people who had been persecuted (10:32–34). The writer knew them personally and was hoping to visit them shortly (13:19 and 23). They had leadership potential but were not making progress (5:12).

They were people who spoke good Greek: the letter is written in perhaps the best Greek of the New Testament. So almost certainly they were not Jews living in Judea. But just as certainly they **were** Jews. Gentiles would never have understood the details of Jewish law.

They probably lived in Rome. This would explain the greetings in 13:24 from Italian Christians.

WHY WAS HEBREWS WRITTEN? There are two possibilities. If the group receiving the letter were Christians, the letter was to warn them of the danger of apostasy, of abandoning Christ.

But perhaps the group were still Jews, undecided, hesitating between decision for Christ (going on) and returning to their old ways.

DATE. Clement of Rome knew this letter, so it must have been written before AD 95. And since 10:1–3 implies that sacrifices are still being offered it was probably written before AD 70 when the Temple was destroyed. If the persecution mentioned in chapter 10 was due to Nero, then the letter was written after the fire of Rome, AD 64.

Outline

1 **THE SON: SUPERIOR TO ANGELS 1:1–2:18**

1:1–14 A contrast
2:1–4 A warning
2:5–18 The humility of the Son

2 **THE SON: SUPERIOR TO MOSES 3:1–19**

3:1–6 Son and servant
3:7–19 A warning

3 **THE SON: SUPERIOR TO JOSHUA 4:1–13**

4 **THE SON: A SUPERIOR HIGH PRIEST 4:14–10:39**

4:14–5:14 Superior to Aaron
6:1–20 A warning and an appeal

Superior to Melchizedek:
7:1–10 The greatness of Melchizedek
7:11–19 A new priesthood
7:20–25 A permanent priesthood

7:26–28 A perfect Son
8:1–13 A superior covenant

A superior sacrifice:
9:1–10 The limitation of the old
9:11–28 The perfection of the new
10:1–18 The body of Christ
10:19–39 An appeal and a warning

5 **THE LIFE OF FAITH 11:1–13:17**

11:1–3 A definition of faith
11:4–22 From Abel to Exodus
11:23–31 From Egypt to Canaan
11:32–38 Judges, kings and prophets
11:39–40 A better future
12:1–2 An example: look to Jesus
12:3–11 Living as God's family
12:12–24 Holiness: **not** an optional extra
12:25–29 A warning
13:1–6 Practical holiness
13:7–17 Leadership and discipleship

6 **CONCLUSION 13:18–25**

HEBREWS

Message

1. An exhortation.
Hebrews is an appeal, a reminder that we are expected to go on, grow up, mature. The Christian is always tempted to stand still, to consolidate instead of venturing even further into the life of faith.

2. A warning.
The exhortation to go on is consistently backed by a warning of the serious consequences that follow from standing still or slipping back. Note especially the five warning passages:
- ☐ No escape! 2:1–4
- ☐ Hold fast! 3:7–19
- ☐ No turning back! 6:1–20
- ☐ No other sacrifice! 10:19–39
- ☐ No escape! 12:25–29

3. A comparison.
The writer is concerned to show us the value of the Old Testament in understanding the New Testament. Today many Christians neglect the Old Testament. Hebrews shows us the **continuity** and the **contrast** between the two covenants.

4. A tent and not a temple.
Although the Temple in Jerusalem is almost certainly still standing, the writer here takes the tent, described in Exodus 25–27, as the purest picture of worship from which to illustrate Christian worship. The tent was appropriate for people on the march, the Temple for people who had settled down. Hebrews challenges our comfortable settled lives, offering instead a pilgrimage (11:16).

Application

Hebrews raises the question of the security of the Christian. Can a Christian be saved today and lost tomorrow? Verses such as John 10:29 seem to suggest that this is impossible. And yet we do meet people who once seemed to be Christians but now deny Christ.

The warning passages in Hebrews seem to suggest that the Christian is still free to go back to his old ways:

'We have come to share in Christ if we hold firmly till the end the confidence we had at first' (3:14).

'It is impossible for those who have once been enlightened . . . to be brought back to repentance . . .' (6:4–6).

'If we deliberately keep on sinning after we have received the knowledge of the truth, no sacrifice for sins is left, but only a fearful expectation of judgment' (10:26–27).

If the letter was sent to Jews who had attached themselves to a Christian church but would not commit themselves to Christ, then the teaching is clear: go on or get out! But if it was written to Christians the letter would seem to confirm that even after becoming Christians we remain free to opt out again. This is difficult to accept as the teaching of Hebrews, because it goes against Jesus' own words (as in John 10:29), against the various analogies of salvation (can the Christian be 'unborn'?) and strikes at God's power to keep his sheep safe.

So: the teaching of Hebrews is:
- ☐ There's no half-way house in Christianity. Go on or get out!

HEBREWS

□ Faith has always been the key to the life demanded by God. Faith, however, is not merely belief **about**, but **is** obedient action.

□ The Old Testament can legitimately be used to light up the teaching of the New Testament. The whole Bible is the word of God.

Key themes

1. The superiority of Christ.
This is an obvious theme of the first part of the letter (1–10). Go through these chapters and list all the ways in which Christ is said to be 'superior'. Start with 1:4, Jesus has a better name. What does this mean?
Work out the significance of these 'superior' characteristics of Christ.

2. Melchizedek.
Melchizedek is mentioned only in Hebrews 5–7 in the New Testament, and in Genesis 14 and Psalm 110 in the Old Testament. Study these passages. Use a Bible dictionary to find out more about him and the significance of his name. Who was he? What did he do? And what is the importance of Melchizedek for the argument being developed by the writer to the Hebrews?

3. The Old Testament.
List all the direct quotations from the Old Testament which you can find in Hebrews. Note also the many indirect references to the Old Testament. Examine the principles which seem to be observed in using the Old Testament. What does this suggest about our approach to the Old Testament?

4. Faith.
Read through Hebrews 11. List everything that the various people are said to have done. How does this emphasis on 'faith which acts' relate to the definition of faith in verse 1?
Study verses 32-38 of the faith chapter. What faith-actions of the people named would you 'write in' to this chapter? How many of the acts and experiences mentioned can you relate to incidents or people mentioned in scripture?

✓ Refer to the K. of the Holy.

JAMES

A letter about practical Christianity

THE AUTHOR AND HIS PURPOSE.
 1. The author. The writer is simply called James without any further introduction (1:1). He was the brother of Jesus. During the lifetime of Jesus he was an unbeliever (John 7:2–5) but he saw Jesus after the resurrection (1 Corinthians 15:7) and was present on the Day of Pentecost (Acts 1:14). He then became the leader of the church in Jerusalem (Acts 12:17, 15:13). He became widely respected for his devotion but was martyred in AD 62.

 Note that he calls himself 'servant' of his brother.

 2. The purpose. James writes as a pastor both to encourage Christians (eg. 5:7) and also to rebuke them. He stresses the importance of faith being put into practical action.

SPECIAL FEATURES. James is different from any other letter in the New Testament in its style. It only refers to Jesus twice (1:1 and 2:1) and apart from that could almost be a Jewish tract. Even so it is full of indirect references to the Sermon on the Mount and other teaching of Jesus. The writer also makes frequent reference to the Old Testament.

 The letter is short and punchy; it sees issues in black and white terms; it switches from topic to topic rapidly and is full of graphic illustrations.

HIS READERS. 1:1 tells us that they are the 'twelve tribes scattered among the nations' and 2:2 says that they meet in a synagogue. So they were almost certainly Jewish converts to Christianity. In view of what James says about wealth most of them may have been quite poor.

DATE. It must have been written before James' death in AD 62 and probably was written as early as AD 50 making it one of the earliest letters in the New Testament.

Outline

1 ADDRESS
1:1

2 A GUIDE TO TRUE RELIGION
1:2–27

1:2–4 The purpose of trials
1:5–8 The way to wisdom
1:9–11 The poverty of wealth
1:12–15 The origin of temptations
1:16–18 The gifts of God
1:19–21 The renouncing of evil
1:22–25 The importance of obedience
1:26–27 The definition of religion

3 THE IMPARTIALITY OF LOVE
2:1–13

2:1–7 An illustration
2:8–13 An application

4 THE PROOF OF FAITH
2:14–26

2:14–16 Probing questions
2:17–26 Basic principles

5 THE CONTROL OF THE TONGUE
3:1–12

The reasons and difficulties involved

6 THE WISDOM OF HEAVEN
3:13–18

3:13–16 The world's view of wisdom
3:17–18 The Lord's view of wisdom

7 THE BATTLE FOR PURITY
4:1–10

4:1–7 The enemies: flesh, world and devil
4:8–10 The resources: the grace of God and how to obtain it

8 THE APPLICATION OF FAITH
4:11–5:12

4:11–12 To a destructive tongue
4:13–17 To confident ambition
5:1–6 To selfish exploitation
5:7–11 To joyful patience
5:12 To verbal integrity

9 THE PRACTICE OF PRAYER
5:13–18

5:13 Prayer and its variety
5:14,15 Prayer and suffering
5:16 Prayer and confession
5:17–18 Prayer and faith

10 THE CARE OF THE UNSTABLE
5:19–20

JAMES

Message

James has three main themes:

1. The fatherhood of God.
James says of God that:
- [ ] He answers prayer generously. 1:5
- [ ] He promises life to persecuted Christians. 1:12
- [ ] He never tempts. 1:13
- [ ] He never changes his attitude to Christians. 1:16–18
- [ ] He chooses the poor. 2:5
- [ ] He makes man in his likeness. 3:9
- [ ] He opposes the proud. 4:6
- [ ] He is always available with grace when we need it. 4:6,8

2. The horror of sin.
- [ ] Sin has its origin in man's flesh. 1:14; 3:6,16; 4:1–3,5
- [ ] Sin starts small but quickly develops. 1:15; 3:5

- [ ] Sin means we have offended God and merit his judgement. 2:10–13; 4:12; 5:1
- [ ] Sin must be treated with due abhorrence. 4:9,10
- [ ] Sin can be forgiven by the grace of the Lord. 2:13; 4:6; 5:11,20

3. The development of Christian behaviour and character.
- [ ] Among the means God uses to develop a Christian character James speaks of:
  - Trials and suffering. 1:2–4
  - The word of God. 1:21
  - Practical obedience. 1:22–25
  - Submission and humility. 4:8,10
- [ ] Christian character is described in 3:13–18; 4:13–17; 5:7–11
- [ ] Christian behaviour is described in 1:26,27; 2:1–26; 3:1–12; 4:11–12; 5:12–20

Application

1. For all Christians.
The message of James is so clear and practical that there is much for all Christians to apply to their lives. Go through the epistle and work out for yourself how each topic relates to you.

But there are also some passages which apply to Christians who are in particular circumstances:

2. For Christians under pressure.
Look to the purpose these trials play in your life. 1:2–4

3. For Christians who are wealthy.
Remember that your material wealth will not last (1:9–11) and make sure that you do not come under the condemnation of 5:1–6.

4. For the Christian as a church member.
Do you equally welcome all into your church? 2:1–9

5. For Christians in leadership.
Don't be too quick to speak. 3:1

6. For Christians who are wavering.
There is a welcome waiting for you on your return to the Father. 5:19–20

JAMES

Key themes

1. Find the illustrations.
James uses vivid picture language to put across his teaching. Look at the illustrations he uses and think about what they communicate to you. They can be found in 1:6,11,17,23,26; 3:3,5,7,12; 4:14; 5:1–2,7.

2. Find the sermon
There are many references to the Sermon on the Mount in this letter. Try to fit the following verses to the words of Jesus in Matthew 5-7; James 1:2,4,5,20,22; 2:10,13; 3:18; 4:4,10,11,12; 5:2,3,10,12.

3. Find the teaching.
James also indirectly mentions other parts of the teaching of Jesus. Where can you find in James similar teaching to the following? Matthew 12:36,37; 21:21; 22:39; 23:8–12; 24:33.

4. Find the Old Testament.
Several Old Testament characters are used to illustrate James' message. Who does he mention and what lesson does he draw from each?

Some themes, such as the law, relate to the Old Testament. How does James develop the Old Testament view of the law (2:8–13)?

Many other verses from the Old Testament find an echo in this letter as well. A good reference Bible will help you track them down.

1 PETER

A letter to suffering Christians

WHY THE LETTER WAS WRITTEN. Peter wrote this letter to encourage Christians who were bewildered because they were being persecuted. He gives them practical guidance as to how they should react even when their suffering was not deserved (3:13–17) and urges them to stand firm. The advice is based upon rich teaching about the nature of their salvation and the example set by their Saviour.

SPECIAL FEATURES. It reads like a sermon rather than an essay. It is lively, full of crisp commands and is written from the heart. Some think Peter took a sermon which was in wide use to prepare candidates for baptism and adapted it to his own ends, but this is doubtful.

The letter breathes the atmosphere of one who had been close to Jesus during his lifetime. References to Peter's days as a disciple are never far below the surface. He vividly recalls the death of Jesus (2:22–25) and writes about leadership as if re-living the scene at the last supper (5:5, see John 13:1–20) and his encounter with Jesus after the resurrection (5:2, see John 21:15–23).

THE READERS AND THEIR SITUATION.

    1. The readers: We do not know how the churches in the four Roman provinces of northern Asia Minor to whom Peter wrote were founded – possibly through some who were present on the Day of Pentecost (Acts 2:9) or through Peter or Paul's missionary activity. It is not certain that Peter had ever visited them.

    Peter calls them 'exiles of the Dispersion' (1:1, RSV) not because they were Greek-speaking Jews living away from home but to remind them of their place as Christians in the world. The churches had both Jews and Gentiles in them.

    2. Their situation: They were dominated by the thought of suffering. Persecution was an imminent threat to them (1:6; 3:9–22; 4:12–19), as it was to Christians across the world (5:9). Local persecutions were beginning to take place, fanned by mob feeling, and reflecting the newer hard line policy of Rome itself towards the Christians.

THE AUTHOR AND HIS SITUATION. The apostle Peter says he was writing from Babylon (5:13) which is a code-name for Rome. He wrote around the year AD 64 as Nero's vicious persecution of the Christians was getting underway. Peter was to lose his own life shortly afterwards.

Outline

1 **ADDRESS AND GREETING**
1:1–2

2 **CHRISTIAN SALVATION**
1:3–2:10

1:3–9 Its present blessings
1:10–12 Its prophetic inquirers
1:13–17 Its practical consequences – holiness
1:18–21 Its secure basis – Christ
1:22–2:3 Its practical consequences – love
2:4–10 Its corporate nature

3 **CHRISTIAN RELATIONSHIPS**
2:11—3:12

2:11–12 In pagan society
2:13–17 In political life
2:18–25 In employment
3:1–7 In the family
3:8–12 In unfair circumstances

4 **CHRISTIAN SUFFERING**
3:13–4:19

3:13–17 How to react: even when wronged
3:18–22 Who to imitate: at all times
4:1–11 How to behave: with an eye to the future
4:12–19 The joy of suffering for Christ

5 **CHRISTIAN COMMUNITY**
5:1–14

5:1–4 Principles for leaders
5:5–11 Principles for everyone
5:12–14 Closing greetings

1 PETER

Message

1. God wins through.
Peter makes constant reference to God's
- [ ] Mercy and grace. 1:3,21; 2:9–10; 3:4; 5:10,12
- [ ] Power and justice. 1:17; 2:12; 3:22; 4:5,17; 5:5,6
- [ ] Holiness. 1:16
- [ ] Will and purpose. 2:15; 3:17
- [ ] Gifts. 4:10–11

2. Look at Jesus.
- [ ] The suffering Saviour. 1:18–21; 2:21–25
- [ ] The great Shepherd. 2:25; 5:4
- [ ] The Christian's example. 2:21; 3:17–18; 4:13

3. The dividing line is obedience.
People are divided on the basis of whether or not they obey God.

Christians obey:
- [ ] Jesus. 1:14
- [ ] The truth, word or gospel. 1:22; 3:1; 4:17

Non-Christians do not. 3:1; 4:17

4. Accept your situation.
The Christian reaction to a raw deal is to accept it, not fight back. Peter says this in several ways:
- [ ] Leave it to God. 4:19; 5:6,7
- [ ] Submit, or in other words accept your God-given place without protest, in all your relationships. 2:13,18; 3:1; 5:5
- [ ] Don't retaliate. 3:9

5. The truth about the church.
Men see the church as a despised and feeble minority. But Peter spells out its real significance. 2:9–10

Application

1. For all Christians.
- [ ] This salvation is yours too! 1:3–9
- [ ] Let the future shape the present. 1:13
- [ ] Live radically. 1:14; 4:2–5
- [ ] Keep on growing. 2:2
- [ ] This world is not your home. 2:11
- [ ] How to behave in society. 2:12–17; 3:9
- [ ] How to behave in the church. 3:8; 4:7–11; 5:1–9

2. For persecuted Christians.
- [ ] Hold on and stand firm. 5:9

- [ ] Suffering has a purpose. 1:7
- [ ] Make sure you suffer for the right reason. 2:19,20; 3:13–17; 4:15
- [ ] Be prepared when it comes. 3:15
- [ ] Think what comes next. 1:3–5,13; 4:13; 5:10
- [ ] Focus your mind on Jesus. 2:21–25; 4:1
- [ ] What a privilege to be like Jesus. 4:13

3. For leading Christians.
- [ ] This is how to lead. 5:1–4

1 PETER

Key themes

Peter keeps coming back to certain words which sum up what is on his mind. Look up the references and summarise what he teaches. Here are Peter's top ten.

1. Hope.
1:3,13,21; 3:15

2. Grace and mercy.
1:2,3,10,13; 2:10; 3:7; 4:10; 5:5,10,12

3. Salvation.
1:5,9,10; 2:2

4. Love.
1:8, 22; 2:17; 3:8,10; 4:8; 5:14

5. Joy.
1:6,8; 4:13

6. Sober.
1:13; 4:7; 5:8

7. Fear.
1:17; 2:16,17; 3:14

8. Humility.
3:8; 5:5,6

9. Precious.
1:7,19; 2:4,6,7; 3:4

10. Glory.
1:7,11,21,24; 4:11,13,14; 5:1,4,10

For further study.
- [ ] Make a list of all the descriptions you can find of the Christian, eg. an exile (2:11).
- [ ] Make a list of all the commands Peter gives to his readers. Most of them are very brief eg. fear God (2:17). There should be over 30 in your list.

2 PETER

Hang on to your faith!

WHY DID PETER WRITE? It is a mistake to think that they had no problems in the New Testament churches. The readers of this letter were in real danger.

1. They needed to go on as they had begun and not to give in to the temptation to sit back. There was tremendous room for growth.

2. In their part of the world there was some vicious false teaching going around. Those who were pushing it said they were Christians, but their lifestyle was far, far away from anything to do with Jesus. It looks as though they said they had special knowledge which allowed them to do away with the rules. Because of this they were encouraging wild sexual excesses and doing it in the name of Christ! They had lost all sense of shame, and did not care who they dragged down with them. As life was pretty permissive in those days anyway, this sort of thing would attract a good number who did not really want to give up the old life.

3. Another lot were getting very cynical about Jesus' promise to come back. The years had gone by and nothing had happened, so they began to doubt if it ever would.

All this was very disturbing for young Christians, and Peter is writing to set the record straight on a number of points as well as to encourage them to go on with the Lord.

WHO WERE HIS READERS? We do not know – because they are not named anywhere in the letter. They might have been the same group who got the first letter, but we cannot be sure. It does look, though, as if he felt that his death was near when he wrote. He says he feels that it will not be long before he leaves them, and that is one of the reasons why he wants to get something down on paper while he can.

SOME UNSOLVED PROBLEMS. 2 Peter is a peculiar letter in that it is written in some of the strangest, flowery language in the New Testament. This might have been Peter's own way of putting things, or it might have been the work of his secretary at the time. Another strange thing is that when we read his second chapter and then look through Jude's letter, we find a good deal in common. Who used what we do not know. Peter might have been adapting his friend's work – or Jude might have been picking Peter's brains! The problem remains unsolved.

Outline

Message

1. You need to go on.
There is
- ☐ more to know. 1:5–7
- ☐ more to prove. 1:8–11
- ☐ more to grow. 3:11,12,18

2. Jesus was no myth.
Eyewitness evidence. 1:16–18
An answer for the false teachers. 2:1; 3:1–2

3. God has it in for some.
He has dealt with wicked people in the past.
2:4–8

He will spare those who love him. 2:9
He will judge the sinners. 2:9–10

4. Don't be impatient.
Jesus did promise to return. 3:2
God brought the world to an end once before.
3:5–6
This present world is doomed to destruction.
3:7,10,11
God sees time differently. 3:8
Longer wait, more Christians! 3:9
We have a wonderful future. 3:13

Application

2 Peter asks some questions . . .

1. Are you growing as a Christian?
- ☐ Still keen to prove his promises?
- ☐ adding to your faith?
- ☐ and not just marking time?

2. Are you confident?
- ☐ You have
  - – God's word
  - – a growing experience
  - – eyewitness evidence
  - – a glimpse of the future

3. Are you on guard?
- ☐ Can you
  - – recognise false teaching?
  - – avoid damning errors?
  - – remember the truth?
  - – watch your behaviour?

4. Are you hanging on?
- ☐ In spite of error?
- ☐ In spite of the scornful?
- ☐ In the light of the past?
- ☐ In the light of the future?
- ☐ Because you have so much to gain and so much to lose?

2 PETER

Key themes

1. The Bible.
It is surprising how much Peter refers to what we know nowadays as the Bible for his teaching. He actually says that it is even surer than what he had seen.

See what you can find out about
- [ ] the Old Testament (1:20–21; 2:4–7, 15–16,22; 3:2,5–6,8,13)
- [ ] the life and teaching of Jesus (1:4,8,17; 2:1,20; 3:2,9,10,18)
- [ ] the teaching of the apostles (1:12–18; 2:21; 3:2,15–16)

2. Eyewitness evidence.
Like some other New Testament authors, Peter could say that the message about Jesus was true because he had been with him and had seen him in action. He also saw how important it was to let people know about this before he died. Mark's Gospel may owe a lot to Peter.

Why do you think that Peter selects the story of the time when they saw something of Jesus' glory? (1:17–18) How do you think this ties in with 'the power and coming of our Lord Jesus Christ'? (1:16)

3. Error.
There is no room in Peter's thinking for false teaching or for stupid questioning of God's word. Christians have no excuse when they play with things which contradict what they already know about Christ and the Christian life.

How does Peter describe the false teachers? What risks were they running? How does it apply to us today?

4. The end.
There was no uncertainty in Peter's mind about Christ's return and the end of the world. Although delayed, it would surely come.

What can we learn from this letter:
- [ ] about a Christian's attitude to death and
- [ ] about the end of the world and what comes next? How should this affect the way we live?

1, 2 & 3 JOHN

How to be sure

WHO WROTE THESE LETTERS? These three short letters tell us very little about their author. The nearest we get is the title 'the elder' (2 John 1; 3 John 1). Still, there are certain things about them which give us some clues just as they did years ago when the early Christians claimed that they had been written by the Apostle John.

1. The style and ideas of all three are the same. Whoever wrote the first seems to have written the other two. What is more, we find the same words and ideas in John's Gospel. As we have seen there, although John is not named, there is a good deal which suggests that he might well have been behind it. In 1 John the author claims to have been an eyewitness of Jesus' life (1:1–3).

2. At the same time, there is that strong, clear authority about these letters which marked out Jesus' special representatives, the apostles. There is a tradition going back a long way that John spent his last years as an old man in Ephesus. If this is so, these letters might have come from this time. In fact he might even have been known as 'the elder' in the sense of 'the respected old man'.

WHO WERE THEY TO? The first letter has no address at all or any reference to anyone in particular. It could well have been a circular letter written for a number of churches which had the same sort of problem.

The second letter was sent to 'the chosen lady' (2 John 1), and the most natural way of seeing this is that it went to a Christian woman whose children were also keen believers (2 John 4). However, some have held that this was John's way of speaking about a church.

The third letter was to a friend named Gaius, a man who was doing a particularly good job putting up and looking after Christian workers (3 John 5–8).

WHAT WAS THE PROBLEM? It was a double one. Like other Christian communities they were plagued with false teachers who were leading others astray. As a result, the faith of the true Christians was being shaken. How could they be sure that they really were Christians? How could they tell truth from error? It seems that the false teachers, as so many others have done, were rejecting the apostles' claim that Jesus was both truly God and truly man. Nowadays we get used to people saying that he was just a man. Strange to say, in those days they questioned whether he really was human. Some found it hard to believe that God's Son could actually live among us in a real body. John tells us that when you start devaluing Jesus in any way you miss out on the good news altogether.

Outline

1 JOHN

1 'WE SAW JESUS' 1:1–4

1:1 Eyewitnesses
1:2–4 Preachers

2 'WHAT FELLOWSHIP IS ALL ABOUT' 1:5–2:2

1:5 God is light
1:6–10 Three impossibilities
2:1–2 Forgiveness available

3 'OBEYING AND LOVING' 2:3–17

2:3–6 Knowing is obeying
2:7–11 Obeying is loving
2:12–14 You are his
2:15–17 Do not love the world

4 'HOW TO DEAL WITH HERETICS' 2:18–29

2:18–20 Learn to discern
2:21–25 Apply the test
2:26–27 Rely on the Spirit
2:28–29 Watch their behaviour

5 'WE ARE GOD'S CHILDREN' 3:1–10

3:1 Privilege
3:2–3 Potential
3:4–10 Possibilities

6 'SHOW THE FAMILY LIKENESS' 3:11–24

3:11–18 Love and hatred
3:19–24 Love and assurance

7 'TEST THEIR TEACHING' 4:1–6

4:1–3 True to the facts?
4:4–6 Or accepted by the world?

8 'THE PROOF OF LOVE' 4:7–21

4:7–12 True Christians love
4:13–21 We can be sure

9 'BE REASSURED . . .' 5:1–12

5:1–5 The change in our lives
5:6–12 Solid grounds for believing

10 'TRUST IN GOD' 5:13–21

5:13–15 He hears
5:16–17 He forgives
5:18–19 He keeps
5:20–21 He satisfies

2 JOHN

1 'THE ELDER TO THE LADY . . .' 1–3

Greetings

2 'LOVE ONE ANOTHER' 4–6

No new commandment

3 'THERE ARE ROGUES ABOUT' 7–11

7 Who devalue Jesus
8 Who need watching
9 Who are not Christian
10–11 Who should not be encouraged

4 'I HOPE TO SEE YOU SOON' 12,13

3 JOHN

1 'DEAR GAIUS . . .' 1–4

2 'YOU HAVE A GREAT REPUTATION' 5–8

5–6 Hospitality
7–8 Supporting God's servants

3 'NOT ALL ARE LIKE THIS' 9–10

4 'GO ON WITH GOD' 11–12

5 'GREET EVERYONE' 13–15

Message

Assurance – and tests for false teaching

We have:

1. The true and original gospel.
☐ God's Son really came. 4:2,15; 5:1,6–10
☐ Those who saw and heard. 1:1–4; 4:6
☐ Deny one, deny both. 2:22–24; 5:10–12; 2 John 9

2. God's promise of forgiveness.
☐ This is quite clear. 1:9; 2:12
☐ Because Jesus died. 2:1,2; 4:10
☐ In spite of our feelings. 3:19–22

3. A new way of living.
☐ Power to break with sin. 3:4–10; 5:4

☐ And to overcome Satan. 2:13,14; 3:8,9; 4:4
☐ Doing what God wants. 2:17,29; 3:3
☐ You can't have it both ways. 1:6,7; 2:3–6

4. The Holy Spirit indwelling.
☐ God-given understanding. 2:20,27
☐ Real assurance. 3:24; 4:13; 5:7–10

5. New love for one another.
☐ Real Christians love others. 3:14,23,24; 4:7,12,16,21; 5:1–3
☐ Loving is self-giving. 3:16; 4:9–11
☐ When we don't. 2:9–11; 3:14,15,17; 4:8,20
☐ Get on with it. 3:11,18, see 2 John 5,6

1, 2 & 3 JOHN

Application

1. You can be sure you are God's child.
You can know
- fellowship with him and with others
- a complete joy
- answered prayer
- a deep sense of belonging

2. Real faith leads to a different kind of life.
It will mean
- a break with habitual sinning
- a new love for others
- being ready to do what God wants

If we haven't got these things, are we really Christians?

3. You will stand out from the rest.
The world is under Satan's control
- ☐ You must shun its ways
- ☐ It will hate you for it

4. There are false teachers about.
- ☐ You can recognise them by
  - what they teach
  - how they live
- ☐ You have the antidote because you
  - have the truth
  - can test the error by it

Key themes

1. Life.
As with the gospel, God's gift to the believer is life. See 1:1,2; 2:25; 3:14; 4:9; 5:11,12.

2. Light and truth.
Christ came to show us God and his ways, to give us light (1:5–7; 2:8–11). This means we know the truth about things (1:8; 2:21,27; 5:20 see 2 John 1,2,4; 3 John 1,3,4,12). Notice, however, that it is more than just knowing the truth; we have to **do** it.

3. Sin.
Notice how John describes sin. In his mind the issues are quite clear-cut. See 1:6,8–10; 2:1; 3:4–6,8; 5:16–18.

4. The world.
John uses this word in more than one sense. Look up the references (2:2, 15–17; 3:13; 4:1,3–5,17; 5:4,5,19) and note especially those which refer to the hostile and godless atmosphere in which Christians have to live.

5. Abiding.
This word which means 'remaining' or 'staying' speaks about the constant and ongoing relationship we now have with Christ. See 2:6,10,24,28; 3:6,9,15,17,24; 4:12,13,15,16 (See 2 John 2; John 15:1–11).

6. Born of God.
Like Jesus, John speaks about being 'born of God' as the beginning of our Christian lives. See how he describes this 2:29; 3:1,2,9,10; 4:7; 5:1,2,18.

7. Jesus Christ.
Because Jesus is being attacked, John says some very positive things about him. Look through the references describing who he is (1:1–3; 2:1,22–24; 3:5,7; 4:2,3,9,14; 5:5,6,8) and what he did for us (1:7; 2:2; 3:5,8; 4:10).

JUDE

Little letter with a bite!

Here we have one of the shortest letters in the New Testament, but it certainly packs a punch. It reminds us that if we love people, we will sometimes have to be quite straight with them.

WHO WAS JUDE? He tells us himself that he was 'James' brother' (1) or, if you like, the brother of the well-known James. Who then was James? There is only one person who measures up to that description and that was James, the Lord's brother. This, of course, makes Jude the brother of Jesus, too (see Mark 6:3; Matthew 13:55). And yet Jude does not even call himself an apostle (although he talks about them)! All of which means that we are dealing here with a humble and modest man who did not throw his weight around.

WHEN AND WHY DID HE WRITE? From the way in which he talks about the faith and the teaching of the apostles, it looks as though Jude was writing well on into New Testament times, although we cannot be absolutely sure. We also do not know where his friends lived, but we do know what they were up against. Like so many churches in the New Testament, this one was in trouble, and what was worse, the trouble was on the inside. There were some who were making out that they were Christians but who were leading disreputable lives, and spreading around false and filthy ideas. It also looks as though they might have been doing it under the disguise of 'higher' or 'more spiritual' teaching.

Jude had meant to write to them a longer and more leisurely letter about Christian things, but this called for swift action. This may be why Jude and 2 Peter have so much in common. Either Jude snatched up Peter's letter and adapted it or he got hold of some tract which Peter knew, too. The result is urgent, powerful and commanding.

WHAT ABOUT ENOCH? One of the unusual things about Jude is that he not only quotes the Old Testament and the apostles, he also cites books which we do not have in our Bibles.

The Book of Enoch (14,15) was a popular religious book which was quite well known in those days.

The Assumption of Moses (9) was another. (There was a story in it about Michael being sent to bury Moses and meeting the devil who claimed his body because Moses was a murderer. Michael left the decision with God.)

There may be other references, too, but this does not mean

that Jude thought that they were on a level with the Bible. There are other occasions in the New Testament when the authors quote well-known sayings or writings just to make a point, in the same way that preachers today might quote Shakespeare or Pilgrim's Progress.

Outline

1 'JUDE TO HIS FRIENDS'
1,2
You are special people

2 'WRITTEN IN HASTE . . .'
3,4
3a What I wanted to write
3b What I am writing
4 Why I write like this

3 'THREE GRIM REMINDERS'
5–7
5 Egypt
6 Angels
7 Sodom and Gomorrah

4 'WHAT WE ARE UP AGAINST'
8–13
8–9 Kicking over the traces
10 Behaving like animals
11 Cain, Balaam and Korah rolled into one!
12–13 Dangerous and useless

5 'ENOCH GOT IT RIGHT!'
14–16
14–15 The Judge is on the way
16 Pride and passion

6 'THE APOSTLES TOLD YOU SO!'
17–19
17–18 Bad times will come
19 Watch out for the worldly!

7 'GET ON WITH THE JOB!'
20–23
20,21 Reinforcement
22,23 Reaching out

8 'WHAT A GOD WE'VE GOT!'
24,25
Capable and in control

JUDE

Message

1. There are enemies on the inside.
They have
- [ ] Wormed their way in. 4
- [ ] Spoiled the fellowship. 12
- [ ] Divided the group. 19
- [ ] Proved they are counterfeit Christians. 19

2. They deny the faith.
- [ ] Opposing what we believe. 3
- [ ] Living evil lives. 4,11,12,16

3. God will deal with them.
- [ ] He did it before. 4,5,6,7,11
- [ ] He will do it again. 14,15

4. True Christians will be on guard
- [ ] Fighting for the faith. 3
- [ ] Loyal to the Master. 4
- [ ] Remembering the promises. 17
- [ ] Going on and living it out. 20,21
- [ ] Rescuing some. 22,23

5. God will see us through.
- [ ] He called us. 1
- [ ] He loves us. 1,2,21
- [ ] He can give us all we need. 2
- [ ] He can keep us. 24
- [ ] He is in charge. 25

Application

Jude tells us about dealing with error. . .

1. What to look for.
- [ ] False teaching
- [ ] Ungodliness
- [ ] Permissiveness and lust
- [ ] Unbelief
- [ ] Pride
- [ ] Irreverence
- [ ] Scoffing
- [ ] Refusing authority
- [ ] Selfishness
- [ ] Lack of fruit
- [ ] Grumbling
- [ ] Boasting
- [ ] Flattery
- [ ] Divisiveness
- [ ] Worldliness
- [ ] Pretended spirituality

2. How to fight back.
- [ ] Hang on to the Bible
- [ ] Check out their teaching
- [ ] Allow no deviations
- [ ] Realise that it is serious
- [ ] Go on as you began
- [ ] Take hold of God's promises
- [ ] Be careful even when you want to help them

JUDE

Key themes

1. The Bible.
Jude speaks about 'the faith' (3); summing up what we believe. Because this is God-given and because God does not contradict himself, it is tremendously important that we stick to it. We have it written down for us in our Bibles, and Jude assumed that his friends knew it and would stand up for it. See how Jude refers to both the Old and New Testaments (verses 3,5,6,7,11,17,18,20) and look up the following references: 1 Corinthians 10:1–12; Genesis 10:1–12; 6:1–4; 19:1–25; 4:1–16; Numbers 22–23; 25:1–5; 31:15,16; 16:1–35.

2. Life and faith.
What we believe and how we live must match up. The false teachers said they believed in God's grace (4) and may even have claimed special revelation (8, see 19) but their daily living betrayed them.

List out the different pictures which Jude uses to describe these pseudo-Christians. What is the total impression that you get?

3. Sin does not go unpunished.
Even though they seem to be getting away with it, Bible history tells us that one day God will judge them.

Look up the references to God's judgement in the letter.

4. True Christians will come through
Not only is God greatly concerned about his people, he is able to give them all they need to come through.

Think around verses 24,25 and work out what God will do and how he can do it.

REVELATION

What the future holds

AUTHOR. The author is named as 'John' four times (1:1,4,9; 22:8) but he does not claim to be John the apostle, and some have suggested another John as the writer, because:

1. The Greek of Revelation is very unusual, quite unlike the Greek of John's Gospel.

2. In the Gospel, John takes care never to name himself.

3. The characteristic themes of John's Gospel, love and truth, are almost absent in Revelation.

But these objections are easily answered. The Greek is deliberately odd – not mere bad Greek – in the interests of prophecy. Secondly, the Gospel was essentially a biography of Jesus, and John would not want to intrude himself into it. But Revelation is a revelation given to a person, and the name of that person gives authenticity to the revelation. Thirdly, we would hardly expect love to be the key theme of a book which is talking about judgement!

RECIPIENTS. The book includes seven letters to seven churches (more strictly to their 'angels') in Asia. There were other churches in Asia, but these seven are selected, firstly, because the number seven indicates perfection or completeness; the seven represent the entire church in all history, and secondly, because the seven between them typify the whole spectrum of churches through the centuries: from the church of Smyrna, of which nothing bad is said, to the church of Laodicea, of which nothing good is said.

DATE. The book is written at a time when the persecution of the church is about to be intensified. Christians have been persecuted, but now they must prepare to resist to death.

The first major persecution took place under the emperor Nero and seems to be reflected in the book – perhaps the mysterious '666' (13:18),. There was a second, fiercer, persecution, under Domitian, which lasted from AD 91-95 and it is generally accepted that John wrote during this period.

SPECIAL FEATURES. This book represents a special type of Jewish writing. It is apocalyptic; an unveiling, a revealing, but written in a vivid and poetic way. It **is** difficult to understand, but this is a very important book for the Christians to study if he is to relate properly to the history of our times.

Outline

REVELATION

Message

1. Interpreting the book.

The book is built around symbols, of which the most obvious is the number seven:

☐ Seven churches. 1:4
☐ Seven spirits. 1:4
☐ Seven lampstands. 1:12
☐ Seven stars. 1:16
☐ Seven seals. 5:1
☐ Seven horns. 5:6
☐ Seven angels. 8:2
☐ Seven trumpets. 8:2
☐ Seven thunders. 10:3
☐ Seven heads. 12:3
☐ Seven last plagues. 15:1
☐ Seven golden bowls. 15:7
☐ Seven kings. 17:10

And even within the text it is possible to identify other sets of seven which are not specifically identified as such. Seven stands for completeness, perfection. It is God's number, just as six is man's number.

The book must be understood as a book of encouragement for times of persecution. It insists that even the Neros of history form part of God's plan.

And the book emphasises judgement: ultimately God demands a reckoning. The liar, the cheat, the immoral seem to get away with it. And we sometimes get impatient: 'How long?' (6:10). There is a day fixed for judgement.

2. Four patterns of interpretation.

☐ **The historic view** interprets Revelation as being intended for the Christians who received it in the first century. The historical references are to people and events of that time alone. All the secrets of Revelation would have been understood by the first readers, but we should not expect to see any detailed revelation about our own times.

☐ **The prophetic view** sees Revelation as presenting a long-term outline of all history, starting from the first century and advancing steadily to our own times and on to the end.

☐ **The futurist view** discounts all historical allusions, and takes Revelation to refer solely to the end times.

☐ **The symbolic view** sees Revelation as being filled with symbols, each of which must be interpreted individually and apart from any necessary connection with world history.

Probably none of these views is entirely satisfactory. The historic view makes Revelation of little use to us, and the futurist view makes it relevant only to Christians actually living in the end time.

But prophecies often have two points of reference: an event near at hand and an event far off. Isaiah's famous prophecy of a child (7:14) refers both to a young woman of Isaiah's day and to Mary, the mother of the Lord. These prophecies also refer both to events in the time of Domitian and to events of the end time.

3. The mysterious number 666 (13:10).

The riddle depends on the fact that both in Hebrew and in Greek the letters of the alphabet stand also for numerals. So any word has a numerical value and any number may be a code for a particular word. Nero-Caesar, if written in Hebrew, totals 666. Titus is another possible solution, this time working from Greek, and this would refer to the third emperor with the name of Titus Domitian.

REVELATION

Application

The message of Revelation is simple: all history is 'His-story', already written and ending in judgement for all the world. And in this knowledge the Christian ought to find comfort, especially in times of persecution.

Key themes

1. Babylon.
The fall of Babylon is described in great detail in chapters 18,19. Use a concordance to trace the Bible teaching about Babylon. Start from Genesis 11, noting that Babel is Babylon. Note especially Isaiah's prophecies about Babylon.

In 18:1–24 identify the seven laments for Babylon, starting with the angel's lament in verses 1–3.

2. The plagues.
Compare the seven plagues of chapter 16 with the ten plagues of Exodus 7–11. Notice how this section of Revelation is deliberately related to the events of the Exodus (see 15:2–4). Why is this vision of judgement connected to the Exodus which is usually thought of as a salvation event?

3. The two witnesses.
There is a tantalising passage (11:1–13) which describes two witnesses who are also described as two prophets although they are not named. Some interpreters understand these witnesses to be two churches; others prefer to see them as Old Testament prophets back on earth again. Moses and Elijah have been suggested as the two. Why these two?

What further light is cast on the subject by Zechariah 4?

4. The tree of life.
The Bible starts with a garden (Genesis 2:8) and ends with a garden (Revelation 22). Compare and contrast the first two chapters of the Bible with the last two.

5. The Lord Jesus Christ.
Go through the book and make a list of all the names and titles used for Jesus. The Alpha and Omega (first and last letters of the Greek alphabet), the Offspring of David and so on. Notice especially the key title of the Lamb (28 times). What is the significance of this title (see also John 1:29–37; Hebrews 9:1–28; 1 Corinthians 5:7; 1 Peter 1:18,19)?

But notice the beautiful way in which this book, which pictures the majesty of Jesus, closes with a simple reference to the Lord (his majesty) Jesus (his humility). Amen. Come, Lord Jesus!